To John, who knows
that economists are not
the only people who screw
up countries.

*Third World Debt
and International
Public Policy*

Third World Debt and International Public Policy

Seamus O'Cleireacain

New York
Westport, Connecticut
London

Library of Congress Cataloging-in-Publication Data

O'Cleirceacain, Seamus.
  Third World debt and international public policy / Seamus
O'Cleireacain.
    p.   cm.
  Bibliography: p.
  Includes index.
  ISBN 0–275–92520–X (alk. paper)
  1. Debts, External—Developing countries.   2. Debt relief—
Developing countries.   3. International Monetary Fund.   I. Title.
HJ8899.025   1990
336.3'435'091724—dc20   89–16019

Library of Congress Catalog Card Number: 89–16019
ISBN: 0–275–92520–X

First published in 1990

Praeger Publishers, One Madison Avenue, New York, NY 10010
A division of Greenwood Press, Inc.

Printed in the United States of America

♾

The paper used in this book complies with the
Permanent Paper Standard issued by the National
Information Standards Organization (Z39.48–1984).

10 9 8 7 6 5 4 3 2 1

To those who starve
and to those who die young
because of bad policy or sloppy theory

Contents

Tables

Acknowledgments

What started out as a simple attempt to bring to students of international public policy the links between trade, aid, and debt grew along the way into this lengthy text. In the process there were colleagues whose help I drew on and who directed me to other colleagues as well.

I worked on the manuscript for this book in New York, London, and Tokyo.

Special thanks go to the Japan Center for Economic Research and the generous assistance and kindness of Hisao Kanamori, Tadashi Nakao, and Kureha Hanafusa.

Like other crises before it, the Debt Crisis has spawned a whole industry of researchers. It has been much to my benefit to have received help from many others who were working on various parts of the problem throughout the world.

In particular, I want to thank the following people and their institutions for the assistance they provided to me in finding, unraveling, and interpreting the data. At the InterAmerican Development Bank, Jim Bass, Uziel Nogueira, and Francisco E. Thoumi. At the Board of Governors of the Federal Reserve System, Sandy Clayton, Deborah Danker, Mary McLaughlin, Linda Rosenberg, and Martin Wolfson. At the International Monetary Fund, Peter Keller, Russell Kincaid, and Peter Quirk. At the United Nations Secretariat, Barry Herman. At the World Bank, Eric Manes.

In addition, William Cline of the Institute for International Economics. Thelma Friedes, Librarian SUNY at Purchase. Derek Hargreaves at Morgan Guaranty Trust Company. Ron Helman of the Bildner Center, CUNY Graduate Center. Atsushi Nishimura of the Long Term Credit Bank of Japan. Kohji Okawa of the Industrial Bank of Japan. Eisuke Sakakibara of the Japanese Ministry of Finance. Akira Shigeta of the Japan Bond Research Institute. Hajime Shinohara of the Bank of Tokyo. Toru Yanagihara of the Japan

Institute for Developing Countries. Catherine Valltos of AID. Norbert Wieczorek of the Bundestag, Federal Republic of Germany.

Finally, many thanks for the editorial and production help provided by Carol O'Cleireacain and Carol Thomas.

*Third World Debt
and International
Public Policy*

The Plunge into Debt

The debt crisis of the 1980s presents a fascinating study in international political economy. It also raises some basic questions of international public policy. These include (1) the appropriate development strategies for Third World countries; (2) the role of multilateral lending agencies; and (3) the role of commercial banks as lenders to sovereign governments.

The crisis emerged over a weekend in mid-August 1982, when Mexico informed the United States and the International Monetary Fund (IMF) that it was unable to meet its debt payments. Soon, the crisis had engulfed other developing countries. It stalled forty years of economic growth in the Third World, producing the worse recession in Latin America since the 1930s. As the development process slowed, education and child welfare were among the budget items slashed in many countries, causing UNICEF to include the debt crisis among the factors contributing to a slowing in the decline in infant mortality.[1] UNICEF estimated that the slowdown in development had cost the lives of an additional half-million children, raising to fourteen million the number of under five-year-olds who die every year. The debt crisis also inflicted costs on developed country taxpayers and shareholders.

This book uses a sample of debtor countries to seek to understand the economic forces within developing countries and the external conditions outside that led to the build-up of debt and the inability to carry it.[2]

In doing so, it raises a number of longer-term questions about international public policy, the role of multilateral lending agencies, and the economic policies of developing countries.

A key issue of international public policy is the sustainable level of Third World debt and the appropriate market and nonmarket organs to be responsible for providing that debt. The rising level of developing country external indebtedness since 1980 is detailed in Table 1.1. The table also shows the main sources of financing. One indicator of the growing debt crisis was the number of countries falling into arrears in their external payments. This doubled between 1975 and

1979 even before the mid-August 1982 Mexican difficulties. Close to one third of the members of the international community were in arrears on their payments from 1983 through 1986. By the end of 1987, 56 countries were in arrears.[3] Despite the pervasiveness of arrears, both creditors and debtors avoided declaring debtors in formal default. It was not until 1987 that the first formal default occurred, when North Korea, an insignificant debtor, was declared in default by its creditors.[4] The value of payments in arrears rose rapidly from SDR 5 billion in 1980 to a peak of SDR 45 billion in 1986. Although the number of countries in arrears continued to mount through 1986, the number of them relying on IMF adjustment programs fell continuously after 1983 until rebounding in 1987. Even the IMF found a growing number of its members in arrears. Liberia, Peru, and Sudan were declared ineligible to use the Fund's general resources after they fell into arrears on Fund loans in 1984; Vietnam and Guyana joined them in 1985; Zambia in 1987; Somalia and Sierra Leone in 1988; and Panama in 1989. The World Bank listed a slightly different list of eight countries as in arrears in 1988. They were Guyana, Liberia, Nicaragua, Panama, Peru, Sierra Leone, Syria, and Zambia.[5]

The growth and persistence of arrears reflected the rising burden that debt levied on developing countries' economies. The burden of

Table 1.1   External Debt of Developing Countries, 1980–88 ($ billion)

	1980	1982	1984	1986	1988
Long-term Debt	437	562	687	894	1020
Official Lenders	165	203	238	365	450
Private Lenders	272	359	449	529	770
Short-term Debt	133	169	132	119	140
Use of IMF Credit	9	21	33	40	40
Other*	77	86	81	99	120
Total	656	838	933	1152	1320

Source: World Bank, World Debt Tables various years.

* Other consists of the debt of countries not included in the World Bank's Debtor Reporting System or countries reporting in non-standard forms.

servicing debt increased as interest and principal repayments consumed a rising proportion of the foreign exchange generated by exports. Eventually, in many cases, this burden, which exceeded that of German reparations after World War I, became insupportable. While German reparations payments averaged approximately 14 percent of exports from 1925 to 1931, debt servicing payments during the 1980s consumed between a quarter and a half of debtor country export earnings.[6] Although measures such as the Brady Plan have reduced the size of the annual resource transfers from debtor countries, present payments remain a severe constraint on economic development. Combining adequate growth with debt repayments has emerged as the most severe task facing debtor countries. This is a task from which the rest of the international community cannot remain immune.

WHAT HAPPENED?

In 1970, the total external debt of the Third World was roughly $100 million. By 1988 it was $1.3 trillion. There are serious questions as to how much of this debt was put to good purpose. Future generations in developing countries face the real burden of lower living standards to pay interest on a debt that allowed an earlier generation a short-lived and unsustainable burst of economic growth. Current and future governments face widespread political difficulties as they seek to unwind a debt crisis created by their predecessors and financed by too easy commercial bank credit.

In the years from 1980 through 1987, developing countries paid more than $10.5 trillion in interest on their external debt.[7] Brazil and Mexico paid more than $70 billion each. The twelve largest developing country borrowers paid $325 billion in interest. These are stupendous sums. And they represent interest alone. Since 1984 there has been a real transfer of resources—wealth—from poorer countries to richer ones, from the developing world to the developed world. The cumulative net transfers in the five years from 1984 through 1988 amounted to $143 billion.[8]

Much of the interest paid by debtor countries was paid because governments had preferred to borrow at higher commercial rates from banks rather than from lower cost lending agencies such as the IMF or the World Bank. At times, this avoidance of the lowest cost lenders caused governments to pay as much as eleven additional percentage points for their loans. Some countries borrowed at commercial rates of just under 18 percent in 1981 when IMF rates averaged 7 percent. Why would governments place such additional burdens on their countries? The explanations lie not only in a failure to anticipate the extent to which interest rates could (and would) rise but also in the deteriorating state of relations between sovereign nations and some of the international organizations to which they belong.

From the onset of the first oil shock in 1973 to the debt crisis in 1982, commercial bank lending supplanted lending from traditional multi-lateral lending agencies, for example, the IMF, the World Bank, and regional development banks such as the InterAmerican Development Bank. The crisis of 1982, provoked by this approach, showed the limits of privatization. It had encouraged poor economic policies in the debtor countries and saddled lenders with bad debts and borrowers with unnecessary interest payments. Most tragically, the unwinding of the crisis imposed heavy burdens on citizens of debtor countries.

The era of privatization of international capital flows to developing countries effectively came to an end with the shut-off of credit to most, though not all, of the debtor countries in 1982 and 1983. The years thereafter saw some more money provided by commercial banks, but often only under duress. These years saw a gradual reassertion by the multilateral lending agencies of their traditional roles in funding economic development programs and balance of payments deficits, culminating in the Miyazawa-Brady debt-reduction plan of 1989.

The crisis also had significant effects on the economies of developed countries. Much of the immediate adjustment in debtor country balance of payments disequilibria was accomplished through savage import compression. For example, import restrictions by debtor countries caused a sharp reduction in U.S. exports to Latin America. Between 1981 and 1983, U.S. exports to Latin America fell by 39 percent, dramatically faster than the general decline in U.S. exports from the overvaluation of the dollar. At end-1987, they were still 17 percent below 1981 levels.[9] According to one estimate, the $9 billion decline in U.S. merchandise exports to Latin America between 1981 and 1983 cost the U.S. economy approximately 225,000 jobs in 1982 alone.[10]

The cumulative effect of the changed trade position of debtor countries is illustrated in Table 1.2 for the sample of twenty-four debtor countries used throughout the book. The table shows the cumulative changes from 1980–81 levels in debtor country trade with the United States, the European Community (EC), and Japan. In six years (1982–87), the Major Borrowers reduced their imports from these three groupings by $32 billion, including a $36 billion reduction in imports from the United States. The Heavily Indebted Countries reduced their imports from the three groupings by $161 billion. In this case, the largest reduction was felt by the EC, which experienced a cumulative reduction of $70 billion. But, as the table also shows, the United States is the only one to which both Major Borrowers and

Heavily Indebted Countries increased exports in this period. Falling European and Japanese imports from debtor nations are largely explained by falling oil imports from Indonesia and Nigeria.

CRISIS MANAGEMENT

The years since 1982 were characterized by a large number of ingeniously designed plans to resolve the crisis.[11] By the middle of 1989, only the 1985 Baker Plan, and the 1988–89 Miyazawa-Brady voluntary debt-reduction proposals, stood out. In the interim, debtors and creditors had muddled through, without any agreement on an

Table 1.2 Cumulative Impact on Trade of the Debt Crisis, 1982–87. ($ billion)

	Change in Imports From*:			Change in Exports To*:		
	EC	Japan	US	EC	Japan	US
Major Borrowers	-1.5	5.1	-36.2	15.7	0.3	88.2
Argentina	-9.1	-3.4	-8.6	-2.1	1.0	0.5
Brazil	-3.8	-2.5	-4.8	1.7	1.7	15.7
Chile	-2.1	-2.1	-3.7	-1.2	-0.1	1.9
Egypt	-0.2	0.0	2.8	1.2	0.7	-1.2
India	6.5	3.4	-0.7	3.9	1.2	6.7
Indonesia	0.3	-4.0	-1.3	-1.2	-19.9	-7.5
Israel	6.6	0.7	0.7	-0.5	0.3	5.0
S. Korea	6.0	16.0	8.4	7.0	9.2	36.2
Malaysia	-0.9	0.8	1.8	0.5	4.4	0.1
Mexico	-9.8	-2.9	-25.3	4.4	3.5	28.0
Turkey	8.4	1.1	2.8	9.4	0.2	1.9
Venezuela	-3.4	-2.0	-8.5	-7.4	-2.0	1.0
17 Heavily Indebted Countries**	-70.3	-26.2	-64.2	-19.8	-2.4	16.2
Bolivia	-0.6	-0.3	-0.4	-0.6	-0.1	-0.3
Colombia	-0.3	-0.3	-1.5	0.9	0.1	2.4
Costa Rica	0.0	-0.2	0.0	0.1	0.0	1.0
Côte d'Ivoire	-2.8	-0.2	-0.5	-1.4	0.0	0.6
Ecuador	-0.3	-0.6	-1.3	-0.2	-1.7	3.4
Jamaica	0.2	0.1	0.5	-0.4	0.0	-0.4
Morocco	-1.3	0.1	0.2	-0.4	0.2	0.0
Nigeria	-30.3	-7.8	-3.9	-14.2	-1.3	-39.9
Peru	-1.7	-0.7	-3.2	-0.2	-0.8	-1.6
Philippines	-0.6	-2.8	-1.6	-0.9	-2.9	1.5
Uruguay	-0.9	-0.3	-0.4	-0.6	0.1	1.9
Yugoslavia	-3.7	-0.2	-1.3	2.5	0.0	0.7

Source: IMF, Direction of Trade Statistics Yearbook 1980-86, 1981-87. Data are developed country data. * Total 1982-87 changes compared to 1980-81 averages. ** The 17 Heavily Indebted Countries category includes the following Major Borrowers: Argentina, Brazil, Chile, Mexico and Venezuela.

overarching solution. Their limited success, suggests that a fundamental redesign of the postwar international financial machinery is needed. Too little attention has been paid to the mechanisms that govern resource transfers between developed and developing countries. In particular, the future role of the international lending agencies, established under the Bretton Woods system more than forty years ago, needs to be reexamined. A new burden has been placed on these institutions by the large number of countries unable to convince banks that they are suitable risks for commercial loans.

Although the debt crisis posed a serious threat to the stability of U.S. banks, their share of global commercial bank lending is smaller than we might commonly suppose. Despite hemispheric ties, U.S. banks' exposure in Latin America was only a little in excess of 25 percent of Latin America's total bank debt and about one third its private sector bank debt when the crisis began.[12] Although less than might be expected, this share left U.S. banks quite vulnerable compared to their international competitors. The total exposure of U.S. banks in nonoil exporting developing countries ($107.3 billion in 1982) was 150 percent of their capital. The exposure of the top nine U.S. money center banks amounted to 229 percent of their capital. By the end of 1988, the exposure of the U.S. banking system in nonoil developing countries had been reduced to $72.9 billion, 54 percent of bank capital, while the exposure of the top nine money center banks had been cut to 91 percent of capital.[13] This was the result of new bank lending's having slowed to a trickle and the banks' defensive measures to increase their reserves.

Since 1982, the debt crisis has moved through very distinct stages involving two broad sets of debt renegotiations. For many debtor countries, commercial bank debt has been restructured in several rounds of negotiations between individual governments and steering committees of twelve to fifteen banks representing the several hundred bank members of a typical loan consortium. Debt owed to governments through loans provided under the bilateral foreign aid programs of OECD governments belonging to the Development Assistance Committee (DAC), has been restructured in negotiations between creditor governments and individual debtor governments under the auspices of the Paris Club, a debt renegotiation forum that predates the current crisis.

Stage I of renegotiations consisted of emergency reschedulings. These were replete with considerable central bank arm-twisting of commercial banks to provide additional finance under an IMF "concerted lending" strategy in which all members of a bank consortium would agree to provide new money equiproportionate to their existing exposure. Disbursement of the new money was usually contingent on a debtor country's compliance with the terms of an IMF-supported adjustment program. This strategy combined policy changes in debtor countries with new funds from both the commercial banks and the multilateral lending agencies. On occasion, these funds were preceded by bridging loans from developed (and developing country) central banks or treasuries while more formal arrangements were put in place. Within the debtor countries, there were savage reductions in imports and, often, in living standards.

In 1984, Stage II began with the appearance of multiyear restructuring agreements (MYRAs) and an effort to adopt a medium-term approach to the problem. These negotiations provided a greater lengthening of maturities and reductions in both the country spreads and the bank renegotiation fees that had been charged during the first round of renegotiations. Stage II also coincided with a general decline in interest rates and an emerging bridge between IMF adjustment policies and World Bank development loan approaches.

This bridge was strengthened in Stage III, which may be dated from the U.S. government initiative known as the Baker Plan, introduced at the IMF annual meetings in Seoul in 1985. The Baker Plan sought to construct policies which would allow economic growth to resume in debtor countries. It received a luke-warm reception in debtor countries since the plan did not include debt write-down provisions. The reception from commercial banks was equally chilly as banks resisted providing the new money it called for.

Stage IV, precipitated by Brazil's indefinite suspension of interest payments on $67 billions of bank debt and by the deepening difficulties of the poorest African debtors, began in 1987. It was marked by banks' aggressive build-up of loan-loss provisions and the emergence of some write-offs of official creditor debt. The worldwide banking system had been under threat of a major default since 1982 and had been quietly building up bad debt reserves or writing off loans. But, prior to 1987, the build-up of U.S. bank reserves had been slow. The U.S. banking industry had been in turmoil, coping simultaneously with deregulation of banking practices that had been in place since the aftermath of the Great Depression, a wave of mergers and acquisitions that came to characterize the U.S. economy of the 1980s, and close to 200 bank failures annually. Although these bank failures were mainly confined to small banks and were due to problem domestic loans (in real estate, energy, and agriculture), large money-center banks were not unscathed and several of them collapsed.

The 1987 U.S. banks' decision to reduce profitability sharply by building up loan-loss provisions presaged a hardening of their negotiating stance in the future. It also indicated that the earlier stage centered on the Baker Plan had come to an end. The Baker Plan had been premised on the assumption that considerable new money would be provided by commercial banks to permit debtor countries to "grow out from under" their debt burdens. The banks' decisions of early 1987 signaled that new money would not be forthcoming for a number of countries in arrears on existing loans. By end-1988, commercial bank exposure in developing countries had been reduced through a combination of different economic policies in debtor countries, loan write-offs, swaps, and limitation of new loans to a trickle. Yet, it was clear that further debt reduction would be required if developing countries were to be able to grow and, ultimately, keep repaying. In the United States, the incoming Bush Administration recognized that there was a need to take a fresh look at the US approach to the crisis.

The strengthening of commercial bank balance sheets and the rising threat to democracy in debtor countries laid the ground for Stage V, the Miyazawa-Brady voluntary debt reduction program introduced in 1989. This stage called for close IMF-World Bank cooperation, together with Japanese "parallel financing" to permit debtor countries to reduce their bank debt while providing multilaterally supported interest guarantees to commercial banks for outstanding bank loans.

THE POLITICS OF DEBT

The political nature of the debt crisis has been no less formidable than its economics. It has called into question the ability of a number of international organizations to do their jobs. The years since 1982 have strained the institutional machinery that handles international economic relations. It has shown the limits to cooperation among developed countries, among debtor countries, and between these two blocs. The debtor countries have argued for political rather than economic solutions, with the Cartagena group of Latin American countries in the forefront. However, political solutions still involve resource transfers. As late as mid-1989, all efforts at global political solutions had failed. Such political solutions as had been attempted were often on an ad hoc, temporary basis, such as the original mid-1982 Mexican rescue by the United States. The extra efforts taken by the U.S. administration in this case reflected the political importance of Mexico to the United States.

For the debtor countries, there have been internal political crises. Governments have sought to avoid being unseated as they introduce unpopular austerity measures. The decline in living standards has been drastic in many, though not all, cases. As we shall see, some debtor countries continued to grow. Particularly in Latin America and the Philippines, the crisis coincided with a movement from military (or other) dictatorships to democratic governments. In some instances, the run-up in debt may have resulted when unpopular regimes attempted to buy political support through financing higher living standards than could be achieved from national income. Later, as living standards fell, now largely democratic governments faced an erosion of the political support that had brought them to power.

Although there is a very obvious political dimension to the debt-development dilemma, the crisis remains at heart an economic one: limited resources and the need to make choices. It is, too, the crisis of appropriate economic development strategies in countries with severe income inequalities. By 1987, a letter from the Presidents of the eleven Latin American countries forming the Cartagena Consensus to the seven heads of government of developed countries attending the Venice economic summit suggested that "in all likelihood, Latin America will enter the next decade with a standard of living similar to, or below the levels existing at the beginning of the 1980s."[14] Such was the fearsome price paid for the debt crisis.

Throughout the crisis, a number of countries declared that economic growth would take precedence over repayment of debt. Early declarations were often accompanied by a denunciation of the policies of the IMF. As mentioned earlier, a strategy of using bank credit rather than the IMF produced a situation in which some governments found themselves paying almost 18 percent interest to commercial banks rather than 7 percent to multilateral banks. This is a high price to pay for the protection of national sovereignty which comes from avoiding the more searching questions likely to be asked by the international institutions. The burden imposed by unexpectedly high interest rates and the closing off of alternative financing eventually brought most debtors back to the IMF and IMF-supported adjustment programs. IMF financing of a Brady Plan debt-reduction requires countries to have an IMF arrangement.

The search for economic growth through unsustainable development strategies had been a cause of the crisis. Domestic political pressure to meet immediate needs produced macroeconomic and pricing policies that were inconsistent with stable economic growth in an international environment of volatile interest rates, exchange rates, terms of trade, and incomes. As Eduardo Wiesner, Director of the IMF's Western Hemisphere Department, described it, the debt crisis originated in the internal policies of the debtor countries and was not created by the recessions and high interest rates of the developed countries. Wiesner sees the origins of the crisis in the excessive public and private spending of the debtor countries, and points to the sharp rise in the public sector deficits from 6 percent to 15 percent of GDP between 1979 and 1982 in the three biggest Latin American borrowers.[15] For Wiesner, although the fiscal imbalance became an exchange rate and foreign debt crisis, the public sector deficits that caused them were the outcome of an unresolved political struggle over income shares.

The struggle over income shares is found in all economies and is manifested in part through government spending priorities and tax policies. The debt crisis coincided with an intensification of the ideological battle over the role of the state in furthering economic development. This is a battle over state intervention versus market forces. During the 1980s, the conservative governments of a number of developed countries, particularly the United States, Britain, and Germany, vigorously pushed their point of view in a number of international organizations including the IMF and the World Bank, in regional banks such as the InterAmerican Development Bank, and in the GATT and UN agencies. The network of these agencies, established in the great conferences during and after World War II, is a major component of contemporary international economic relations. There has been from the beginning a tension in the charters or articles of agreement of these organizations between reliance on market forces or state intervention.

The postcolonial era has seen the membership of these organizations grow from a cozy group of highly developed countries to a diverse membership similar to that of the UN. The resurgence of the defeated nations of World War II altered the balance of power among the developed country members within these organizations. With changes in membership came changes in prevailing opinions concerning the policies of members. In the case of the IMF, there has been a heightening of a debate over the appropriateness of IMF policies when applied to developing countries. In the case of the GATT, developing countries complain about developed country protectionism while developed countries respond in kind, attacking the willingness of developing countries to hide behind special exceptions which grant them GATT privileges without GATT responsibilities. Several of these struggles have influenced attitudes on how individual countries, as well as international organizations, should respond to the debt crisis.

There have been a number of more short-term battles directly related to the debt crisis. Several of these have involved battles over burden sharing. The variety of debt renegotiations has displayed the relative bargaining powers of sovereign debtors when arrayed against either banks or official creditors. There will be continuing debt even after the debt crisis has been resolved. The obvious battle between debtor governments and commercial banks over the terms of debt restructurings has occurred within a larger interbank struggle for survival in an era of crumbling capital controls, global financial markets, and a wave of mergers and acquisitions.

SOME QUESTIONS

The experience with the debt crisis raises a number of obvious questions. Did the fault lie with developing country governments that pursued unsustainable domestic economic policies fated to grind to a halt when the funding dried up? Or with young commercial bank lending officers possessed of little or no country experience, whose career advancement depended on the volume of loans placed in an era of explosive international lending and who hoped to be well up the corporate ladder before loans went sour?

How much of what happened was the result of vulnerable economies receiving two oil shocks in the 1970s, an interest rate shock, and a savage deterioration in the terms of trade? How different would things have turned out if Third World governments had resisted the blandishments of commercial bank loan officers and relied instead on the old-line multilateral lending agencies such as the IMF and the World Bank, with their relatively fixed rate loans?

To what extent did the dismal growth experience, growing protectionist mood, and monetarist policies of developed economies contribute to the onset of the crisis and delay resolutions of the crisis? Are the conditions attached to IMF loans unreasonable, ineffective, impractical, wrong? In getting out of the debt crisis, how much of the burden should fall on the taxpayers of developed countries, on the shareholders of commercial banks, on the citizens (and particularly the poor) of the heavily indebted developing countries? And finally, in a period in which democracy is on the resurgence in much of Latin America, to what extent should special efforts be made to resolve the crisis in a way that does not destroy the political base of fledgling democratic governments?

The chapters that follow seek to help the reader answer these questions. They are organized into three main sections, the theoretical underpinnings that link economic development, trade, and macroeconomic policy; factors external to the developing world that contributed to the crisis; and responses to and failures to end the debt crisis.

Chapters 2, 3, and 4 provide the theoretical underpinnings for the subsequent discussion. A particular effort is made to place the causes of the debt crisis within the wider context of the choices governments face in development strategy and in open economy macroeconomic policy. Chapter 2 sketches the main forces at work on a country's balance of payments and shows how indebtedness grows. Chapter 3 is concerned with the role of debt in financing economic development. Chapter 4 surveys established theory on lending and credit limits.

The theoretical section is followed by a section examining some proximate factors that contributed to the debt crisis. Chapter 5 provides estimates of the relative importance of a number of external shocks facing all economies since the 1973 oil shock. These shocks are commonly mentioned as major causes of growing indebtedness in a large number of studies. Chapters 6 and 7 focus on the changing relationship between governments and multilateral lending agencies, particularly the IMF. Chapter 6 describes the evolution of the international financial system over the past forty years, concentrating on changes in the roles of the IMF, the World Bank, and the regional development banks. It is followed by a closer look at the theory and practice of conditional lending pursued by the Fund and the Bank. Chapter 7 examines the success of IMF conditionality, which has long been controversial and is often seen as a major reason why developing countries turned from reliance on multilateral lending to borrowing variable rate loans from commercial banks.[16]

The final section of the book focuses on the responses to the crisis since 1982. Chapter 8 examines the adjustment that has occurred within debtor countries. Chapter 9 looks at the response of the United States, separating the response of the government from that of commercial banks. Chapter 10 outlines the changing terms of restructuring agreements, debt reduction methods, and the changing attitudes of debtor countries and creditor banks. The final chapter contains some thoughts on future prospects.

NOTES

1. UNICEF, *The State of the World's Children 1989* (New York: United Nations, 1988).

2. This sample comprises two categories used by the World Bank: the twelve "Major Borrowers," each with long-term debt in excess of $17 billion each at the end of 1985; and seventeen "Highly Indebted Countries," commonly termed the "Baker 17" because they were to benefit from the so-called "Baker Plan." This latter category includes a number of Major Borrowers. The two groups account for almost half of all developing country debt.

3. IMF, *Annual Report on Exchange Arrangements and Exchange Restrictions, 1987*, pp. 17–18. Arrears on external payments are not restricted to debt arrears but include a variety of payments difficulties.

4. Nicholas D. Kristof, "North Korea, in Default, Said to Relent on Debt," *New York Times*, September 17, 1987, p. D18.

5. World Bank, *Annual Report 1988*, p. 173.

6. C. R. S. Harris, *Germany's Foreign Indebtedness*, 1935, reprinted (New York: Anno Press, 1978) reported by Arminio Fraga, *German Reparations and Brazilian Debt: A Comparative Study*, International Finance Section, Princeton Essays in International Finance No. 163, July 1986, p. 20.

7. World Bank, *World Debt Tables 1988–89*, Vol. I, p. 2, and author's estimates of payments on short-term debt.

8. World Bank, *World Debt Tables 1988–89*, p. xii.

9. IMF, *Direction of Trade Statistics Yearbook 1981–87*, p. 407.

10. Dhar Sanjay, "US Trade with Latin America: Consequences of Financing Constraints," in Federal Reserve Bank of New York, *Quarterly Bulletin*, Autumn 1983, pp. 14–8.

11. See William R. Cline, *Mobilizing Bank Lending to Debtor Countries* (Washington, D.C.: Institute for International Economics, June 1987), Appendix B, for a summary of proposals.

12. Department of State, *Report to Congress on Foreign Debt in Latin America*, December 1985, Table 4.

13. United States Federal Financial Institutions Examination Council, *Country Exposure Lending Survey, Statistical Release E 16 (126)*, various years.

14. Reprinted in *Capitulos del SELA*, No. 16, April/June 1987, pp. 75–76.

15. Eduardo Wiesner, "Latin American Debt: Lessons and Pending Issues," *American Economic Review*, Vol. 75, No. 2 (May 1985), pp. 191–95.

16. IMF interest rates are adjusted from year to year. World Bank loans have carried variable rates since 1982.

2

Debt and the Balance of Payments

Today's Third World debt is the result of a need to finance past balance of payments deficits. This chapter examines the relationship between annual balance of payments flows and the stock of indebtedness.[1] After establishing a conceptual framework, the chapter concentrates on three of the main sources of demand for foreign borrowing: current account deficits, the accumulation of domestically held foreign exchange, and capital flight. The chapter's analysis is static, stressing a number of basic balance of payments and national accounting identities. These will be placed in the more dynamic context of development strategy in Chapter 3.

The chapter is organized as follows: after some brief remarks on the supply of credit, a conventional treatment of relationships among components of the balance of payments is provided. This is followed by a closer look at the financing alternatives available for deficits in the current account. Attention is then directed to the three sources of demand for debt mentioned above, with separate sections devoted to the demands for current account financing, borrowed reserves, and capital flight. Capital flight receives an extensive treatment as numerous studies have shown that it was a major contributory factor in the debt difficulties of a number of countries. Capital flight is also a useful yardstick against which to evaluate domestic economic policies.

THE SUPPLY OF DEBT

A precursor of the debt crisis was the change in the mix of financing flows between commercial banks and multilateral lending agencies. While the Fund, the Bank, and other multilateral agencies had dominated Third World financing in the period up to the mid-1970s, the commercial bank liquidity created by OPEC petrodollar deposits produced a reversal of roles from then onward. As developing countries shifted the public/private mix of their financing flows toward greater reliance on private short-term variable interest-rate loans, and away from multilateral lending sources, the international trade and payments system was subjected to some additional shocks that might have been avoided.

The bulk of the stock of debt owed by developing countries is a mix of debt owed to the world's commercial banks, to developed country governments, and to multilateral lending agencies. The latter is provided at below-market interest rates but with explicit strings attached in the review of loan applications. Traditionally, less strings were attached to commercial bank lending although the need to maintain acceptable international credit ratings has always imposed some restrictions on a country's long-run choice of economic policies. With the emergence of the debt crisis, debtor countries found the disparity between commercial bank conditionality and multilateral agency conditionality drastically narrowed.

In contrast to voluntary commercial bank lending, the flows of financing provided by international agencies, are, in some sense, a "club" response to ensure the continued provision of a public good. This public good may be viewed as a smoothly functioning international trade and payments system. Some public sector financing flows, such as foreign aid and export credit, are available at the bilateral level. There is also a small amount of hybrid financing involving the joint participation of the private sector and multilateral agencies. Perhaps the most significant hybrid financing of recent years has been the "concerted lending" of a number of debt restructurings in which commercial banks were forced to make new loans side by side with credit extended by multilateral agencies. A growing source of hybrid financing is the co-financing schemes of the World Bank.

Developed country monetary policy influences the supply of private credit flows internationally just as it does domestically. This was particularly evident in the recycling of petrodollars during a time of depressed demand for money in OECD countries in the aftermath of the first oil shock of 1973–74. Flush with OPEC dollar and sterling deposits, developed country commercial banks faced very depressed loan demand at home because of recessions induced by the oil shock. They responded by moving their loan sales forces toward the market where loan demand was strong—developing countries with persistent current account deficits. In some instances these deficits were the result of the absence of energy conservation programs. At the time, the commissions and spreads on loans to developing countries appeared to make this lending very lucrative. Few conditions were attached by the lenders.

Public sector lending, on the other hand, particularly lending by multilateral lending agencies, is driven by political rather than commercial factors. A political process in developed countries determines the lending capacities of such agencies as the International Monetary Fund (IMF); the World Bank, more formally known as the International Bank for Reconstruction and Development (IBRD); the International Development Association (a soft loan subsidiary of the World Bank), or regional multilateral lending agencies such as the Inter-American Development Bank (IDB). The periodic replenishment of these agencies and the increases in the capital of both the Bank and the Fund occur only after intense negotiation, not only among developed countries, but also between developed and developing countries.

In addition to determining the overall lending capacities of these agencies, political considerations also influence the size and direction of these noncommercial flows. Particularly in the case of the IMF, domestic political considerations sometimes prevent governments from adopting the economic policies necessary to obtain Fund approval of loans to which members are otherwise entitled. In the case of the development agencies, the disbursement of funds is also not completely free of political influence. Disbursement may be prevented or delayed indefinitely by the threat of a veto on the part of a country or group of countries possessing veto power in the weighted voting arrangements of the Executive Boards of the agencies. With these reservations, it is probably fair to say that once overall agency lending limits are established, multilateral agency lending is a long way from being as political as might be envisaged. Technical considerations dominate staff analyses of loan applications. But, as we shall see in later chapters, the technical criteria by which loan applications are judged are often the subject of political debate.

THE BALANCE OF PAYMENTS

The build-up of a stock of external indebtedness occurs through annual flows of borrowing.[2] These flows are reflected in a country's balance of payments. At any time, a country's indebtedness represents the summation of its history of balance of payments deficits (including interest on the outstanding debt) in the same manner that a country's domestic national debt represents the summation of its history of government budget deficits. In seeking explanations of how a country's foreign indebtedness grew, or how to cope with it, it is necessary to analyze balance of payments flows. This section examines some of the fundamental tautologies of balance of payments accounting.

The basic identity of the balance of payments (BOP) consists of four fundamental elements, two involving trade and two involving capital flows—exports (X) and imports (M); capital inflows (K_{in}) and capital outflows (K_{out}). The total of these four determines what happens to a country's exchange rate or, if the exchange rate is fixed, what happens to the country's reserves of foreign exchange. The change in reserves will be denoted by $\dot{R}$.

$$BOP: X - M + K_{in} - K_{out} = \dot{R} \tag{2.1}$$

Exports and capital inflows earn foreign exchange for a country. Imports and capital outflows deplete foreign exchange. If the sum of the four items is negative, that is, if there is a balance of payments deficit, the central bank's net holdings of foreign exchange must decline by the amount of the deficit, or the exchange rate must fall.

The limit on a country's ability to continue *financing* balance of payments deficits is set by its initial level of reserves, its ability to borrow reserves, and the lower limit to which it is prepared to see these fall. At some point, when reserves have fallen low enough and poor creditworthiness rules out further borrowing to bolster reserves, financing the balance of payments disequilibrium becomes impossible and steps must be taken to *correct* it. This is accomplished by policies that influence the four components of the identity in equation 2.1 above. The policies may include adoption of a more realistic exchange rate.

The balance of payments (equation 2.1) may be rearranged to reflect a number of other definitions. For example, the current account (CA) of the balance of payments consists of total trade in goods and services. Services include net factor income, which includes income earned on investments.

$$X - M = CA \tag{2.2}$$

Similarly, the net capital flow component of the balance of payments is the balance on the capital account (KA).

$$K_{in} - K_{out} = KA \tag{2.3}$$

Thus, in the case of a fixed exchange rate,

$$BOP: CA + KA = \dot{R} \tag{2.4}$$

The four elements of the balance of payments may be arranged in a variety of configurations to produce overall payments surplus, deficit, or equilibrium. A current account deficit need not produce a balance of payments deficit if it is offset by a capital account surplus.

Let us look a little more closely at the capital account of the balance of payments. The following analysis will assume a fixed exchange rate. Capital inflows may be short term or long term. The latter may consist of direct private investment or of portfolio investment. Direct private investment inflows represent the purchase or creation of non-financial assets such as factories, mines and so forth. In general, portfolio investment in developing countries is very small because of their limited capital markets, but it is a growing source of interest. Portfolio capital inflows involve the sale of domestic financial assets for foreign exchange and an increase in net foreign claims. Except in the case of equity investment flows, the domestic assets sold will involve borrowing. The sale of such financial assets as government securities obviously involves borrowing. Both private sector and public sector borrowing may also occur through a variety of other forms of loan agreements. Public sector borrowing may include borrowing for the purpose of bolstering foreign exchange reserves. In summary,

$$K_{in} = DPI + B \tag{2.5}$$

where DPI is direct private investment, and B is borrowing.

Capital inflows have their counterparts on the other side of the capital account. When the two sides of the capital account are netted out, yielding net capital inflows (negative if net outflows),

$$Net\ K_{in} = net\ DPI + net\ Borrowing \tag{2.6}$$

and from equation,

$$Net\ K_{in} = \dot{R} - (X - M) \tag{2.7}$$

Therefore,

$$Net\ Borrowing = \dot{R} - (X - M) - net\ DPI \tag{2.8}$$

This last equation shows that, with a fixed exchange rate, borrowing builds up reserves, finances a current account deficit, finances private capital outflows, or finances some combination of all three. The level of outstanding debt will represent the accumulation of borrowing over a number of years, that is, the cumulative impact of efforts at reserve build-up, of current account deficits, and of capital outflows. These three factors may be reduced to two: current account deficits and the accumulation of foreign assets. The accumulation of foreign assets may occur through the public or private sectors. Public sector accumulation will include central bank accumulation of foreign exchange reserves. Private sector accumulation will include capital flight.

The preceding has merely established an accounting framework. It has shown that a search for explanations of why some countries have heavy indebtedness, and others do not, must begin with the balance of payments and the policies that influence reserves, current account deficits, and capital outflows. At its most basic level, the debt crisis is the result of the manner in which these three were allowed to develop over a period of years.

CURRENT ACCOUNT DEFICITS

Typically, developing country balance of payments deficits have their origin in current account deficits. At early stages of economic development, countries usually have structural trade deficits requiring financing through the savings of the rest of the world. The limit on a country's ability to continue financing a current account deficit, without altering its exchange rate or other policies, depends on both the size of its net capital inflows and on the lower limit to which it is prepared to let its foreign exchange reserves fall. Because net capital inflows consist of gross capital inflows minus gross capital outflows, the borrowing accompanying net capital inflows may be reduced to the extent that a country is able to attract direct foreign investment or equity investment, or to attract home capital flight.

Direct foreign investment usually means multinational corporation investment. Many governments have been reluctant to produce the conditions that would encourage it, fearing the loss of sovereignty as more control of the domestic economy passes into foreign hands. From the corporate viewpoint, the bulk of LDCs have economies that are too regulated and too lacking in market processes to be attractive to firms seeking offshore assembly locations. As a result, direct private investment inflows are a relative rarity for many developing countries. For those countries that have actively sought it, the international competition among governments for such investment is particularly intense. Extremely generous tax and financing incentives are offered to corporations in an effort to attract jobs. In a world of no easy choices, the perceived costs of permitting the operations of multinationals may be avoided only by accepting the alternative costs of higher indebtedness and lost income and employment opportunities.

Although current account deficits may be financed through net capital inflows, there is a limit on the debt component of these inflows.

A continual stream of annual current account deficits, which require financing through annual additions to the existing stock of foreign indebtedness, will become unsustainable if the annual interest payments on the debt use up too much of the foreign exchange that has been earned by exports. The ratio of debt service charges to export earnings is a critical guideline used by international creditors to decide whether or not a country has reached the limit of its debt servicing capacity. As a number of countries discovered, once a country has been perceived to reach this limit, the required changes in its current account will be as abrupt and drastic as if its central bank had run out of foreign exchange. The exact relationship between interest payments, export earnings, and debt dynamics will be examined with greater detail in Chapter 3.

There is a close connection between current account deficits and the factors influencing the internal economy. Export flows represent domestic production not absorbed at home. Import flows represent domestic absorption without domestic production. These relationships may be expressed in terms of the fundamental equilibrium condition that injections to aggregate demand equal leakages from it, that is,

$$X + I + G = M + S + T \qquad (2.9)$$

where X = exports, I = investment, G = government spending, M = imports, S = savings, T = taxes.

This may be rewritten as:

$$(X - M) = (S + T) - (G + I) \qquad (2.10)$$

or

$$(X - M) = (S - I) + (T - G) \qquad (2.11)$$

Equation 2.11 shows that a current account deficit has a counterpart in either insufficient domestic savings and/or a fiscal deficit. A current account disequilibrium cannot exist unless there is simultaneously a disequilibrium in the domestic sector of the economy. Twenty years ago economists developed "two-gap models" using expressions similar to equation 2.9. This literature posited that developing countries faced a foreign exchange gap and a savings gap and that both gaps needed to be closed by capital inflows to ensure economic growth. Insofar as borrowing is the result of a need to finance a current account deficit, equations 2.10 and 2.11 show that the deficit, and the consequent need to borrow, will continue as long as the sum of investment and government spending exceeds the sum of the savings generated domestically, either voluntarily (savings) or forced (taxes). If the private sector generates *net* savings, that is, if private savings exceed private investment, equation 2.11 shows that a current account deficit will occur if the public sector deficit exceeds the private sector's net savings. If domestic savings is less than investment, the financing of a budget deficit cannot be accomplished through borrowing at home, but requires borrowing abroad.

Annual domestic savings shortfalls and budget deficits will continue to be mirrored in ongoing current account deficits and, *ceteris paribus*, will produce a continuing need to borrow. Each year's incremental borrowing adds to the total stock of external indebtedness. To prevent the debt from *growing*, a year must pass in which there is no current account deficit. It is not necessary that budgets be balanced to obtain a current account balance. Equation 2.11 shows that a budget deficit is consistent with a balanced current account as long as the budget deficit has a counterpart in a surplus of domestic savings over investment. As Harry Johnson showed thirty years ago, to remove a current account deficit, domestic absorption must be brought down to the level of domestic production while production must be switched from domestic uses to exports and consumption must be switched from consumption of imports to consumption of home goods.[3] We shall see in subsequent chapters that the fierce debates over IMF "conditionality" have ultimately been debates over which policy instruments most appropriately are to be used for this purpose.

At the macroeconomic level, economic policy influences the current account balance through the impact of monetary and fiscal policy, the real exchange rate, and expectations about the future. Monetary and fiscal policy directly affect the level of GNP and hence imports. Monetary and fiscal policy also influence nominal interest rates, actual and expected inflation, and hence real interest rates. Differentials between domestic risk-adjusted real interest rates and world real interest rates influence the current account through their effects on domestic savings and investment and hence on overall economic activity. For a given level of activity, the real exchange rate is an important determinant of the split between absorption of domestic and foreign goods.

From the above, it is apparent that among the factors that will cause a current account deficit and a resultant increased indebtedness will be a high rate of inflation without an offsetting depreciation of the nominal exchange rate and increase in nominal interest rates; anticipation of a nominal devaluation; and increases in real GNP in an economy whose economic structure causes imports to outpace exports. These three possible explanations of persistent current account deficits, and resulting possible persistent needs to borrow, involve inappropriate levels of the real interest rate or real exchange rate in the first two instances and economic structure in the third case. Of course, a structuralist view of economic development may conclude that deficits produced by a combination of overvalued real exchange rates and low or negative real interest rates are also structural in character and that it may be naive to expect governments not to run deficits and to expect low income countries to finance domestic investment out of domestic savings.

A number of interested groups may wish to view current account deficits as structural in nature and not amenable to correction through short- or medium-term policy changes. These groups will include incumbent governments afraid of the political backlash from unpopular policies, trade unions opposed to the reduction in real wages produced by anti-inflation programs, those who face increased taxation, beneficiaries of government spending programs (the military as well as those benefiting from such programs as food subsidies), and, finally, business groups who fear reductions in profits from the dislocation of the inflationary status quo.

This is a rather formidable list of interest groups. Many may prefer a continuation of the current account deficit and its financing through an increase in external indebtedness. In searching for arguments to bolster their opposition to measures aimed at correcting current account deficits, these groups turn naturally to those analysts whose training makes them most amenable to viewing all deficits as structural in nature. Although some economists may show that Latin America's surreal inflation rates are directly the result of irresponsible rates of monetary expansion, for many, the implication that a noninflationary development path is readily available if only Latin American central bankers would slow down their printing presses flies in the face of social and political reality on that continent.

Some of the current account deficits of the countries that went on to experience debt difficulties stemmed from their response to the oil shocks of 1973–74 and 1979. In an era of North-South economic confrontation, the two oil shocks were hailed by oil-importing developing countries as an example of the new-found muscle of primary producers, even as their own import bills were raised, laying the foundations for later debt difficulties. Of course, the debt difficulties of oil-exporters such as Mexico, Nigeria, and Venezuela have other roots.

In the aftermath to the first oil shock, overall domestic consumption was not reduced immediately within the oil-importing developing countries to reflect the need to switch more domestic output into exports to pay for each barrel of oil. Living standards and consumption patterns were kept high through borrowing, mirroring the shortfall of savings relative to investment. At the same time, in an effort to shield the poor from the inflationary effects of the increase in the world price of oil, domestic energy prices were kept artificially low. Conservation was limited. In countries where oil retailing was in the hands of a state-owned energy utility, the difference between the domestic currency equivalent of the price paid for oil and that received from consumers was met from the government budget. However, because world oil prices are set in hard currency, usually dollars, the need to borrow abroad in key currencies to pay for dollar-invoiced oil, increased. When the second oil shock occurred in 1979, oil-importing developing countries were finally forced to follow the pattern already adopted by the oil-importing developed countries. Adjustment to an energy-scarce world required policies that would end the annual borrowing to pay for oil.

Borrowing to finance current account deficits is the main reason for foreign borrowing by developing countries. Few non-oil producing developing countries earn current account surpluses with any regularity. In a sample of 74 developing countries other than high-income oil exporters, only 6 reported a current account surplus in 1983. They were China, Chad, Panama, Uruguay, Yugoslavia, and Venezuela (an oil exporter).[4] Table 2.1 gives some indication of the role of recurrent merchandise trade deficits or current account deficits in the run-up of debt between 1974 and 1982.

The stock of debt that had been amassed by 1982 represented, in part, the cumulative need to finance earlier years of current account deficits. As Table 2.1 shows, the cumulative merchandise trade deficits of the Major Borrowers between 1974 and 1982 amounted to $64 billion, while their cumulative current account deficits totaled $222 billion. Comparable figures for the group of 17 Heavily Indebted Countries were $19 billion and $227 billion. The trade deficit totals for both groups are lowered by the cumulative trade surpluses run by net petroleum exporters as well as surpluses run by Argentina, Bolivia, the Côte d'Ivoire, and Malaysia. Among the Major Borrowers, countries that ran cumulative trade deficits actually amassed a total of $152 billion in deficits over the period. In the absence of other factors, these cumulative deficits would require an equal amount of financing, producing a growth in external indebtedness. The totals for the current account deficits in Table 2.1 include the effects of interest payments on existing debt as well as invisible trade. As the current account totals show, Venezuela was the only one of the 24 countries to avoid the need to finance a cumulative current account deficit over the period. For the Major Borrowers as a group, the financing needs

Table 2.1 Cumulative Deficits, 1974–82   ($ billion)

	Current Account	Trade Balance
Major Borrowers	-222.4	-63.7
Argentina	-9.9	10.0
Brazil	-84.6	-15.5
Chile	-12.5	-3.2
Egypt	-10.2	-24.9
India	-1.5	-18.5
Indonesia	-4.9	35.6
Israel	-10.0	-26.5
S. Korea	-22.1	-21.5
Malaysia	-5.4	9.8
Mexico	-49.1	-14.1
Turkey	-16.3	-27.6
Venezuela	4.1	32.6
17 Heavily Indebted Countries*	-227.4	-18.7
Bolivia	-1.5	1.0
Colombia	-4.5	-1.6
Costa Rica	-3.2	-1.4
Côte d'Ivoire	-7.3	4.4
Ecuador	-4.7	1.1
Jamaica	-1.8	-1.1
Morocco	-11.6	-10.5
Nigeria	-6.9	26.6
Peru	-7.1	-0.9
Philippines	-12.8	-13.2
Uruguay	-2.4	-1.4
Yugoslavia	-11.4	-31.7

Source: IMF, International Financial Statistics Yearbook 1986 and IFS, May 1988.   * The 17 Heavily Indebted Countries category includes Argentina, Brazil, Chile, Mexico and Venezuela.

produced by their current account deficits were triple the financing needs produced by trade deficits.

RESERVE BUILD-UPS

A second source of demand for foreign loans originates in the search of central banks for larger reserves of foreign exchange. Instead of viewing changes in reserves as a residual, determined by balance of payments flows, an alternative approach would consider them to be a target of policymakers. From this vantage, central bankers are concerned with holding an optimal level of reserves and an optimal mix of currencies, and may borrow to achieve their objectives.

Since the 1973 collapse of the Bretton Woods exchange-rate regime produced floating exchange rates, central bankers have become much more active managers of both the level and currency composition of their foreign exchange reserves. They have also become more active managers of their liabilities. Traditionally held in the form of gold and dollars, reserves now held by central banks consist of a much wider mix of currencies as central bankers hedge against the exchange risk associated with holding only one currency.

A central bank's reserves of foreign exchange may be seen as a cushion permitting a country to run balance of payments deficits while avoiding policies that would correct the deficit. Reserves are also a cushion against temporary balance of payments disequilibria, such as shortfalls in export earnings through crop failures or sudden changes in world prices of commodities. As a cushion, they act as a buffer between the domestic economy and shocks to the balance of payments.

A major cost attached to build-up of reserves consists of the imports foregone from not using the foreign exchange. Therefore, the optimal level of reserves depends on the amplitude of fluctuations in export earnings and on the costs to the economy if it is forced to adjust suddenly to a lower level of imports. The gain, or return on having adequate reserves, may be measured by the forced reduction in GNP which would have occurred from export shortfalls in the absence of adequate reserves. This implicit rate of return on reserves may then be compared with the cost of borrowing.[5]

Ideally, reserves should be borrowed only if the interest cost of the borrowing is less than the benefits gained through postponement of the internal adjustments that a balance of payment disequilibrium would otherwise require. These benefits are both economic and political. Governments have an obvious interest in being able to postpone taking the unpopular actions needed to correct a balance of payments disequilibrium, especially if the disequilibrium is temporary and reversible.

Prior to the debt crisis, some central banks of developing countries took advantage of declines in world interest rates to build up reserves through borrowing. In most cases, the optimal level of reserves appropriate for a developing country is likely to be extremely low. Countries with low levels of per capita income cannot afford to tie up reserves in any form of savings, domestic or foreign exchange. Furthermore, for countries with extremely poor international credit ratings, the risk premium on borrowing will be very high. Accordingly, it might be expected that only a very limited number of developing countries will have engaged in international borrowing for the purpose of building up reserves to socially optimal levels. It is more likely that some governments borrowed reserves in the 1970s and early 1980s to avoid the political costs to themselves of balance-of-payments adjustment programs.

Foreign exchange reserve levels may be viewed as a policy target of policymakers rather than as a residual determined by the balance-of-payments consequences of other policies. Because the primary role of reserves is to finance balance of payment deficits, a commonly used yardstick of reserve adequacy is the number of months of imports that could be sustained by reserves. Such a calculation gives some indication of how long an economy can endure disruption to export earnings without requiring a cutback in imports and the associated disruptions of the domestic economy. In a less extreme example, the calculation provides useful information on the adequacy of reserves to cope with fluctuations in export earnings. Table 2.2 provides some data on international differences in reserve levels. It shows, with only a few exceptions, the run-up in reserves of the late 1970s before their depletion in the 1980s.

CAPITAL OUTFLOW

A third demand for foreign borrowing is the result of capital flight. Borrowing to compensate for capital flight was an integral part of the Bretton Woods exchange-rate regime long before the Third World debt crisis. The network of swap arrangements among the major developed country central banks is but one example. There is no parallel developing country network yet, though Mexico has a swap arrangement with the United States. The developed country swap network was designed to provide short-term borrowing when a country's exchange rate comes under pressure from speculative selling flows of short-term capital. The capital outflow problem of developing countries is not a short-run problem. It is considerably more endemic and has assumed major proportions in some instances.

The issue of capital flight from developing countries and the extent to which it contributed to the debt crisis are fraught with political as well as measurement problems. Disputes over the impact of capital flight are, at heart, disputes over income and wealth distribution, and, of course, the distribution of political power. For some, capital flight is antisocial; for others it is a discipline on irresponsible government policies. Government officials condemn the flight as starving the country of scarce resources that might contribute to national development; those engaging in flight see their actions as protection from

Table 2.2 Foreign Exchange Reserves Expressed in Months of Imports, 1975–87

	1975	1978	1980	1981	1982	1983	1984	1985	1986	1987
Major Borrowers										
Argentina	2.1	11.8	6.6	3.5	4.3	2.7	2.5	4.9	4.5	3.5
Brazil	2.9	6.8	2.3	2.3	1.2	1.7	4.7	4.7	2.7	3.0
Chile	1.2	4.0	5.9	4.5	4.1	5.2	4.8	5.8	5.4	5.2
Egypt	1.2	1.9	2.2	1.5	1.5	1.2	1.0	1.1	1.5	2.0
India	3.9	10.6	8.1	5.5	5.8	5.5	5.4	5.5	6.0	5.9
Indonesia	0.9	2.5	4.2	2.9	2.0	2.2	2.8	3.2	3.1	3.9
Israel	2.1	3.6	3.6	3.2	3.5	3.2	2.7	3.3	3.9	3.9
S.Korea	1.2	1.8	1.3	1.0	1.1	0.9	1.0	1.0	1.1	0.9
Malaysia	4.2	5.3	4.6	3.7	3.2	2.8	2.6	3.7	5.1	5.5
Mexico	2.2	1.8	1.5	1.3	0.6	2.4	3.4	2.3	3.1	6.2
Turkey	3.3	3.8	4.3	2.8	3.0	2.8	2.2	1.9	2.5	2.4
Venezuela	15.4	6.4	9.4	7.6	6.0	11.3	11.1	12.3	10.0	10.6
17 Highly Indebted Countries*										
Bolivia	3.7	3.6	6.0	3.4	6.0	5.4	5.8	5.4	5.3	5.2
Colombia	3.2	8.7	12.5	10.1	8.2	5.8	3.0	3.8	5.9	5.2
Costa Rica	0.8	1.8	1.2	1.0	2.1	2.7	3.1	3.9	3.9	3.3
Côte d'Ivoire	0.7	1.6	0.1	0.1	0.1	0.1	0.1	0.1	0.1	0.1
Ecuador	2.7	3.5	4.1	2.4	1.5	3.5	2.8	3.1	3.0	2.4
Jamaica	1.1	0.6	0.8	0.5	0.7	0.4	0.7	1.1	0.7	1.1
Morocco	1.7	2.2	1.7	1.0	1.1	0.9	0.6	0.8	1.1	1.6
Nigeria	7.6	1.6	5.8	2.0	1.2	1.0	1.7	2.0	2.5	2.3
Peru	2.1	2.8	6.8	3.4	4.0	4.6	5.7	7.5	6.0	3.2
Philippines	4.0	4.0	4.6	2.9	1.8	0.9	1.0	1.6	3.9	2.7
Uruguay	8.9	13.2	12.5	9.2	8.8	9.3	7.5	8.5	11.8	12.0
Yugoslavia	1.4	2.5	1.5	1.3	1.0	1.2	1.2	1.3	1.4	1.2

Source: IBRD, World Debt Tables 1988-89, 1986-87. * The 17 Highly Indebted Countries category includes the following Major Borrowers: Argentina, Brazil, Chile, Mexico, and Venezuela.

particular government policies that they view as antisocial. Opponents of incumbent governments point to capital flight as indicators of loss of confidence in government policies; incumbent governments point to capital flight as the unpatriotic response of its opponents. What is capital flight to one observer is international diversification of portfolios to another.

Borrowing to offset the exchange rate or balance-of-payments effects of capital flight appears to involve an increase in national indebtedness to compensate for what some will see as the antisocial act of capital flight. However, because capital flight by residents involves the acquisition of foreign-denominated assets, these assets offset the increased liabilities that occur with borrowing. Thus, no increase in *national* indebtedness is necessary. However, public sector foreign liabilities increase to finance the larger private sector foreign assets.

Capital flight has damaged the credibility of a number of debtor country governments. Developed country commercial bankers participating in debt renegotiations have argued that they should not be expected to provide new lending to countries that cannot even persuade their own citizens to repatriate their savings. Although the term "capital flight" evokes images of capital leaving countries, in many instances the "flight" consists of not repatriating income that has been earned abroad. In some middle-class instances of "capital flight," consulting fees earned by professionals during overseas stays are deposited in foreign bank accounts for use during subsequent trips abroad.

Capital flows are motivated by relative post-tax real rates of return. Although governments may attempt to ignore the extent to which their policies produce gaping disparities in real rates of return, the growth of international banking in the past twenty years has made it easier for private citizens around the planet to take advantage of these disparities. Because relative post-tax real rates of return are an amalgam of domestic and foreign tax rates, nominal interest rates, inflation rates, and expected depreciation rates, a variety of policies induce capital flight.

Policies that produce expectations of high domestic inflation without corresponding changes in the nominal exchange rate will lead to capital flight. Inflation produces automatic reductions in the value of assets that are denominated in national currency. It is also often accompanied by negative interest rates; that is, the real income stream produced by these assets is negative. The erosion in international competitiveness produced by domestic inflation ultimately requires a devaluation of the exchange rate to restore competitiveness. This devaluation will produce a foreign-currency capital loss for domestic currency–denominated assets and a domestic currency capital gain for foreign currency–denominated assets.

Large budget deficits and a reduction in the ability to rely on external financing for budget deficits clearly presage either tax increases or inflationary increases in money growth to finance the deficits. Domestic asset holders can easily see the future implications for any assets not moved out of the reach of the future inflation or taxation. Capital flight may be illegal in some countries, but it is not irrational. The effects of overvalued exchange rates, negative real interest rates, and high inflation are quite predictable even in instances in which the more obvious factors associated with political risk, for example, expropriation and, confiscatory taxation, are absent.

Capital-scarce developing countries should have high risk–adjusted real rates of return for capital to reflect the relative scarcity of capital. Too often, however, monetary, fiscal, and exchange rate policies have presented private asset holders with real risk–adjusted after-tax rates of return that are dramatically negative. Deppler and Williamson have argued that differing international rates of return were an important source of both capital outflows and capital flight from capital-importing developing countries from 1979–82, the years just before the outbreak of the debt crisis.[6] They suggest that real interest rates for the aggregate grouping of countries were negative in every single year from 1975 to 1984, while the black market premium over the official exchange rate never fell below 40 percent and sometimes exceeded 300 percent. This combination produced 1979–82 estimates of a minus 5 percent annual average real rate of return in capital-importing developing countries at a time when a positive 17.5 percent return on foreign assets was available. The likely capital flow response is all too predictable.

Capital controls are widely used in most developing countries. They are usually ineffective. They reduce but do not eliminate capital flight. Cuddington argues that Brazilian controls held down capital flight from levels that might have been expected, given Brazilian rates of inflation.[7] However, more commonly, residents are too ingenious for regulators or it becomes politically impossible to maintain draconian controls for more than a short period of time. As a result, the threat of potential outflows presents a discipline on governments which they are unable to escape completely through the imposition of capital controls.

Overvalued exchange rates coupled with controls on trade and capital flows invariably produce opportunities for vast profits for those prepared to break laws. In Nigeria, the maintenance of an overvalued exchange-rate in the mid-1980s discouraged non oil exports and led to a proliferation of import controls to stem the demand for undervalued imports. Controls breed corruption. Although the payment of "dash" was not unheard of previously in Nigeria, the 400 percent margin between official and market exchange rates for the *naira* is reported to have led to some dramatic scams. In one reported instance, Nigerian politicians with the authority to implement the country's foreign exchange controls borrowed sterling in London on the pretext that it would be used to buy imports, converted the sterling into *naira* at the market exchange rate and then (circumventing foreign exchange controls) bought sterling at the official exchange rate. This transaction produced a fourfold increase in sterling holdings.[8]

A similar scheme in Paraguay was reported to involve $100 million. Central Bank officials allegedly provided dollars to holders of falsified import invoices at the official exchange rate of 240 *guaranis* at a time when the free market exchange rate for the dollar ranged up to 1,100 *guaranis* per dollar.[9] Under the scam, dollars purchased to pay for the non-existent imports were either deposited in bank accounts abroad or resold for *guaranis* at the free rate.

The interest in capital flight as a contributory factor to debt difficulties has been intense. Although accurate statistics on capital flight do not exist, some estimates suggest that capital flight made a staggering contribution to the balance-of-payments and debt problems of a number of the major debtors. Argentina, Mexico, and Venezuela have been particularly susceptible to capital flight.

In 1985, *The Economist* reported that "roughly half the foreign capital lent to the big Latin American debtors since 1979 left them again as soon as it arrived."[10] It reported estimates for the period 1979–82 which showed that Venezuela, Argentina, and Mexico were particularly subject to capital flight.[11] In the case of Venezuela, *The Economist* reported capital flight in excess of $20 billion, amounting to 136 percent of gross capital inflows. Its figures for Argentina were just under $20 billion, that is 65 percent of gross capital inflows, while those for Mexico were in excess of $25 billion (48 percent). Capital flight did not appear to figure prominently in Brazil, for which a figure of approximately $5 billion over the period (8 percent) was reported.

A 1986 Morgan Guaranty study estimated that, for a sample of 18 countries, *net* capital flight over the decade 1976–85 amounted to almost $200 billion at a time when these countries were increasing their foreign indebtedness by $450 billion.[12] Argentina and Mexico were cited by the Morgan study as particular examples of countries where capital flight had been responsible for most of the increased debt burden. The Morgan estimates of capital flight from Mexico amounted to $36 billion between 1976 and 1982, with a further $17 billion in 1983–85. Mexican government estimates were much lower, at $6.8 billion for the 1983–85 period.[13] The Morgan study suggests that, in the absence of capital flight, the observed 1985 debt to export ratios of 493 percent and 327 percent would have been a mere 16 percent and 61 percent for Argentina and Mexico, respectively.

In a very careful study of capital flight from eight heavily indebted countries, Cuddington restricted his definition of capital flight to short-term capital outflows rather than gross capital outflows, and produced two sets of estimates of capital flight between 1974 and 1982.[14] One methodology, relying heavily on the "net errors and omissions" entries in each country's balance-of-payments accounts, suggested that capital flight accounted for 47 percent of the increase in external debt of Argentina, and 40 percent of the increase in debt of Mexico and Venezuela. A second methodology, devised by Dooley et al., produced even higher estimates for these countries and suggested that 12 percent of Brazilian increased indebtedness and 29 percent of Peruvian could be accounted for by capital flight.[15]

A 1987 study by Williamson and Lessard obtained estimates of resident capital outflows that were not as large as some earlier estimates of capital flight, but were still considerable.[16] Eschewing the term "capital flight" and constructing a preferred measure of resident capital outflows through further adjustments to Cuddington's methodology, Williamson and Lessard report 1976–84 total capital outflows for six countries amounting to $86 billion. This total included $30 billion from Venezuela, $27 billion from Mexico, and $16 billion from Argentina.

The concept of capital flight is beset with measurement and definitional difficulties. The motivations that distinguish capital flight from normal capital outflows include efforts to escape large discrete losses through expropriation, debt repudiation, confiscatory taxation, or exchange rate depreciations. Measuring motivations is impossible. There are other difficulties. Dooley argues that capital flight not only must be distinguished from other capital outflows by the motivations that produce it, but also may occur without any current capital outflow at all, for example, when foreign assets previously purchased for ordinary commercial reasons are retained because of fear of what would happen if they were repatriated.[17] As mentioned above, Williamson and Lessard find it more productive to concentrate on measuring resident capital outflow, however motivated, rather than capital flight.

Measurement difficulties in determining the motivations behind observed flows and even greater difficulties if capital flight can occur, have not deterred analysts. Deppler and Williamson provide a survey of the approaches that have been adopted.[18] Their estimates of capital outflows from capital importing developing countries between 1975 and 1985 range from $200 to $300 billion, of which capital flight is estimated to be between $150 and $200 billion.[19]

These estimates are a significant percentage of the increase in external debt of these countries over the period, leading Deppler and Williamson to view foreign lending as a process of intermediation of capital flight. There is considerable regional variation in the importance of capital flight in capital outflows. According to Deppler and Williamson, approximately 80 percent of the capital outflows from Africa and Latin America from 1975–85 could be considered to be capital flight, while the proportions for Asia and the Middle East were one quarter to one third.[20]

An unknown fraction of capital flight from developing countries is included in nonresidents' deposits in the international banking system. Both the IMF and the Bank for International Settlements (BIS) report bank deposits by country of nonresidents. Table 2.3 presents the data on the deposits of nonresident nonbanking entities in the banking systems of the IMF/BIS reporting countries. The table also relates these overseas deposits to the size of total external debt in 1987.

The most startling result is for Venezuela and Uruguay, where overseas deposits could have paid off 35 percent and 55 percent of total external debt. Of course, cross-border bank deposits by nonbanks may occur for a variety of ordinary business reasons unrelated to capital flight. Money deposited in banks abroad—even if the result of capital flight—is but one component of capital flight, for bank deposits are but one of the many assets likely to be held. Moreover, the IMF/BIS data will not capture bank deposits held through third parties, for example, by relatives who are residents of the country in which the bank is located.

CONCLUSION

This chapter has briefly treated the main differences between public and private supplies of international credit and examined three sources of demand for borrowed foreign funds that cause increases in the stock of external indebtedness. Central banks' efforts to treat foreign exchange reserves as a policy target rather than a balance-of-payments residual balancing item may produce an increase in external indebtedness rather than a reduction in foreign exchange reserves. A variety of expansionary macroeconomic policies will also produce current account deficits and will increase external debt. Finally, policies that lead to capital flight will also increase indebtedness. Because countries have only limited ability to insulate themselves from external economic shocks, long-term efforts to keep external debt within sus-

Table 2.3 Debtor Country Bank Deposits Held Abroad by Nonbanks, 1981–87 ($ billion)

	1981	1982	1983	1984	1985	1986	1987	% of Debt (1987)
Major Borrowers	**46.1**	**43.9**	**52.3**	**54.6**	**64.0**	**64.9**	**71.3**	**11.6**
Argentina	6.4	7.1	7.9	7.6	8.5	8.5	9.7	17.1
Brazil	3.5	4.1	8.1	8.2	9.8	12.0	11.3	9.1
Chile	1.2	1.5	2.1	2.0	2.2	2.4	2.4	11.4
Egypt	1.6	2.2	2.1	2.4	3.4	3.1	3.5	8.7
India	1.6	1.6	1.8	1.4	2.6	2.3	3.5	7.6
Indonesia	0.5	0.5	0.5	0.5	0.8	0.8	1.2	2.3
Israel	2.8	2.7	2.9	2.6	2.8	3.1	3.2	12.1
S. Korea	0.3	0.5	0.3	0.4	0.7	0.7	0.6	1.5
Malaysia	1.2	1.1	1.2	1.3	1.2	0.6	0.7	NA
Mexico	9.4	10.4	12.7	14.3	16.1	16.3	19.6	18.1
Turkey	2.0	2.2	2.1	1.8	1.9	2.3	2.5	6.1
Venezuela	15.6	10.0	10.9	12.0	14.0	12.9	13.0	35.5
17 Highly Indebted Countries*	**NA**	**NA**	**52.2**	**55.4**	**63.7**	**66.1**	**71.6**	**16.4**
Bolivia	NA	NA	0.4	0.4	0.4	0.2	0.3	5.4
Colombia	NA	NA	2.6	2.4	2.7	2.9	3.0	17.3
Costa Rica	NA	NA	0.5	0.7	0.7	0.6	0.6	13.1
Côte d'Ivoire	0.4	0.4	0.3	0.3	0.5	0.5	0.7	4.9
Ecuador	0.6	0.9	1.0	1.2	1.5	1.4	1.4	13.3
Jamaica	0.1	0.1	0.1	0.1	0.2	0.4	0.3	5.8
Morocco	0.6	0.4	0.4	0.5	0.6	0.7	0.8	3.9
Nigeria	1.5	1.4	1.4	1.2	1.5	1.7	2.3	7.8
Peru	0.6	1.0	1.2	1.4	1.6	1.8	2.0	10.8
Philippines	0.5	0.5	0.8	1.1	1.1	1.3	1.4	4.6
Uruguay	0.9	1.1	1.5	1.7	1.9	2.2	2.3	54.8
Yugoslavia	0.3	0.3	0.3	0.3	0.4	0.4	0.6	2.6

Source: IMF, International Financial Statistics Yearbook 1987, Table 7xrd, pp. 81-83; IFS December 1988, pp. 63-65; IBRD, World Debt Tables 1988-89.

* Includes Argentina, Brazil, Chile, Mexico and Venezuela.

tainable limits require policies that address the three sources of demand for borrowing. These demands must be restrained if countries are to avoid the contractions that occur when they bump up against global lending limits set by lenders.

To the extent that foreign borrowing has financed capital flight, it raises fundamental political as well as economic questions concerning the appropriate adjustment to any subsequent debt crisis. Although policy adjustments should be aimed at removing the fundamental causes that give rise to capital flight, because capital flight is a middle and upper class economic response inevitable equity questions arise. One such question will be the extent to which the burden of adjustment should fall on the working class when the crisis has occurred in part because of borrowing made necessary by the capital flight of the upper and middle classes.

Debtor country governments face choices. Implementing adjustment programs, without at the same time making capital flight less attractive, amounts to a ratification of the "portfolio diversification" strategies of the upper and middle classes. Opposing tougher adjustment programs demanded by international creditors, because of a concern for its impact on low income workers, means entering into greater conflicts with creditor banks.

Similar choices face both private and official creditors. They may ratify capital flight, by providing fresh funds with the certainty that a large portion of it will be recycled back into their own banking systems, or they may oppose it, by restricting further lending putting greater pressure on governments to adopt policies that make capital flight less desirable.

The simultaneous willingness of foreign banks to buy developing country assets in the form of loans while domestic residents were engaging in capital flight requires an explanation. It may be explained either by differences in the information available to the two sets of asset holders or by differences in the risks they bore. An explanation based on asymmetric information would suggest that capital flight represented the bailing out of domestic assets by domestic residents and should have been seen by foreign lenders as an early indicator of a coming debt crisis. This explanation suggests that banks accepting foreign deposits do not talk enough to their foreign depositors before making loans to governments.

The alternative explanation of differences in risk may be used to argue that developing country citizens recognize that it is much easier for governments to engage in a virtual default on its domestic debt but that there are high costs attached to declared defaults on its external debt.[21] The virtual default on domestic debt may take any of the forms that motivating capital flight which were mentioned earlier.

As Ize and Ortiz argue, governments committed to making interest payments on their external debt may paradoxically cause capital flight if domestic asset holders believe that the external payments are to be made by higher taxes on domestic residents or by reductions in the servicing of domestic debt.

NOTES

1. Dornbusch provides a framework for examining the relationships between the balance of payments and the stock of foreign indebtedness while stressing the need for consistency between exchange rate policy and monetary and fiscal policy. See Rudiger Dornbusch, "External Debt, Budget Deficits and Disequilibrium Exchange Rates," in Gordon W. Smith and John T. Cuddington (eds.), *International Debt and the Developing Countries* (Washington D.C.: The World Bank, 1985), pp. 213–25.

2. Net claims by foreigners will be considered to be indebtedness.

3. Harry G. Johnson, "Towards a General Theory of the Balance of Payments," in Harry G. Johnson, *International Trade and Economic Growth* (London: George Allen and Unwin, 1958), pp. 153–68.

4. World Bank, *World Development Report 1985*, Table 14.

5. The optimal level of reserves would be that at which the social rate of return on reserves (as measured by the discounted value of the GNP losses avoided) would be equal to the interest paid on the borrowing needed to bring actual reserves up to the level of optimal reserves.

6. Michael Deppler and Martin Williamson, "Capital Flight: Concepts, Measurement, and Issues," IMF, *Staff Studies for the World Economic Outlook*, August 1987, p. 49.

7. John T. Cuddington, *Capital Flight: Estimates, Issues, and Explanations*, International Finance Section, Princeton Studies in International Finance No. 58, December 1986, p. 33.

8. *The Economist*, December 21, 1985, pp. 12–13.

9. *New York Times*, January 14, 1986, p. A7.

10. *The Economist*, November 23, 1985, p. 17.

11. *The Economist*, August 2, 1985.

12. Morgan Guaranty Trust Company, *World Financial Markets*, March 1986, pp. 13–15.

13. *New York Times*, June 9, 1986, p. D4.

14. John T. Cuddington, *"Capital Flight."*

15. Michael Dooley et al., "An Analysis of External Debt Positions of Eight Developing Countries through 1990," *Journal of Development Economics*, No. 21 (May 1986), pp. 283–318.

16. John Williamson and Donald R. Lessard, *Capital Flight: The Problem and Policy Responses*, Policy Analyses in International Economics, No. 23 (Washington D.C.: Institute for International Economics, November 1987), p. 7.

17. Michael P. Dooley, "Country-Specific Risk Premiums, Capital Flight and Net Investment Income Payments in Selected Developing Countries" (IMF,

mimeo, 1986), cited by Michael Deppler and Martin Williamson, "Capital Flight: Concepts, Measurement, and Issues," IMF, *Staff Studies for the World Economic Outlook*, August 1987, pp. 39–58.

18. Michael Deppler and Martin Williamson, "Capital Flight: Concepts, Measurement, and Issues," IMF, *Staff Studies for the World Economic Outlook*, August 1987, pp. 39–58.

19. Deppler and Williamson, "Capital Flight," p. 46.

20. Deppler and Williamson, "Capital Flight," p. 47.

21. Alain Ize and Guillermo Ortiz, "Fiscal Rigidities, Public Debt, and Capital Flight," *International Monetary Fund Staff Papers*, Vol. 34, No. 2 (June 1987), pp. 311–32.

3

Debt and Development Strategies

The previous chapter demonstrated that there are three general sources of demand for borrowing produced by balance of payments deficits and that these demands are influenced by a variety of economic policies on exchange rates, taxation, trade protection, wage and price controls, subsidies, budget deficits, monetary expansion, and so forth. These policies, in turn, are influenced by the longer-term economic development strategies of governments. The present chapter examines the relationship between these development strategies and foreign borrowing, concentrating, in particular, on the trade component of development strategies.

The first section of the chapter outlines the links between debt and trade in development strategy and makes some general points about the choice between import substitution and export promotion strategies. This is followed by a review of a more general debate on whether it is correct to view international trade as an engine of economic growth. The determinants of a country's capacity to assume and service external debt is examined next. The chapter concludes with some measures of debt burden in recent years.

DEBT AND TRADE IN DEVELOPMENT STRATEGY

The international trade component of any country's development strategy lies somewhere on a spectrum between the two poles of import-substitution policies and export promotion policies. Advocates of the former seek to create a domestic industrial base that will produce products presently imported. The approach inevitably calls for the use of tariffs, quotas, or other "buy national" commercial policy instruments to provide protection for the domestic industries. Advocates of the latter stress the fact that an ability to compete in export markets will ensure that domestic industries can also hold their own against imports.

Extreme cases of self-reliance in the design of development strategies are represented by the paths followed by Albania, Burma, and Maoist China. In these instances, foreign influences—economic, political, social, and so forth—are minimized. The minimalist strategy has little to recommend it. Apart from the politically abhorrent features of a closed, command society, the economic costs of a strategy that produces a stagnant, backwater economy are extremely high.

Just as the Albanian and Maoist China trade prescriptions make little sense in the long run, similar policies with respect to capital flows are also unlikely to produce rapid economic growth. The experience of the past quarter-century shows clearly that economic development is almost impossible without some reliance on foreign indebtedness. High growth targets require capital accumulation. If income levels are so low that capital cannot be generated from domestic savings, it must be imported. For a given savings rate, there is no ducking the choice between a reliance on foreign resource transfers (which represent the savings of other countries) or the acceptance of a less ambitious growth target. Population growth spurs governments to attempt high GDP growth paths, if only to prevent per capita income from falling. Foreign indebtedness is the inexorable result.

It is probably no accident that the debt crisis of the early 1980s was centered in the region that was the home of import substitution polices—Latin America. Import substitution as a development strategy was a major cause of the debt crisis. The countries in the twenty-four debtor country sample which appear to have had the least difficulties have been those pursuing export-led growth strategies. The difference in trade strategies between Latin America and some Asian exporters may account for the relative absence of Asian, and the preponderance of Latin American, countries on the list of seventeen Heavily Indebted Countries. The Philippines is Asia's only representative on the list. The arrival of the debt crisis contributed powerfully to the further discrediting of import substitution as a viable, long-term development strategy. Import substitution has a venerable tradition in economic growth strategies. Latin American economists such as Raoul Prebisch had argued in the 1950s that even if developed economies are booming, developing economies must expect sluggish growth in their exports of primary products. Meanwhile, economic growth in developing countries would drive their demand for imports up. The intervening years have shown that the outcome has not been as disastrous as "primary export pessimists" such as Prebisch had suggested over thirty years ago.[1] Despite their volatility, primary product exports rose sufficiently in the interim to provide many countries with a breathing space to diversify their export structure into the export of manufactures.[2] As Lloyd Reynolds points out, developing country export earnings since 1950 have increasingly been used to pay for investment goods needed for further economic growth. With the exception of food, imported consumer goods represent a small and declining share of total imports in most developing countries.

Import substitution strategies reduce the foreign exchange bill previously spent on some imports. Whether they reduce the long run foreign exchange needs of the economy is more problematical. Most empirical evidence suggests otherwise. Import substitution provides domestic producers with monopoly power by shielding them from import competition. As a result, domestic production costs rise inexorably as protection breeds inefficient industries incapable of competing internationally. These high costs also affect the costs of doing business in the nontraded sector of the economy.

There is another difficulty with import substitution. It tends to generate budget deficits. The inefficient, high-cost economic structure produced by import substitution often requires state subsidization because of political limits on the extent to which high costs can be reflected in the price level. As a result, state subsidies are often an integral complement to the commercial policy component of import substitution strategies. This additional annual charge on the budget adds to any existing budget deficit and to the domestic financing needs of the state.

Economic development strategies regarding export promotion, on the other hand, favor the creation of industries that will produce for the export rather than the home market. The foreign exchange earned from exports is then available to pay the country's import bill. Moreover, successful export promotion strategies generate an industrial structure capable of facing world competition in both domestic and export markets. Industries serving the domestic market reap the benefits of lower costs when they use inputs from the export-oriented sector, putting them in a better position to compete with imports.

In general, export promotion strategies are often more heavily imbued with a laissez-faire ideology than the obviously interventionist import-substitution strategies. However, the interventionist role of the state in export promotion should not be understated. It can be quite extensive through import controls, credit policies, subsidies, planning permission, and so forth. Thus, export promotion strategies can also add to budget deficits. The export promotion strategies of a number of the exported success stories among the Newly Industrializing Countries (NICs), such as South Korea, have involved very considerable state intervention. Under Part IV of the international trading rules of the General Agreement on Tariffs and Trade (GATT), developing countries have considerably more latitude than developed countries to engage in such practices. Some self-imposed limits exist for those countries that adhere to the GATT Subsidies Code drawn up during the Tokyo Round negotiations.

The long-term implications for foreign indebtedness of import substitution and export promotion are quite different. While both may call for reliance on borrowing or direct foreign investment in the "start-up" phase of building factories and installing productive capacity, a major difference between the two strategies is readily apparent when debt payments must be made. Export promotion strategies earn foreign exchange through the specialized export sector and also economize on foreign exchange through the competition provided to imports by an efficient importable sector.

Import substitution strategies, on the other hand, lack foreign exchange earning capacity and must rely on the fact that foreign exchange previously spent on the substituted imports will now be available for debt repayment and for imports of nonsubstitutable products (including raw materials required to produce import substitutes). This assumes that foreign exchange will continue to be earned by whatever export sector previously provided it prior to the introduction of the import substitution strategy. This assumption becomes increasingly unrealistic over time. Cost increases fostered by the protection required for the success of the import substitution strategy will diminish the international competitiveness of the export sector. In the absence of a balanced manufacturing export sector, the export sector of import-substituting economies tends to be a traditional primary product sector. Here, foreign exchange earnings are at the mercy of world commodity markets where prices fluctuate wildly. Finally, as GNP and population grow, the traditional primary product export sector will be unable to keep pace with the foreign exchange demands of the rest of the economy.

The discussion above has suggested that, in designing economic development strategies for particular countries, a path that creates an industrial sector producing import substitutes is more likely to end in balance-of-payments crises than a path that creates an industrial sector based on exports. There are ample reasons why developing countries may experience balance of payment crises irrespective of the strategy they follow. They will always be affected by fluctuating world interest rates and prices, developed country recessions, crop failures, their own (and others') mismanagement of exchange-rate, monetary, and fiscal policy, and so forth. However, one source of a persistent balance-of-payments deficit, and a resulting persistent need to borrow, will be an economic structure created through reliance on an import substitution strategy.

TRADE AS AN ENGINE OF GROWTH

For fifty years, there has been a controversy over the extent to which viable economic growth could be based on international trade flows. Until recently, there was a sharp regional difference between Asia's embrace of export-led growth strategies and Latin America's clinging to the more import-substituting end of the spectrum. Although there are major exceptions to the Asian pattern, for example, India and Pakistan, Asian NICs have generally accepted the proposition that trade may be an "engine of growth" whereas Latin America has a long alternative tradition of limiting dependence on the rest of the world.

The "engine of growth" phrase had been coined by the English economist Dennis Robertson in his pre-World War II analysis of the part played by international trade flows in the growth of the world economy from the middle of the nineteenth century to the outbreak of World War I.[3] In the aftermath of World War II, the Swedish economists Ragner Nurkse and Gunnar Myrdal, the Austrian-born English economist Hans Singer, and the Argentinean economist Raoul Prebisch were the leaders in the development of a pessimistic view that this engine of growth had faltered and should no longer be relied upon because the terms of trade between developed and developing countries could be expected to move against developing countries in the long run. A wide variety of stylized models have been produced by trade theorists to show that the commodity terms of trade, that is, the ratio of export prices to import prices—a crude measure of the purchasing power of exports—could be expected to produce an unequal international distribution of the gains from trade.[4] The Singer-Prebisch writings of the 1950s stressed the need to reduce dependence on trade flows and argued for import substitution.

The global environment in which developing countries must sell their exports today looks a lot less promising than it did twenty years ago. Prior to the 1973 oil shock, the world economy had experienced two decades of unprecedented growth in world trade during which world trade had grown at annual rates of 8 percent in real terms. The oil shock–induced recessions of the 1970s produced a slowdown in OECD economic growth, including import growth from developing countries. The debt crisis has also coincided with rising protectionist pressures in developed countries. A new complication is the danger of overcapacity of manufacturing capacity as industrialization continues throughout developing countries. If the world economy has settled into a long-run trend of lower growth rates in GNP and international trade, the gains from export-led growth strategies will be less than were experienced by an earlier generation of export-oriented developing countries. These difficulties all combine to pose a threat to the ability of debtor nations to continue servicing their debt through export earnings.

Although the international environment may not be as promising as in the past, there are still strong reasons for relying on an export orientation to development strategies. Trade is not the only engine of growth, but it is at least its handmaiden.[5] The responsiveness of nonoil developing country export volume to OECD economic growth remains considerable. Empirical estimates place the cyclical income elasticity between 2 and 3, with the secular income elasticity around 2.[6] The influence of the terms of trade in the long term is less clear. The original Singer-Prebisch hypothesis of a secular deterioration in developing country terms of trade was premised on a commodity composition of international trade in which the center exported manufactured goods and the periphery exported primary products. This pattern has disappeared with the advent of NICs. Recent empirical studies have cast suspicion on the Singer-Prebisch thesis that the terms of trade are strongly related to growth performance.[7]

A wide variety of econometric studies have compared the growth performance of a large number of developing countries and sought to discover factors that account for intercountry differences. Invariably, export orientation has been singled out as one of the strongest explanations.[8] The most obvious manner in which export promotion encourages economic growth is by encouraging cost cutting and efficiency. If an economy's industrial structure is tailored to survive global competition in export markets, this will produce cost-reducing pressures throughout the domestic economy. To the extent that the domestic market uses products produced by the export-oriented sector, domestic prices will reflect the cost reductions associated with the economies of scale of long production runs aimed principally at foreign markets. There will also be spin-offs from the acquisition of technological innovation that will be necessary if the export oriented sector is to *remain* competitive.[9]

Export orientation may be a source of economic growth because of the gains that come from shifting capital and labor out of low productivity sectors and redirecting them into high productivity sectors. A sector capable of withstanding international competition through exports must, of necessity, be a high productivity sector. The low productivity sectors are those producing goods or services which are not exported. Moreover, high productivity export sectors produce ripple productivity effects on other sectors. An export orientation will contribute to economic growth not only because of the higher productivity within the export sector but also because of the "externalities" or ripple effects on other sectors. However, economic development obviously cannot begin with export promotion strategies. A minimum level of infrastructure and industrial structure is required first.

If continued optimism about trade as an engine of growth even in a less favorable global environment is warranted, it has important implications for developing country debt strategy. An appropriate export orientation can yield economic growth and smaller current account deficits. Smaller long-term current account deficits not only add to the existing stock of indebtedness at a slower rate but also make it easier to service it. It is time to examine the critical determinant of debt dynamics—the race between export growth rates and nominal interest rates.

THE CAPACITY TO SERVICE DEBT

Even with appropriate trade policies, rising external indebtedness is usually an inexorable accompaniment to economic development. With rising debt come rising debt servicing charges. The maximum size of a country's sustainable debt is set by its debt-servicing capacity. Indebtedness may continue to grow but will only be sustainable if within the growing debt-servicing capacity of the economy.

The debt-servicing problem is a transfer problem similar to the German transfer problem of making the reparation payments imposed by the Allies after World War I.[10] The transfer burden consists of two separate burdens—a budgetary burden of collecting the sum to be transferred in the local currency and a current account burden of making the payment in foreign currency.[11] The deflationary implications of both burdens were spelled out by Keynes, who opposed the terms imposed on Germany.[12] The current account burden may be measured by relating debt service charges to foreign exchange earnings rather than to GDP. The burden of German reparations payments averaged approximately 14 percent of exports from 1925 to 1931.[13] At the onset of the debt crisis in 1982, debt servicing ratios on public and publicly guaranteed debt for the Major Borrowers averaged 22 percent, while the Brazilian ratio was 43 percent.[14]

The domestic burden, measured by the ratio of debt-servicing charges to GNP, is an indicator of the extent to which the domestic economy must be squeezed, and hence is a measure of the political difficulties faced by governments attempting to make the transfer. It is a somewhat capricious measure since it is sensitive to the choice of exchange rate. The 1982 ratio averaged 4 percent for major debtors, with individual country ratios ranging from 0.3 percent for India up to 11.4 percent for Israel. The 1986 average exceeded 5 percent, with a Chilean ratio of 11 percent and an Indian ratio of 1.3 percent.[15] In many cases these ratios are also substantially above those found with German reparations. Fraga reports a 1929–31 average German reparations ratio of 3.5 percent. and reminds us that, in the German case, a one-year moratorium was announced by President Hoover in June 1931 and that the Lausanne Settlement of 1932 canceled reparations.[16]

The classic work on the factors that determine a country's debt-servicing capacity is the 1964 World Bank study, by Avramovic et al.[17] The Avramovic study used a modification of the Harrod-Domar growth model to show that a steady-state solution of a constant debt-to-GDP ratio depends on the size of such key parameters as the interest rate, the savings rate, the incremental capital-output ratio and the rate of growth of GDP. In Solomon's simplification of Avramovic's approach, he describes debt-financed development strategies as "a race between two variables growing at compound rates: debt and income."[18]

Because the Avramovic-tradition models are not maximization models, they do not consider the question of the *optimal* degree of borrowing to be incorporated in a development strategy. An optimal foreign borrowing strategy might be defined as one that minimized shortfalls between actual and maximum sustainable levels of welfare. Bardhan discussed this issue in a 1967 article and showed that borrowing from abroad, if left to private borrowers, will be excessive because of the cumulative effect of individual borrowing on the interest rate faced by the country.[19]

The foremost current proponent of models of debt-servicing capacity in terms of debt/export ratios has been William Cline of the Institution for International Economics.[20] The Cline approach has been widely followed and expanded upon as numerous investigators examined growing debt burdens and the forces influencing the probability of default. The presentation that follows borrows heavily from, and uses the original notation of, Simonsen's approach to debt dynamics.[21]

Let D be the level of total foreign debt net of foreign exchange reserves; G is the resource gap in the balance of payments, defined as the noninterest current account deficit less direct investment inflows plus capital outflows; a positive G indicates a resource gap, a negative G indicates a surplus on these nondebt components of the balance of payments; i is the nominal interest rate on debt; X is value of exports; x is growth rate of exports; z is the debt/export ratio, D/X; g is the resource gap relative to annual exports, G/X; overdots indicate time derivatives.

The behavior of the debt stock through time may be described by a differential equation in which annual indebtedness changes because of interest payments on the existing debt stock or because resource gaps in the balance of payments require additional financing.

$$\dot{D} = iD + G \tag{3.1}$$

At any time, short of repudiation, the only component in equation 3.1 susceptible to indebted countries' direct influence is G. The level of D is a matter of history, representing the resource gaps of past years. The level of interest rates largely depends on monetary policy in developed countries, although there may be room for some bargaining over spreads.

The percentage growth rate in indebtedness is determined in equation 3.2.

$$\frac{\dot{D}}{D} = i + \frac{G}{D} \tag{3.2}$$

or

$$\frac{\dot{D}}{D} = i + \frac{g}{z} \tag{3.3}$$

The growth rate, $\dot{z}/z$, of the debt-export ratio, is found as follows.

$$z = \frac{D}{X} \tag{3.4}$$

Therefore,

$$\frac{\dot{z}}{z} = \frac{\dot{D}}{D} - \frac{\dot{X}}{X} \tag{3.5}$$

substituting equation 3.3,

$$= \left(i + \frac{g}{z}\right) - x \tag{3.6}$$

$$\dot{z} = z\left(i + \frac{g}{z}\right) - xz \tag{3.7}$$

$$= iz - xz + g \tag{3.8}$$

$$= (i - x)z + g \tag{3.9}$$

Equation 3.9 is the basic equation in the debt dynamics literature. It shows the fundamental race between nominal interest rates and export growth rates and the part played by this race in determining whether debt-export ratios rise or fall. Debt-export ratios will rise explosively if the right-hand terms are positive, that is, if there is both a resource gap ($g > 0$) and if export growth rates fall below interest rates. A continual resource gap is consistent with stable or declining debt-export ratios if exports sufficiently outpace interest rates to make $\dot{z}$ less than or equal to zero. In the event that export growth falls short of the level of interest rates on existing debt, equation 3.9 indicates that a negative resource gap, ($g < 0$), that is, a surplus on the nondebt components of the balance of payments, is necessary to prevent the debt-export ratio from rising.

Equation 3.10 shows the size of a sustainable resource gap consistent with a stable debt-export ratio that is, with $\dot{z} = 0$. It is possible only if exports win the race against interest rates.

If

$$\dot{z} = 0$$

then from equation 3.9,

$$g = (x-i)z \tag{3.10}$$

If export growth lags behind interest rates, equation 3.10 also shows the size of the surplus ($g < 0$) that must be recorded by the nondebt components of the balance of payments if the debt-export ratio is to be kept from rising. Abstracting from capital flows, a permanent noninterest current account deficit may be sustained indefinitely, with rising levels of indebtedness but no change in debt-export ratio, if export growth exceeds the level of interest rates and condition (equation 3.10) is met. How well did debtor countries do in the race between interest rates and export growth? Table 3.1 contains the details since 1978 for the sample of Major Borrowers and Heavily Indebted Countries. The values in the table indicate the annual percentage changes in the debt-export ratio which would have occurred even if the noninterest current account were balanced and there were no capital flight (i.e., if $g = 0$ in equation 3.9). Negative values represent a reduction in debt-export ratios because export growth outpaces interest rates. The choice of the London inter-bank offer rate, LIBOR, plus a spread of one percentage point represents a conservative estimate of the interest rate facing developing countries which borrow from commercial banks. Spreads have varied from a high of 2.5 points for Jamaica in 1984 to ^{13}⁄$_{16}$ of a point for Brazil in 1987 and Argentina in 1988.

The choice of a one point spread overstates the effective interest rate paid by countries, since much of their debt is at the lower rates charged

Table 3.1 The Race Between Interest Rates and Export Growth

(LIBOR plus spread minus annual rate of export growth)
(Percentage points)

	1978	1979	1980	1981	1982	1983	1984	1985	1986	Cumulative 1978-86	Cumulative 1980-86
Major Borrowers	**-5.0**	**-17.2**	**-14.8**	**5.8**	**21.0**	**9.9**	**0.3**	**13.3**	**14.6**	**28.0**	**50.2**
Argentina	-6.1	-13.4	2.1	12.3	32.0	10.8	10.8	5.4	22.2	76.2	95.6
Brazil	3.0	-11.1	-14.3	2.0	27.4	7.2	-11.8	12.6	21.5	36.6	44.7
Chile	-3.6	-45.9	-17.2	28.3	22.8	17.2	12.6	12.7	-4.8	22.0	71.6
Egypt	9.0	-6.7	-33.6	11.3	10.5	10.3	10.7	11.0	20.0	42.4	40.2
India	1.6	-9.3	-3.2	18.7	10.0	4.9	9.5	13.5	7.6	53.3	61.0
Indonesia	6.6	-24.2	-28.0	5.9	29.1	17.5	0.8	18.7	28.5	55.0	72.6
Israel	-10.6	-8.1	-6.9	11.4	17.6	12.3	7.0	5.8	0.3	28.6	47.4
S. Korea	-21.1	-0.7	-0.6	-3.1	10.6	3.8	1.5	11.3	-18.9	-17.1	4.6
Malaysia	-12.4	-34.9	-4.4	24.2	11.6	-2.5	-5.3	16.4	16.0	8.6	55.9
Mexico	-28.9	-26.9	-38.9	-5.9	23.7	7.6	-1.2	18.0	28.0	-24.6	31.3
Turkey	-12.9	7.9	-8.7	-46.2	-17.1	10.7	-10.5	-7.1	12.7	-71.1	-66.2
Venezuela	11.0	-37.1	-21.3	7.4	32.5	24.8	2.8	20.6	41.6	82.4	108.4
17 Heavily Indebted Countries	**1.1**	**-21.7**	**-19.0**	**15.1**	**27.7**	**15.8**	**1.2**	**12.4**	**20.5**	**53.2**	**73.8**
Bolivia	9.3	-10.6	-4.6	20.0	24.7	13.0	18.0	22.7	15.0	107.5	108.8
Colombia	-7.1	-5.0	-5.8	32.2	15.4	28.4	-17.6	23.0	-32.9	30.7	42.8
Costa Rica	4.4	4.7	5.4	19.3	19.3	8.4	0.3	12.9	-5.1	69.5	60.4
Côte d'Ivoire	-0.9	6.5	4.5	37.6	17.1	21.8	-7.7	0.5	-3.0	76.4	70.8
Ecuador	3.3	-29.1	-4.4	16.8	23.9	11.4	1.7	-2.2	29.1	50.7	76.4
Jamaica	-6.0	8.8	-1.4	12.2	23.2	13.8	12.1	14.8	-0.8	76.7	73.8
Morocco	-5.5	-12.2	-5.5	23.4	19.1	11.4	9.4	4.9	-5.3	39.6	57.3
Nigeria	22.7	-41.5	-37.4	46.6	49.1	26.5	-1.6	2.4	55.0	122.0	140.8
Peru	-2.5	-58.3	-2.1	30.7	15.5	19.1	8.9	10.9	21.3	43.4	104.2
Philippines	-5.7	-14.2	-12.8	10.4	21.3	9.3	13.7	10.9	-1.2	31.7	51.6
Uruguay	-3.4	-20.9	-12.6	1.9	23.4	23.4	18.9	13.2	-12.1	31.8	56.0
Yugoslavia	-3.2	-6.5	-19.8	3.6	17.1	24.9	10.6	4.9	-1.4	30.1	39.8
6 month Euro-$ LIBOR	9.2	12.2	14.0	16.7	13.6	9.9	11.3	8.6	6.9		

Source: IMF, International Financial Statistics Yearbook 1987 and IFS, May 1988.
Interest rate is IFS 60lde plus a one percentage point spread. Exports are IFS 77aad+77add.

by official creditors. Accordingly, the results need to be treated with caution. Had all external debt been private creditor debt, the last columns of Table 3.1 would indicate the cumulative increase in the debt-export ratio which would have occurred in the absence of other balance of payments resource transfers. More accurately, the columns indicate the cumulative increase in the ratio of private creditor debt to exports had no effort been made between 1978–86 to substitute official creditor debt for the 1978 level of private creditor debt.

As Table 3.1 shows, 1981 marked a sharp break from the past. Although interest rates had been rising continuously since 1976, it was not until 1981 that the race against them was lost. Even dynamic South Korea was unable to keep pace beyond 1981, although rates were already moving down. Reductions in export earnings (i.e., negative growth in exports) are an important factor in producing positive values for some countries in Table 3.1, particularly for oil exporters. In the three years 1981–83, there was only a single instance in which export growth of a heavily indebted country outpaced interest rates. The sole exception was Mexico in 1981. Of all the countries in the sample, only four (Korea, Malaysia, Mexico, and Turkey) won the race in any of these three years. Cumulatively, over the 1980–86 period, only Turkey won the interest-exports stakes, while over the longer 1978–86 period it was joined by South Korea and Mexico. All other countries in the sample reported increases in their commercial bank debt-export ratio of between 2 percent and 92 percent.

The conditions for a stable debt/export ratio even with the typical current account deficit of developing countries were set out in equation 3.9. Examining Table 3.1 in the light of this equation, we can see that while it had been conceivably possible to live with trade deficits and/or capital flight without rising debt-export ratios in the years prior to 1981, this slim and rarely realized possibility disappeared once exports lost the interest-exports growth race.

We can use the information in the last columns of Table 3.1 to estimate the extent to which the failure to win the exports-interest race would have produced increases in the level of indebtedness to private creditors even without trade deficits or capital flight. Table 3.2 shows how the race between export growth and interest rates affected the debt-export ratio of each of the sample countries. The results are obtained by comparing two hypothetical levels of 1986 private creditor debt. One hypothetical level is obtained by applying the actual 1978 debt-export ratio to actual 1986 exports. This produces an estimate of 1986 debt if the interest-export race had ended in a draw. The second hypothetical level of 1986 debt is obtained by applying actual 1986 exports to the hypothetical 1986 debt-export ratio that

Table 3.2 Effects of the Race Between Interest Rates and Export Growth

	1978 Debt-Export Ratio	1978-86 % Change in Ratio Produced by Race	1978-86 Resulting Increased Debt ($ billion)	As % of 1978 Debt (%)
Major Borrowers	0.74	28%	17.0	11.9
Argentina	0.65	76	4.4	76.2
Brazil	1.68	37	15.6	36.6
Chile	0.83	22	1.0	22.0
Egypt	0.36	42	1.0	42.4
India	0.04	53	0.3	53.3
Indonesia	0.42	55	3.7	55.0
Israel	0.53	29	1.8	28.6
S. Korea	0.36	-17	-2.6	-17.1
Malaysia	0.17	9	0.2	8.6
Mexico	1.93	-25	-11.3	-24.6
Turkey	0.32	-71	-2.5	-71.1
Venezuela	0.59	82	5.4	82.4
17 Heavily Indebted Countries*	0.85	53%	26.2	20.6
Bolivia	1.18	108	0.9	107.5
Colombia	0.19	31	0.4	30.7
Costa Rica	0.42	70	0.4	69.5
Côte d'Ivoire	0.65	76	1.8	76.4
Ecuador	0.63	51	0.8	50.7
Jamaica	0.47	77	0.5	76.7
Morocco	1.23	40	1.7	39.6
Nigeria	0.12	122	1.0	122.0
Peru	1.18	43	1.7	43.4
Philippines	0.47	32	1.3	31.7
Uruguay	0.58	32	0.3	31.8
Yugoslavia	0.05	30	0.2	30.1

Sources: World Bank, World Debt Tables 1987-88; IMF, International Financial Statistics Yearbook 1987 and IFS various issues. Note: Debt is private creditor debt outstanding and disbursed. The estimate of increased debt due to the race is obtained by applying the changed debt-export ratio to 1986 exports.
6 month $LIBOR is IFS 60lde. Exports are IFS 77aad+77add.
* The 17 Heavily Indebted Countries category includes Argentina, Brazil, Chile, Mexico and Venezuela.

would have existed after a race from 1978 to 1986. It is calculated from equation 3.9, assuming $g = 0$.

$$\dot{z} = (i-x)z + g \qquad\qquad (3.9)$$

If

$$g = 0 \qquad\qquad (3.10)$$

then

$$\frac{\dot{z}}{z} = (i-x) \qquad\qquad (3.11)$$

$$z_1 = [1+(i-x)]z_0 \qquad\qquad (3.12)$$

$$D_1 = z_1 X_1 \qquad\qquad (3.13)$$

where D_1 and X_1 are debt and export levels at t_1.

Table 3.2 shows race-induced increases in indebtedness for all cases except South Korea, Mexico, and Turkey—the three winners of the export-interest race. For the losers, the largest growth rates in debt are imputed to Nigeria, Bolivia, Venezuela, Jamaica, the Côte d'Ivoire, and Argentina.

THE PATTERN OF DEBT BURDEN

It is now time to examine the behavior of actual rather than hypothetical levels of debt-export ratios and debt service-to-export ratios for our sample of debtor countries. There is clearly a limit to the amount of annual export earnings that may be set aside to pay for annual debt service. The limit on the debt-to-export ratio sets a ceiling on the amount of external debt that is sustainable. The suspension of voluntary lending to a number of debtor countries which occurred after mid-1982 showed that the economic limits on sustainable debt levels had been reached. Moreover, the delays in repayment of debt-servicing charges after 1982, and the widespread restructuring of loans, showed that the political limits to which citizens might be subjected so that existing debt might be serviced had also been reached.

As a rough rule of thumb, a debt-export ratio under two has been widely used as a criterion of creditworthiness.[22] In 1978, only six of the Major Borrowers and seven of the seventeen countries in the Heavily Indebted Country category had ratios in excess of this level. As Table 3.3 shows, there have been marked differences in the behavior of the debt-export ratio for individual members of the two groups of borrowers, although the aggregates have behaved in a similar manner. The table contains two dramatic, but opposite cases, Nigeria and Turkey. While Turkey's debt ratio fell from over 3 to under 2 between 1980 and 1984 (before relapsing thereafter), Nigeria's rose twelvefold, from a ratio of a third to 3. Between 1980 and 1983 the number of Major Borrowers with debt-export ratios in excess of two rose annually until nine of the group had reached that level. By 1986, seven countries listed in the table had ratios close to, or exceeding, a

Table 3.3 Debt to Export Ratios, 1980–87*

	1980	1981	1982	1983	1984	1985	1986	1987
Major Borrowers	1.7	1.9	2.2	2.4	2.3	2.5	2.8	2.5
Argentina	2.3	2.9	4.3	4.6	4.7	4.7	5.5	6.6
Brazil	3.0	3.0	3.9	4.0	3.5	3.6	4.5	4.3
Chile	1.9	2.8	3.4	3.7	4.1	4.4	3.8	3.3
Egypt	1.8	2.2	2.2	2.1	2.3	3.0	3.5	3.4
India	1.3	1.4	1.8	1.9	1.9	2.4	2.5	2.4
Indonesia	0.9	0.9	1.2	1.5	1.4	1.8	2.7	2.7
Israel	1.8	2.0	2.2	2.3	2.3	2.2	2.1	1.9
S. Korea	1.3	1.2	1.3	1.3	1.3	1.4	1.1	0.7
Malaysia	NA	NA	NA	NA	NA	NA	NA	NA
Mexico	2.3	2.6	3.1	3.3	2.9	3.3	4.3	3.6
Turkey	3.3	2.3	2.0	2.1	1.9	2.0	2.6	2.5
Venezuela	1.3	1.3	1.6	2.2	1.9	2.1	3.1	2.8
17 Highly Indebted Countries**	1.7	2.0	2.6	3.0	2.8	3.0	3.5	3.6
Bolivia	2.6	3.2	3.6	4.5	5.1	6.5	8.1	9.0
Colombia	1.2	1.7	2.0	2.7	2.2	3.0	2.2	2.2
Costa Rica	2.2	2.7	3.2	3.6	3.0	3.4	3.1	3.1
Côte d'Ivoire	1.6	2.3	2.7	3.0	2.7	3.1	3.0	3.7
Ecuador	2.0	2.6	2.9	2.8	2.8	2.6	3.5	4.4
Jamaica	1.3	1.5	2.0	2.4	2.5	2.8	2.7	2.6
Morocco	2.2	2.6	3.3	3.4	3.6	3.9	3.8	3.8
Nigeria	0.3	0.6	1.0	1.7	1.5	1.5	3.5	3.7
Peru	2.1	2.4	2.9	3.1	3.3	3.6	4.7	5.0
Philippines	2.1	2.3	2.9	2.9	3.0	3.3	3.3	3.2
Uruguay	1.0	1.2	1.6	2.2	2.4	2.9	2.5	2.6
Yugoslavia	1.0	1.0	1.0	1.2	1.2	1.2	1.1	1.5

Source: World Bank, World Debt Tables 1988-89.
* Total external debt (EDT) to exports of goods and services (XGS).
** Includes Argentina, Brazil, Chile, Mexico and Venezuela.

ratio of four—Argentina, Bolivia, Brazil, Chile, Morocco, Peru, and Mexico.

As debt-to-export ratios climb, so too (unless interest rates fall sufficiently) do interest-to-export ratios. Table 3.4 shows the manner in which interest payments on foreign debt rose dramatically as a percentage of the revenue received from exports of goods and services in the years after 1980. It also provides estimates of the cumulative interest paid between 1980 and 1987.

There are considerable differences in country experiences within the sample. Many countries saw their interest-to-export ratio double in the early years of the crisis. Thereafter, a considerable number of them were able to reduce their ratios. In addition to export performance and changes in LIBOR, the ratios show the influence of debt rescheduling as well as the unilateral actions of countries such as Brazil and Peru. Rescheduling affected not only the level of interest rates but also the maturity structure of a country's debt. The dramatic decline in Brazil's ratio after 1982 is due to reductions in interest payments on a rising level of long-term debt and a sharp fall in the level of short-term debt, some of which was converted to long-term debt in debt restructuring.

Debt servicing consists not only of interest payments but also of principal repayments. The debt-service ratio for total long-run debt is found in Table 3.5. The exclusion of short-term debt underestimates the total servicing burden considerably. The influence of debt rescheduling is apparent in the sharp decline of the ratio for Brazil after 1982, but the impact on other countries, such as Mexico, is not very obvious. However, the unilateral action of Peru which limited debt servicing to 10 percent of exports is quite noticeable. In 1986, the Peruvian debt service ratio was the lowest Latin America ratio in the sample. By 1987, it was the lowest of all sample countries. Many of the other ratios were clearly intolerable in the long run.

The debt-servicing ratio depends on the stock of debt, its maturity distribution, interest rates, the bunching of repayment schedules, and the level of exports. The variability of three of these variables—interest rates, export earnings, and maturity bunching—is very much out of the control of debtor countries. Export variability may be reduced by reducing dependence on primary products, but this is a long-term structural solution. Interest rate variability may be minimized by limiting the floating rate component in the stock of external debt. This may be accomplished by maximizing the multilateral agency component in the debt stock, but there will be many instances in which multilateral lending is not available or is inappropriate.

Since the debt servicing ratio fluctuates because of fluctuations in a variety of variables other than the level of the debt stock, a debt stock that appears sustainable at one level of interest rates or export earn-

Table 3.4 Estimated Total Interest Payments as a Percentage of Exports, 1980–87

	1980	1981	1982	1983	1984	1985	1986	1987	Interest 1980-87 ($ billion)
Major Borrowers	**15.7**	**19.5**	**23.7**	**21.6**	**20.1**	**19.9**	**19.6**	**15.4**	**324.8**
Argentina	19.8	31.3	43.2	43.6	42.9	51.7	46.4	47.3	33.0
Brazil	33.8	38.4	49.5	39.8	29.8	28.8	32.9	22.9	71.9
Chile	19.0	33.4	46.2	36.6	48.4	39.0	28.6	23.7	14.4
Egypt	9.5	12.6	9.0	8.8	9.8	10.3	10.5	10.1	9.5
India	3.6	4.2	5.5	6.5	6.5	8.4	8.5	8.7	8.4
Indonesia	6.9	7.7	9.6	11.0	11.3	12.1	17.2	16.7	18.6
Israel	14.6	16.7	22.0	19.5	18.8	19.6	17.7	15.5	15.7
S. Korea	12.2	14.3	13.9	12.3	12.0	11.7	8.7	5.5	29.0
Malaysia	NA	NA	NA	NA	NA	NA	NA	NA	NA
Mexico	25.0	29.6	41.4	39.1	35.6	33.7	34.4	25.4	75.1
Turkey	21.3	16.7	14.8	15.2	12.7	12.4	14.9	14.8	13.0
Venezuela	14.5	17.6	22.4	22.2	20.0	15.8	26.0	20.6	27.9
17 Highly Indebted Countries	**17.0**	**22.9**	**30.2**	**28.9**	**27.1**	**25.3**	**25.4**	**21.2**	**302.8**
Bolivia	21.5	23.0	25.8	25.9	29.9	27.8	21.8	19.9	1.7
Colombia	10.6	17.1	22.1	23.7	19.2	24.2	17.3	16.9	8.3
Costa Rica	19.3	19.8	17.5	52.8	23.3	29.5	17.1	11.8	2.4
Cote d'Ivoire	14.2	21.7	25.6	25.6	22.8	22.7	22.2	18.2	5.4
Ecuador	19.4	27.5	37.5	26.4	31.7	25.9	27.8	13.4	6.0
Jamaica	9.1	8.1	10.6	12.2	16.3	17.3	15.8	14.3	1.5
Morocco	16.6	19.8	19.3	17.7	17.4	14.4	16.8	13.1	5.8
Nigeria	3.5	6.6	11.8	12.0	15.2	14.2	10.1	10.9	10.4
Peru	20.3	24.6	25.3	23.2	18.2	15.9	11.9	11.5	6.1
Philippines	17.4	24.4	27.9	27.1	26.1	23.0	22.6	20.4	16.0
Uruguay	9.8	11.1	15.0	20.4	25.0	24.3	19.7	19.3	2.2
Yugoslavia	7.4	9.3	10.1	10.4	15.0	9.5	9.7	11.4	14.7

Notes: Includes interest on public, publicly guaranteed and private non-guaranteed long-term debt and estimates of interest on short-term debt. Estimates obtained from interest payments on long-term debt from World Bank, World Debt Tables 1988-89, plus interest on short-term debt estimated from (LIBOR + non-OPEC country spread) multiplied by lagged short-term debt from World Debt Tables. Exports of goods and services are XGS in World Debt Tables.

Table 3.5 Long-Term Debt Service as a Percentage of Exports, 1975–87

	1975	1980	1981	1982	1983	1984	1985	1986	1987
Major Borrowers	**22.8**	**23.7**	**25.5**	**29.9**	**26.8**	**26.4**	**30.0**	**32.8**	**29.3**
Argentina	59.8	26.6	32.1	37.1	38.0	39.7	51.5	63.4	52.0
Brazil	43.2	56.5	57.0	71.9	46.2	38.6	35.0	42.7	33.2
Chile	33.4	37.9	57.3	62.0	47.4	51.7	44.3	34.7	26.4
Egypt	23.2	13.8	19.5	17.5	16.4	17.0	19.5	17.9	14.8
India	12.8	7.9	8.1	10.6	11.9	11.6	17.5	21.2	21.6
Indonesia	14.3	12.6	12.9	16.5	18.4	18.9	24.9	32.6	33.3
Israel	24.3	19.5	27.9	30.0	27.3	23.9	27.7	28.1	25.3
S. Korea	12.7	14.1	14.8	16.1	16.3	15.9	21.7	24.0	27.5
Malaysia	5.1	4.6	6.8	9.2	10.2	12.8	28.9	19.7	20.0
Mexico	41.1	38.0	34.9	44.5	45.4	49.0	48.8	51.9	38.4
Turkey	8.7	19.0	20.9	23.3	25.3	20.3	28.1	28.0	29.8
Venezuela	5.9	20.0	16.9	22.0	21.9	20.2	16.4	38.4	32.0
17 Highly									
Indebted Countries	**23.2**	**26.2**	**29.7**	**37.5**	**33.8**	**33.8**	**33.3**	**36.7**	**30.6**
Bolivia	16.1	30.7	30.4	34.3	34.6	43.4	45.7	30.2	22.1
Colombia	14.3	9.7	16.3	21.8	29.7	24.1	34.3	30.0	33.4
Costa Rica	23.1	27.4	26.1	20.1	56.8	29.0	38.1	29.2	14.4
Côte d'Ivoire	9.5	25.9	36.3	41.1	44.8	34.5	38.6	41.6	40.8
Ecuador	8.5	30.5	45.1	70.0	26.3	33.9	31.1	34.3	21.9
Jamaica	27.2	15.1	18.1	17.6	20.3	20.7	30.4	30.6	26.7
Morocco	6.3	28.0	32.2	37.9	33.4	20.2	24.9	29.8	24.2
Nigeria	3.0	2.8	6.6	13.2	20.0	28.0	32.0	19.0	11.7
Peru	49.0	36.8	52.0	44.2	29.0	25.6	25.2	18.3	12.9
Philippines	13.2	13.5	17.4	22.7	21.3	17.5	19.0	26.0	25.2
Uruguay	54.1	15.8	13.6	27.9	23.5	32.3	35.8	22.6	25.7
Yugoslavia	18.6	19.3	16.9	18.9	19.0	23.5	15.7	17.4	19.4

Source: World Bank, World Debt Tables 1988-89.

ings may be unsustainable at another. As we shall see when we examine the origins of the debt crisis, two severe shocks to debtor countries have been large fluctuations in interest rates and large fluctuations in export earnings.

CONCLUSION

While the previous chapter had examined some of the components of the balance of payments which are responsible for the demand for international borrowing, the present chapter has concentrated on the dynamics of debt through time. Growing indebtedness is an inevitable accompaniment to economic growth. It need not be unsustainable. One of the factors contributing to increased external indebtedness is a failure to win the race between export growth and the level of interest rates. Trade, in the sense of a sufficient export orientation, remains not only an engine of growth, but also a way of avoiding unsustainable debt. As relatively capital-scarce economies, developing countries should expect to be recipients of net transfers of resources from the rest of the world. In the years leading up to the debt crisis, much of this resource transfer occurred through excessive borrowing rather than equity forms of capital inflows. The inevitable result was the period of negative resource transfers from 1984 onward as debt service exceeded new lending.

The performance in the exports-interest race of each of the countries in the sample of twenty-four countries has been compared with the observed build-up in actual debt-export ratios and debt-servicing ratios. There were few race winners. As debt-export ratios and debt-servicing ratios rise, the ability to engage in further borrowing is eroded as lenders begin to look more closely at the eroding probability of repayment.

What is a sustainable level of debt? At what level of the debt-export ratio should lenders become nervous? At what level of the debt service-to-exports ratio should lenders decide the burden has become unbearable? As Table 3.3 showed, there are a considerable number of countries with debt-export ratios well in excess of two. This raises the question: to what extent were the debt difficulties of a number of countries predictable? To what extent were they the result of unpredictable exogenous forces? Chapter 4 will take up some of these issues by examining some theories of how private lenders treat sovereign borrowers and how an ongoing supply of credit can abruptly cease. Chapter 5 will concentrate on an empirical investigation of external factors that contributed to the difficulties of debtor nations.

NOTES

1. Raoul Prebisch, "Five Stages in My Thinking on Development" in Gerald M. Meier and Dudley Seers (eds.), *Pioneers in Development* (Oxford: Oxford University Press for the World Bank, 1984), pp. 175–91.

2. Lloyd G. Reynolds, "The Spread of Economic Growth to the Third World," *Journal of Economic Literature*, Vol. XXI, No. 3 (September 1983), p. 974.

3. D. H. Robertson, "The Future of International Trade," *Economic Journal*, Vol. 48 March 1938, pp. 1–14, quoted by Ronald Findlay, "The Terms of Trade and Equilibrium Growth in the World Economy," *American Economic Review*, Vol. 70, No. 3 (June 1980), pp. 291–99.

4. United Nations Economic Commission for Latin America, *The Economic Development of Latin American and Its Principal Problems* (New York: United Nations, 1950); Hans W. Singer, "The Distribution of Gains Between Borrowing and Investing Countries," *American Economic Review*, Vol. 40, May 1950, pp. 473–85; and Ronald Findlay, "The Terms of Trade and Equilibrium Growth."

5. Irving B. Kravis, "Trade as the Handmaiden of Growth: Similarities Between the Nineteenth and Twentieth Centuries" *Economic Journal*, Vol. 80 (December 1970), pp. 850–72.

6. William R. Cline, "Comment" on Rudiger Dornbusch, "Policy and Performance Links between LDC Debtors and Industrial Nations," *Brookings Papers on Economic Activity*, No. 2 (1985), p. 364.

7. William Tyler, "Growth and Export Expansion in Developing Countries: Some Empirical Evidence," *Journal of Development Economics*, Vol. 9, No. 3 (August 1981), pp. 121–30.

8. Bela Belassa, "Exports and Economic Growth: Further Evidence," *Journal of Development Economics* Vol 5, No. 2 (June 1978), pp. 181–89; Peter S. Heller and Richard C. Porter, "Exports and Growth: an Empirical Re-investigation," *Journal of Development Economics* Vol. 5 No. 2 (June 1978), pp. 191–93; Tyler, "Growth and Export Expansion."

9. Gershon Feder, "On Exports and Economic Growth," *Journal of Development Economics*, Vol. 12 (1982), pp. 59–73.

10. See, among others, Stephen A. Schuker, *American "Reparations" to Germany, 1919–33: Implications for the Third-World Debt Crisis*, International Finance Section, Princeton Studies in International Finance No. 61, July 1988.

11. Fritz Machlup, "The Transfer Problem: Theme and Four Variations," in Machlup, *International Payments, Debts, and Gold* (New York: Scribners, 1964), pp. 374–95.

12. John Maynard Keynes, *The Economic Consequences of the Peace* (London: Macmillan, 1919); Keynes, "The German Transfer Problem," *Economic Journal*, March 1929.

13. F. R. S. Harris, *Germany's Foreign Indebtedness*, 1935, reprinted (New York: Anno Press, 1978) reported by Arminio Fraga, *German Reparations and Brazilian Debt: A Comparative Study*, International Finance Section, Princeton Essays in International Finance No. 163, July 1986, p. 20.

14. World Bank, *World Debt Tables 1986–87*.

15. World Bank, *World Debt Tables 1987–88*.

16. Arminio Fraga, *German Reparations and Brazilian Debt: A Comparative Study*.

17. Dragoslav Avramovic et al., *Economic Growth and External Debt* (Baltimore: Johns Hopkins Press for the International Bank for Reconstruction and Development, 1964), pp. 188–92.

18. Robert Solomon, "A Perspective on the Debt of Developing Countries," *Brookings Papers on Economic Activity*, No. 2, 1977 pp. 485.

19. Pranab K. Bardhan, "Optimum Foreign Borrowing," in Karl Shell (ed.), *Essays on the Theory of Optimal Economic Growth* (Cambridge, Mass.: MIT Press, 1967).

20. William R. Cline, *International Debt: Systemic Risk and Policy Response* (Washington D.C: Institute for International Economics, 1983).

21. Mario Henrique Simonsen, "The Developing-Country Debt Problem," in Gordon W. Smith and John T. Cuddington (eds.), *International Debt and the Developing Countries* (Washington, D.C.: The World Bank, 1985), pp. 101–28.

22. William R. Cline, "Comments" on Rudiger Dornbusch, "Policy and Performance Links." *Brookings Papers on Economic Activity*, No. 2, (1985), p. 366.

4

Sovereign Debt and Private Lenders

The last two chapters have examined demand influences on debt levels. It is now time to turn to supply influences, and, in particular, to the supply of loans from private creditors. The debt run-up of the 1970s and early 1980s was characterized by a growing reliance of sovereign borrowers on private creditors. The resulting change in the mix between public and private creditor debt can be shown to have contributed to the debt crisis.

The first section of the present chapter concentrates on the relative importance of private credit to sovereign borrowers. The types of risk borne by private creditors engaged in international lending are defined in the second section. The nature of the long-run relationship between private creditors and sovereign borrowers under conditions of risk is examined in the third section through a discussion of a number of theoretical models of how private creditors set credit ceilings. The fourth section contains a brief review of the manner in which banks measure sovereign risk.

THE ROLE OF PRIVATE LENDERS

The years preceding the debt crisis saw a change in the composition of developing country debt as borrowers reduced the share of official creditor debt and increased the share of private creditor debt. A profound change in the reliance on private sector loans occurred in the years between 1975 and 1980. A similar change had taken place in the previous five years. This change occurred not only because international banks expanded their supply of sovereign lending but also because debtor countries sought it. For some countries seeking to avoid the tough questions normally asked by official creditor agency staffers, the plentiful supply of private credit was seen as a desirable substitute to multilateral official loan credit.

Table 4.1 displays the changing pattern of debtor country dependence on public and private creditors. There are wide differences

Table 4.1 Private Creditor Long-Term Debt as a Percentage of Total Debt, 1975–87

	1975	1980	1981	1982	1983	1984	1985	1986	1987
Major Borrowers									
Argentina	46	59	60	62	66	67	65	63	61
Brazil	64	81	82	88	89	90	88	87	85
Chile	71	83	83	83	83	82	79	76	73
Egypt	43	71	72	77	79	85	84	79	75
India	19	15	16	18	19	19	19	18	18
Indonesia	2	4	4	7	8	13	15	15	18
Israel	37	36	37	40	45	45	43	43	40
S. Korea	47	33	33	31	30	30	29	28	27
Malaysia	53	60	61	60	59	62	64	63	52
Mexico	54	63	71	78	83	80	78	77	76
Turkey	80	87	88	87	90	90	88	85	81
Venezuela	56	95	96	97	97	98	96	97	96
17 Highly Indebted Countries									
Bolivia	61	74	75	76	78	78	75	72	68
Colombia	40	49	48	46	40	41	40	32	24
Costa Rica	27	41	48	50	49	51	45	44	40
Côte d'Ivoire	43	54	59	55	56	56	51	50	45
Ecuador	59	72	74	72	67	61	56	52	44
Jamaica	46	60	57	58	69	72	71	69	65
Morocco	73	36	29	24	20	19	19	17	16
Nigeria	33	46	41	40	35	33	30	29	27
Peru	33	78	83	86	84	83	82	67	55
Philippines	64	50	50	56	56	57	54	51	49
Uruguay	57	70	76	79	85	85	84	83	79
Yugoslavia	17	21	24	27	44	51	50	53	53

Source: World Bank, World Debt Tables 1988-89. Total debt defined here as public and publicly guaranteed long-term debt outstanding and disbursed (DOD).

within the twenty-four country sample in the division between public and private creditors. In 1975, only ten countries in the sample relied on private creditors for more than half of their long-run public sector external indebtedness; by 1980 that number had grown to 14. The growing importance of private sector credit meant that borrowers had increased the variable rate component of their external indebtedness.

There were some notable exceptions to the growing dependence on private creditors. The exceptions included the two largest recipients of U.S. foreign aid, Egypt and Israel. Also included were a number of countries, such as Bolivia and Jamaica, with disastrous credit ratings precluding reliance on private sector lending. Low income countries, such as India, qualify for special "soft window" multilateral loan programs such as those of the World Bank's International Development Association (IDA). These loans have a per capita income ceiling which disqualifies middle income developing countries, ruling out most of Latin America.

Table 4.2 shows Bank for International Settlements (BIS) estimates of bank exposure from 1983 through 1987, together with estimates of gross flows corrected for exchange-rate changes. The table illustrates the trend to reduce exposure in almost all countries after 1985. Corrected for exchange-rate changes, end-1987 commercial bank exposure to the two country groupings was $10–12 billion below end-1985 levels.

RISK AND PRIVATE SECTOR LENDING

A wide variety of risks are borne by those engaged in international lending.[1] Lending to foreign governments or state entities involves sovereign risk. Lending across international borders to any borrower, public or private, involves transfer risk. Lending in an era of changing exchange rates involves currency risk. Finally, lending to the private sector involves private risk. Each of these risks is discussed below.

Sovereign risk is the risk that a sovereign state will not meet its obligations. This may be due to insufficient foreign exchange reserves, domestic public finance problems, or political attitudes toward foreign debt. Sovereign risk involves not only the risk that the state may be unable to meet its obligations, but also the risk that it may be unwilling to repay. Unilateral debtor actions, such as debt moratoria or limiting debt servicing to a percentage of export earnings, are political decisions that commitments made to lenders have become impossible to keep or are inequitable.

Transfer risk is the risk that foreign private sector debtors may be unable to obtain the foreign exchange needed to make payments even

Table 4.2 Gross Bank Debt Owed by Developing Countries, 1983–87

	($ billion)					Exchange-Rate Adjusted Flow			
	1983	1984	1985	1986	1987	1984	1985	1986	1987
Non-OPEC Developing Countries	**325.7**	**331.0**	**353.6**	**368.1**	**384.9**	**10.5**	**11.1**	**3.1**	**-1.2**
Latin America/Caribbean	208.8	212.3	218.6	225.0	225.7	5.7	1.7	1.6	-7.1
Middle East	16.2	15.4	16.5	16.6	17.0	1.8	0.2	-0.8	-1.0
Africa	19.8	18.8	21.6	23.0	25.0	0.2	0.9	-0.2	-0.6
Asia	80.8	84.5	97.0	103.4	117.2	4.9	8.3	2.5	7.5
Major Borrowers	**287.3**	**292.8**	**308.3**	**318.1**	**319.9**	**9.2**	**6.6**	**-4.7**	**-7.6**
Argentina	27.4	26.1	28.9	32.4	34.2	-1.0	2.2	-1.0	0.4
Brazil	71.2	76.9	76.9	81.1	81.1	6.6	-1.7	0.0	-1.0
Chile	13.0	13.6	14.3	14.1	12.9	0.7	0.4	-0.3	1.2
Egypt	6.6	6.9	7.4	7.5	7.6	0.6	-0.1	-0.5	-0.6
India	3.1	4.1	6.2	7.3	9.1	1.1	1.8	0.7	1.0
Indonesia	13.7	14.2	15.2	16.8	19.0	0.9	0.0	0.6	0.4
Israel	7.0	6.2	6.5	6.0	5.6	-0.7	0.1	-0.8	-0.6
S. Korea	29.2	30.9	34.4	33.2	28.7	2.0	2.4	-2.2	-5.9
Malaysia	11.4	11.2	11.2	11.6	10.9	0.0	-1.3	-0.2	-1.7
Mexico	72.0	72.3	74.5	74.2	74.4	0.9	0.8	-1.2	-1.9
Turkey	4.5	5.1	7.0	9.0	11.4	0.8	1.5	1.5	1.6
Venezuela	28.3	25.3	25.8	25.1	25.0	-2.8	0.4	-1.1	-0.5
17 Heavily Indebted Countries	**275.6**	**274.8**	**282.6**	**290.8**	**292.2**	**3.1**	**0.9**	**-4.7**	**-5.5**
Bolivia	0.7	0.7	0.6	0.6	0.6	0.0	-0.1	0.0	0.0
Colombia	7.6	7.1	6.5	6.5	6.2	-0.4	-0.7	-0.1	-0.6
Costa Rica	1.1	0.9	0.8	0.9	0.9	0.0	0.0	0.0	0.0
Côte d'Ivoire	3.1	2.6	2.9	3.3	3.5	-0.2	0.0	0.0	-0.2
Ecuador	5.1	4.9	5.2	5.3	5.0	-0.1	0.2	0.1	-0.5
Jamaica	0.6	0.6	0.7	0.5	0.5	0.0	0.0	-0.2	0.0
Morocco	4.4	4.4	4.8	5.2	5.7	0.2	0.0	0.0	0.0
Nigeria	9.3	8.1	9.1	10.0	10.8	-0.6	0.1	0.0	-0.4
Peru	6.5	5.7	5.6	5.3	5.1	-0.7	-0.2	-0.5	-0.5
Philippines	13.7	13.8	13.4	14.1	14.3	0.2	-0.7	0.3	-0.4
Uruguay	1.9	2.0	2.0	2.0	2.1	0.1	-0.1	-0.0	0.0
Yugoslavia	9.9	9.7	10.5	10.3	10.0	0.2	0.1	-0.9	-1.0

Source: BIS, International Banking Developments; BIS, International Banking and Financial Market Developments, various issues.

though they have the domestic currency equivalent. It may be due to foreign exchange controls or a government decision to limit public and private debt service charges. Some governments prevent resident private sector entities from servicing foreign debts despite debtor wishes to remain current. For lenders, there is little practical difference between transfer risk and sovereign risk. Both require negotiations with debtor country governments.

Currency risk is a risk that only occurs when foreign borrowers issue debt instruments in a currency other than that of the lender. This need not be the currency of the borrower, but may be that of other lending countries. For example, French banks that buy dollars to participate in dollar-denominated bank consortium loans run the risk that the debt instruments may experience Franc-denominated capital losses through exchange rate changes. Some currency risk may be covered through forward cover in forward exchange-rate markets or through build-up of offsetting foreign currency liabilities.

Private credit risk is the normal risk to all lenders that private borrowers may not be able to repay because of poor commercial conditions or poor business decisions.

As commercial bank lending grew in the 1970s, a new component to risk became important. Systemic risk is the risk that the difficulties of an individual country may infect the system, producing defaults not predicted by isolated country risk assessments. Among the forces increasing systemic risk during the debt crisis was the formation of debtors' groups. These did not evolve into formal debtor cartels, a development that would have added substantially to systemic risk. The prime example of a debtors' group has been the Cartagena group. Developed country protectionism and the depressed state of the export markets of debtor countries were further sources of systemic risk. Other factors contributing to systemic risk were the wide variation in regulatory practices of national authorities toward international bank lending and borrowing and the poor quality of information. Efforts to reduce systemic risk included greater coordination among bank regulators of different countries, IMF-led concerted lending programs, and private sector efforts at improving the flow of information to banks.[2]

Risks peculiar to restructuring agreements with sovereign lenders include the risk associated with "moral hazard." Moral hazard refers to the danger of setting precedents in the treatment of one debtor that encourage other debtors to pursue policies that will lead them to seek similar relief. Any impression that a debtor country successfully renegotiated its debts by deliberately creating a situation in which it was incapable of servicing its debts would cause other debtors to pursue similar strategies. Creditors must walk a narrow line in debt renegotiations lest other debtors feel that it is stupid to continue making payments when less responsible debtors appear to benefit from irresponsibility.

Any of the risks cited above may produce repayments difficulties. The most severe difficulty is default. The probability of default was a major factor in the abrupt appearance of credit ceilings and the suspension of voluntary commercial bank lending in 1982. Formal default occurs when creditors declare borrowers in default for not meeting the terms of a loan agreement, and initiate legal proceedings to recover their assets. Although there have been widespread failures of debtor countries to meet their obligations under loan agreements, commercial banks have hesitated to declare defaults. Multilateral institutions such as the IMF had been much less reluctant. It took five years after the 1982 onset of the crisis for the first bank loan default to occur. North Korea was declared in default by European and Japanese bank creditors in August 1987 as they began legal proceedings to seize North Korean assets.[3] United States banks, prevented by law from lending to the defaulter, were not involved.

There are a variety of ways in which deviations from the terms of loan agreements may occur.[4] It is not too useful to label all deviations "defaults." Cline restricts the term to the most severe of the disruptions that may occur along "the continuum of debt disruptions."[5] For Cline, these severe instances are either repudiation or unilateral indefinite suspension of payment of *both* principal and interest. He excludes "temporary payments disruptions and reschedulings." By Cline's definition there have been no recent repudiations by a major borrowing country since those of Cuba and Ghana in the 1960s.[6] Brazil's February 1987 unilateral indefinite suspension of interest payments did not include principal and hence escaped Cline's definition. Eaton, Gersovitz, and Stiglitz limit their definition of default to the formal declaration by the lender that "the borrower has violated a certain condition of the loan," stressing that lenders need not exercise their option to make such a declaration.[7] Broader definitions of default have been used by others. Feder and Just defined defaults as "any case in which public or publicly guaranteed payments to lending institutions are delayed or rescheduled with or without the consent of creditors."[8] Similarly, Kharas considers any failure to fulfill obligations to service outstanding debt to be a default.[9]

In at least one important respect, the bank debt crisis of the 1980s differed from that produced by repudiation of bond issues in the 1930s. Bank lending involves loan syndicates containing hundreds of banks. Syndicate members share some common objectives, have legal relationships between each other, and possess the capability for concerted action. However, the interdependence between members of a syndicate also introduces new elements of risk. For Sachs, default risk in syndicated lending takes the form of either the risk of insolvency or "panic" risk, the latter referring to financial panics among the members of a loan syndicate.[10] Panic risk incorporates an important distinction between single lender action and the collective action involved in syndicated loans.

The risks that have been described above are risks of repayment difficulties. Most, though not all, debt repayment difficulties occur because a country is either unwilling or unable to service its debts. Unwillingness produces repudiation. Inability may be due to either illiquidity or insolvency.[11] Illiquidity is a short-run condition in which a country lacks sufficient foreign exchange earnings or reserves to service its debt even though its long-term outlook may be very promising. Insolvency, produced by unsound long range investment strategies which use borrowed funds in ways which prevent their repayment, will occur if debt cannot be repaid out of income but requires asset sales.[12]

Much of the early literature on limits to international borrowing had focused on insolvency. The long-run limit on a country's borrowing, its long-run credit ceiling, is set by its capacity to service debt out of income rather than future borrowing. This capacity depends on the present value of the discounted stream of net foreign exchange earnings. The expected future income stream from abroad must exceed the value of the debt, otherwise the lender's asset (i.e., the debt) has no value. A well-known property of early debt-cum-growth models was the requirement that the long-run economic growth rate of the borrower exceed the real interest rate.[13]

The solvency requirement is unlikely to be the first, or binding, constraint faced by countries. Solvency is an irrelevant criterion in international lending to governments, since national sovereignty limits the assets that may be seized as surety for loan repayment. The liquidity limit is of more immediate relevance. Illiquidity is probably the most pervasive risk in international lending. It occurs when amortization payments plus interest payments exceed foreign exchange reserves.

Lenders have a vested interest in ensuring that credit is not extended beyond a level at which a liquidity constraint would bind. The probability that a credit ceiling will be reached increases as the stock of debt and its associated servicing charges approach the highest level supportable by reserves and net foreign exchange earnings. Debt-to-export ratios reached 3.13 in 1987 for countries with recent debt problems.[14] Countries without debt servicing problems had a ratio of 1.12 in the same year. The details for the twenty-four countries in the sample have already been presented in Table 3.3. In 1985, eleven countries had ratios in excess of 3, with three having ratios in excess of 4.

A binding liquidity constraint may be relaxed if imports can be squeezed to free up foreign exchange to service the debt. After 1982, import compression was an immediate response as debtor countries reached credit ceilings. Much depends on the structure of the economy and on domestic politics. Some level of imports is needed as intermediate products in the production of exports. Moreover, lenders recognize that there are political limits on the ability of debtor governments to compress imports. There are also limits on a government's ability to use taxes as a way of squeezing domestic consumption in order to service foreign debt.[15] In short, illiquidity may be the result of the political infeasability of domestic adjustment programs.

The current debt crisis' bargaining over repayment terms represents a crucial development over past international debt crises. The external debt crises of the nineteenth century and the 1930s involved a multitude of bond holders rather than bank loans. During the present crisis, cohesive bank steering committees representing hundreds of banks have negotiated with debtors. The ongoing bargaining nature of debtor-creditor relationships includes the possibility that each side can impose some sanctions or penalties and that debtor-creditor relations will continue over a time horizon extending beyond the maturity of the present debt.[16]

The long-run relationship between sovereign borrowers and commercial bank lenders is ultimately a cooperative one of mutual benefit.[17] The mutual gains produced by the relationship include the smoothing of consumption paths and the pooling of risk. How these gains are to be shared under all future eventualities is never fully described in explicit loan contracts. Unforeseen events produce difficulties in contract enforcement for both sides. In seeking enforcement or a redivision of the gains from the cooperative arrangement, each side has a range of potential sanctions at its disposal. Credit ceilings become the main instrument with which the lender may influence borrower adherence to the contract.

In addition to a shut-off of future lending, lender sanctions may include attempts to seize borrower assets. Borrower sanctions include actions that influence stock market or bank regulator attitudes toward lenders. Borrowers may also attempt to protect themselves against possible lender sanctions. Brazil, in announcing its indefinite suspension of bank interest payments in February 1987, took preemptive action by freezing outstanding short-term credits. These would otherwise have been withdrawn by creditors, provoking an immediate crisis in Brazil's trade relations.

The long-run nature of credit relationships, and the legal difficulties in enforcing explicit loan contracts with sovereign borrowers, suggest that sovereign debt possesses some of the characteristics of labor markets—explicit contracts are supplemented by implicit contracts. These implicit contracts place obligations on both parties based on expectations formed from past experience. Examples of implicit contracts in the credit relationship include an expectation that lenders will continually roll over short-term credit as it matures, that borrowers will not engage in policies that jeopardize their ability to service debt, and that national living standards will not be unduly depressed for the sake of maintaining debt servicing during short-term setbacks.

MODELS OF CREDIT CEILINGS

The arrival of the debt crisis was heralded by the abrupt termination of voluntary lending as countries ran into bank lending ceilings. Since 1982, credit to a large number of debtor countries has been rationed. For them, the concerted lending component of debt restructuring packages has replaced voluntary lending. A characteristic of private creditor lending is the abrupt manner in which it may be terminated even if borrowers are prepared to pay higher interest rates.

In a perfectly competitive framework, market-clearing interest spreads measure creditworthiness and default probabilities. However, both lenders and borrowers may prefer not to allow rates to rise to market-clearing levels. High rates imply low creditworthiness and lower-quality loan portfolios.[18] They also make default a more attractive option.[19] The alternative to market-clearing interest rates is some form of quantity control. The shut-off of credit as a credit ceiling is reached need not be unexpected if both lender and borrower have previously agreed to the height of the ceilings. It becomes abrupt when a large number of lenders have not previously announced country lending limits and all come to the same conclusion that further lending is inappropriate.

A number of analysts explain the appearance of credit rationing as a defensive measure by lenders in the presence of bankruptcy or sovereign risk.[20] Because international lending involves sovereign risk, there is no international equivalent to the property rights provided to creditors under national bankruptcy laws. Lenders do not allow debt to grow to such a level that the borrower's benefits from a default would exceed the costs. In credit markets, as distinct from many other markets, borrowers will not pay the price, that is, the interest rate, if they default.

Credit ceilings are an indicator of a country's creditworthiness. Theories that seek to explain how ceilings are set commonly assume that borrowing countries are rational and inherently dishonest.[21] Rational governments will refuse to pay their debts if the gains from reneging exceed the costs of repayment. In defense, lenders will impose credit ceilings low enough to prevent dishonesty from becoming too appealing, in which case default occurs only as a random event. The notion that borrowers are at heart not to be trusted raises some interesting questions regarding national honor. A number of theorists have included related concepts in their models. For example, national reputation is mentioned by Cooper and Sachs as an important concern of governments seeking to reduce external perceptions of "country risk."[22]

In some instances, credit ceilings are the consequences of imperfect information and lenders' inability to evaluate sufficiently the creditworthiness of clients. High-risk premia cannot be relied upon to weed out high-risk borrowers since low-risk borrowers seeking financing for low return projects will be the first to disappear from credit markets as rates rise. This phenomenon has been used by Stiglitz and Weiss to construct a theory of credit rationing in markets with imperfect information.[23] Stiglitz and Weiss show that even in equilibrium there may be excess demand in credit markets and that the existence of an excess demand for credit need not imply a market failure or a market disequilibrium. We shall examine the Stiglitz-Weiss model below before turning to models that deal explicitly with lending under conditions of default probability.

The Stiglitz-Weiss Model

The Stiglitz-Weiss credit ceiling model stresses the economics of information and shows that it is precisely those borrowers who have the lowest expectation of repaying loans who will agree to pay the highest rates. Their willingness to pay high rates reflects their view that there is a low probability of repaying the loan because of a low probability of success with the financed project. In these circumstances, the absence of a non-price screening device will cause a lender's portfolio to increase in riskiness as interest rates rise. Although traditional theory would suggest that an excess demand for loans will drive up interest rates and call forth an increased quantity supplied, Stiglitz and Weiss show that, with imperfect information, it may be irrational for lenders to respond to higher interest rates if to do so would lower expected returns on their loan portfolio.[24]

Risk may cause the expected return to the bank to have an upper bound even though interest rates continue to increase. This upper bound is termed the bank optimal rate. Banks will not lend to borrowers prepared to pay more than the bank optimal rate. Credit will be rationed rather than provided to those prepared to pay the most for it. In this view, the interest rate at which supply equals demand is not an equilibrium rate because banks could increase both their expected return per dollar loaned and their profits by cutting interest rates to the level of the bank optimal rate and simultaneously restricting lending to the levels sought by all those who wished to borrow at the higher rate. This strategy will leave banks with a higher expected return per dollar loaned.

Although developed for bank financing of commercial investment projects rather than the smoothing of national consumption paths, the Stiglitz-Weiss model is applicable to sovereign lending. Moreover, although developed for cases in which there were no identifiable differences between borrowers, it is also applicable to instances in which there are readily identifiable differences among countries. If lenders are able to distinguish among classes of borrowers based on risk and expected returns for each class, there will be interest rates at which entire classes will be "red-lined." The early 1980s saw clear instances of ceilings, and a fear on the part of individual sovereign debtors that their credit ratings would be tarnished by the actions of others. Individual Latin American governments worried that "country risk" would be contaminated by "area risk." This fear was partly responsible for the failure of a debtor cartel to emerge in the early years of the crisis.

The Stiglitz-Weiss model makes it clear that the sudden shut-off of credit need not be the result of a "market failure" and need not represent either a "disequilibrium" or an exercise in monopoly power. Instead it may be the rational outcome, in competitive markets facing imperfect information, of decisions based on expected rates of return and subjective probability distribution functions. As interest rates rose and the debt servicing burdens became calamitous, borrowers sought new financing while lenders imposed a lending freeze. Gradually, the full extent of country indebtedness to a wide range of international banks became clear. By 1989, banks recognized the need for voluntary debt reduction.

The Eaton-Gersovitz Model

For Eaton and Gersovitz, the level of credit ceilings depends on the probability of default and on a cost-benefit analysis of default. The probability of default, in turn, depends on the probability that the expected gains from default will exceed the expected costs of default. The borrower's benefits from default depend on the size of the debt, since default entails nonrepayment of borrowed resources. The borrower's costs of default stem from a likely inability to borrow further subsequent to a default. Borrowers expect to face future economic shocks. If they default, their inability to borrow will leave them unable to cushion future economic disruptions which might otherwise have been smoothed out had credit been available. Thus, the costs of a putative default are measured by how much higher and how much smoother future economic growth would be with, rather than without, continued access to international credit. An additional cost of default may be the seizure of some assets abroad, but this cost is likely to be minor compared with the costs of being denied future access to financing flows.

Lenders attempt to prevent borrowers from defaulting by limiting the expected benefits to a level below that of the expected costs that could be imposed on the putative defaulter. In practice, this has taken the form of individual banks establishing "country limits." If the credit ceiling has been set correctly, a default would produce an expected net welfare loss to the defaulter because the immediate benefit, that is, confiscation of resources, is exceeded by the expected discounted value of the future costs of credit denial. In addition, the sudden emergence of unexpected threats of default will alter banks' judgment of the likelihood of default and will result in an immediate lowering of credit ceilings.

If all parties are rational in the sense that they do not take courses of action in which the expected costs exceed the expected benefits, and if there is perfect information regarding the probability distribution function of default, expectations are rational. In these conditions, the Eaton-Gersovitz approach would conclude that defaults would never occur deliberately. All observed defaults would be accidental. However, in a world characterized by uncertainty it is not too difficult to find reasons why default, loosely defined, might occur. If the income of the borrowing country contains a stochastic element, defaults may occur as the result of random events. Uncertainty about borrower country income introduces uncertainty, not only about the future demand for credit, but also about the future ability to repay existing debt. With both borrowers and lenders uncertain of future income at the time a loan commitment is made, there are conditions under which it would be evident to both that borrowers could benefit from default on its existing debt even if they then faced indefinite exclusion from credit markets in the future.

SYNDICATED LENDING

The great bulk of debtor country bank debt was contracted through syndicates containing hundreds of participating banks. Syndicates face difficulties in agreeing on collective action. While syndicates diversify risk, individual syndicate members will continue to act in their own self-interests. These may be at variance with the collective interests of the syndicate. The resulting conflicts raise some interesting questions about the behavior of large syndicates containing members with different predilections. The composition of loan syndicates will be discussed in later chapters. As we shall see, the presence of large numbers of small and regional, particularly U.S., banks introduced major complications in debt renegotiations. Larger lenders, with greater exposure and more at stake, have sharper divergences of interest than do smaller lenders. Smaller lenders, with low individual loan exposure, have been more prepared to reduce credit ceilings, declare loans in default, and write them off against bad debts.

The manner in which collective behavior among lenders may influence the supply of credit has been examined by Sachs in a series of papers both alone and with various co-authors.[25] Syndication diversifies risk by reducing the exposure of individual lenders. However, one side effect of diversification will be a greater probability of financial panics because of collective action.[26] The interdependence among syndicate members may produce sudden disruptions in financing flows even though individual syndicate members would have been prepared to continue lending if the actions of other lenders could have been ignored. A lack of information, or a failure to agree on a collective lending strategy, may precipitate a crisis in which the borrower is starved of the funds needed to service interest payments even though it would be perfectly capable of servicing additional debt.

The group dynamics of syndicate lending that produce financial panics are relatively simple. If each bank suddenly believes that, although it was prepared to continue lending, all others in the syndicate are about to stop, all lending will cease. Factors that will precipitate sudden changes in individual lender perceptions include political changes, growing calls for debt repudiation by groups within debtor countries, or evidence that other lenders are building up loan loss reserves. As each lender comes to the conclusion that other lenders will not be forthcoming with further loans, the share of new loans to be taken up by those remaining will increase until, in the extreme, only one bank remains to provide the entire loan. The suspension of lending by some syndicate members will cause the lending-to-capital ratio to rise for the remaining lenders. As this measure of risk rises, so too does the interest rate at which it still makes sense to assume the risk. But higher interest rates raise borrower's servicing costs, increasing the probability of default. What had been a safe situation for a syndicate loan becomes unsafe for any single bank if it becomes convinced that it may be the sole participant in the syndicate with no ability to diversify the risk.

The type of financial panic described above, in which rational behavior for individual lenders is irrational for a collective, is likely to occur when there is already a high outstanding level of debt. When lending stops, it may be difficult to distinguish between credit ceilings imposed because of lender panic and those due to lending's having reached the ceiling on syndicated lending for the existing risks of default or insolvency. As voluntary lending ground to a halt in the mid-1980s, a wider collective than bank syndicates was needed to ward off the likelihood of financial panics. This wider collective was the amalgam of groups involved in the IMF's concerted lending strategy—bank syndicates, the IMF, multilateral development banks, central banks, and finance ministries. Until debt reduction began in 1989, the IMF's "concerted lending" strategy had required further bank exposure as a condition of IMF lending. In dealing with the problem of financial panic, the strategy provided a public good that will be more fully discussed in Chapter 6.

HOW BANKS MEASURE RISK

Practitioners' views on risk were surveyed in a 1982 Group of Thirty study on risks in international bank lending.[27] The report was a companion to a questionnaire survey of banker attitudes and brought out some of the important differences in risk when credit is supplied by private rather than official lenders.[28] In its review of existing systems of Country Risk Analysis (CRA), the Group of Thirty report reviewed eleven systems and questioned the widespread inclusion in CRA systems of such economic indicators as GDP, level and growth, economic diversity, and money supply growth.[29] These are variables whose ability to contribute to the better assessment of risk is not self-evident. For measures that clearly do matter—export growth, debt service ratios, and so forth—the report pointed to the usually long lags before these data are available.

CRA systems also make widespread use of political variables seeking to measure future political stability. In the Group of Thirty survey, these range from "philosophy of rating group," to "minority groups," "religious problems," "external ethnic problems" and "ability of government officers." The manner in which the political and economic elements are combined varies considerably. Some CRA systems tend to rate countries by calculating an overall score for each country, a dubious approach that requires summing quantitative economic indices and political indices. Other systems use a more descriptive approach.

Country risk analysis is also sensitive to the country of residence of the analyst. Risk recognition differs from one financial center to another, in part depending upon closeness of trading ties. There have been systematic regional differences in ratings. Tokyo-based ratings of Asian countries generally exceed U.S.-based ratings. The opposite is true with ratings of Latin American countries. United States banks have sometimes rated Latin American countries below the credit ratings provided by non-U.S. banks.

Clearly, political factors are important in determining sovereign risk. They are usually ignored by the economics literature. For example, the straightforward difference in economics between inability to repay and unwillingness to repay may involve a less clear cut political distinction. The economic distinction is based on the difference between resources in one case (inability), and *preferences* in the other (unwillingness). Unwillingness implies that the resources exist but are not to be used for purposes of debt repayment. Incumbent politicians may feel *unable* to repay though the resources exist because of the political sanctions (e.g., loss of office) to which they will be exposed if they introduce policies that permit repayment. This political dilemma facing policymakers is usually ignored by the economics models. However, it is ultimately the key factor in determining country risk of default. If the economics indicators are to be better matched with the political ones, greater attention needs to be paid to how adjustment costs are spread in a society, and how this distribution affects the political future of the decisionmakers who have ordered up the pain. Too often what appears economically sensible to economists seems politically suicidal to politicians.

Risks unique to the interbank market vastly complicate the analysis of risk in the case of private lending. The 1982 Group of Thirty report pointed to fears among bankers that the interbank market had become more risky because of the growing role of second and third tier banks on the borrowing side of the market.[30] Prior to 1982, developing countries had made use of overseas affiliates of their commercial banks as an additional source of lending to that provided by loan syndicates. Operating in the interbank market, these affiliates placed and received deposits from other banks. When they were net buyers of deposits, they provided an additional funnel of loans to their native country by remitting the proceeds of these deposits to head office. Because the interbank market is a short-term market, it is often the first place in which signs of a country's increasing illiquidity become evident. When a growing percentage of deposits are on loan from less risky to more risky banks, overall risk in the market rises.

There are wide differences in the experience and management skills of many foreign participants in the interbank market. There are also wide differences in the level of support to be expected from their central banks should a bank be in trouble. The Group of Thirty reported that around one third of the banks surveyed reported that their international operations were not subject to the scrutiny of their national banking authorities. The fragility of the interbank market was apparent in 1984 when Continental Illinois, fighting rumors, found its large depositors withdrawing funds and placing them in U.S. government securities. The bank was unable to attract new funds through the sale of CDs while its previously issued CDs sold at very heavy discounts in the secondary market. The 1984 failure of Continental Illinois, the ninth largest bank in the United States, would have had major repercussions had the FDIC not arranged that even large depositors would be protected despite the fact that FDIC deposit insurance is nominally limited to deposits under $100,000.

The Continental Illinois story may be contrasted with the Group of Thirty's description of the 1980 liquidation of Argentina's second largest bank, Banco Intercambio Regional. The Argentinean central bank disclaimed responsibility for interbank claims against the bank's New York branch. As a result, both Argentinean and non-Argentinean banks had difficulty attracting deposits in the interbank market even at high interest rates.

CONCLUSION

This chapter has looked at conditions determining the supply of private credit to sovereign borrowers when lending is subject to a number of forms of default risk including insolvency, illiquidity, repudiation, and lender panics. The shut-off in private creditor lending in the mid-1980s was abrupt, compounding the repayment difficulties of debtor countries. The theories of private creditor behavior examined above show that a shut-off need not be viewed as a drastic change in the rules of the game but merely the application of implicit rules known in advance by both sides.

Under conditions of default risk, the aggregate of individual banks' credit ceilings for a country will be less than the ceilings for collective lending. The role of multilateral lending agencies is not only to supplement the credit flows through its own financing of noncommercial projects, but also to ensure that the applicable private lending ceilings approach the collective lending ceilings. In the case of the debt crisis, this required a strategy that would prevent financial panic among bank syndicates.

When credit ceilings begin to bind, debtor country political institutions face decisions that can no longer be avoided. These decisions ultimately involve budget and current account deficits, requiring changes in a large number of other variables such as growth rates, inflation, wage increases, and the exchange rate. Even if credit cut-offs become likely as a country's explicit or implicit credit ceiling is approached, there are political advantages to those in power to argue that it was unexpected, unfair, and outside their control. In the next chapter we shall examine the extent to which shocks emanating from the external environment were responsible for both the accumulation of debt and the resulting difficulties of each country in the sample.

NOTES

1. The following taxonomy is based on that found in *AMEX Bank Review*, Vol. 13, No. 9 October 28, 1986, p. 3.

2. In one short-lived experiment to diversify risk to the nonbanking private sector, Citicorp was reported to have obtained $900 million insurance coverage for its developing country loans in May 1984. The policy, with Cigna Corporation, was terminated in February 1985 (*New York Times*, February 2, 1985).

3. Nicholas D. Kristof, "North Korea, in Default, Said to Relent on Debt," *New York Times*, p. D18, September 17, 1987.

4. Donogh C. McDonald, "Debt Capacity and Developing Country Borrowing," *International Monetary Fund Staff Papers*, Vol. 29, No. 4 (December 1982), pp. 603–46.

5. William R. Cline, *International Debt and the Stability of the World Economy* (Washington D.C.: Institute for International Economics 1983), p. 87.

6. Group of Thirty, *Risks in International Bank Lending* (New York: The Group of Thirty, 1982), p. 43.

7. Jonathan Eaton, Mark Gersovitz, and Joseph E. Stiglitz, "The Pure Theory of Country Risk," National Bureau of Economic Research Working Paper No. 1894, April 1986, p. 3.

8. G. Feder and R. E. Just, "A Study of Debt Servicing Capacity Applying Logit Analysis," *Journal of Development Economics*, Vol. 4 (1977), p. 30.

9. Homi Kharas, "The Long-Run Creditworthiness of Developing Countries: Theory and Practice," *Quarterly Journal of Economics*, August 1984, pp. 415–39.

10. Jeffrey Sachs, *Theoretical Issues in International Borrowing*, International Finance Section, Princeton Studies in International Finance No. 54, July 1984.

11. James Riedel, "Determinants of LDC Borrowing in International Financial Markets: Theory and Empirical Evidence," World Bank, International Trade and Capital Flows Division, Division Working Paper No. 1983–2, February 1983, p. 23.

12. James Riedel "Determinants of LDC Borrowing." p. A1.

13. Dragoslav Avramovic et al., *Economic Growth and External Debt*, International Bank for Reconstruction and Development (Baltimore: Johns Hopkins Press, 1964).

14. IMF, *World Economic Outlook*, April 1987, p. 186.

15. Jeffrey Sachs, *Theoretical Issues in International Borrowing*.

16. Surveys of recent literature may be found in Jonathan Eaton, Mark Gersovitz, and Joseph E. Stiglitz, "The Pure Theory of Country Risk," National Bureau of Economic Research Working Paper No. 1894, April 1986; and in Vincent P. Crawford, *International Lending, Long-Term Credit Relationships, and Dynamic Contract Theory*, International Finance Section, Princeton Studies in International Finance No. 59, March 1987.

17. Some of these relationships have been examined in a game theory framework by Vincent P. Crawford, in his *International Lending, Long-Term Credit Relationships, and Dynamic Contract Theory*.

18. Daniel McFadden et al., "Is There Life after Debt? An Econometric Analysis of the Creditworthiness of Developing Countries," in Gordon W. Smith and John T. Cuddington (eds.), *International Debt and the Developing Countries* (Washington D.C.: The International Bank for Reconstruction and Development, 1985), p. 190.

19. Richard N. Cooper and Jeffrey D. Sachs, "Borrowing Abroad: The Debtors Perspective," in Smith and Cuddington (eds.), *International Debt and the Developing Countries*, pp. 21–60.

20. Martin F. Hellwig, "A Model of Borrowing and Lending with Bankruptcy," *Econometrica*, Vol. 45 (1977), pp. 1879–1906; Jonathan Eaton and Mark Gersovitz, "LDC Participation in International Financial Markets: Debt and Resources," *Journal of Development Economics*, Vol. 7 (March 1980), pp. 3–21; Eaton and Gersovitz, "Debt with Political Repudiation: Theoretical and Empirical Analysis," *Review of Economic Studies*, Vol. 48 (April 1981), pp. 289–310; Eaton and Gersovitz, *Poor Country Borrowing in Private Financial Markets and the Repudiation Issue*, International Finance Section, Princeton Studies No. 47, 1981; Jonathan Eaton, Mark Gersovitz, and Joseph E. Stiglitz, "The Pure Theory of Country Risk," National Bureau of Economic Research Working Paper No. 1894, April 1986; Jeffrey Sachs and Daniel Cohen, "LDC Borrowing with Default Risk," National Bureau of Economic Research Working Paper No. 925, July 1982, and *Kredit und Kapital*, 1984; Jeffrey Sachs, *Theoretical Issues in International Borrowing*, International Finance Section, Princeton Studies in International Finance No. 54, July 1984, pp. 23–25; Richard N. Cooper and Jeffrey D. Sachs, "Borrowing Abroad: The Debtor's Perspective," in Gordon W. Smith and John T. Cuddington, *International Debt and the Developing Countries*, p. 50.

21. Riedel, "Determinants of LDC Borrowing," p. 15.

22. Richard N. Cooper and Jeffrey D. Sachs, "Borrowing Abroad: The Debtor's Perspective," in Gordon W. Smith and John T. Cuddington, *International Debt and the Developing Countries*, p. 50.

23. Joseph E. Stiglitz and Andrew Weiss, "Credit Rationing in Markets with Imperfect Information," *American Economic Review*, Vol. 71, No. 3 (June 1981), pp. 393–410; Stiglitz and Weiss, "Incentive Effects of Terminations: Applications

to the Credit and Labor Markets," *American Economic Review*, Vol. 73 (December 1983), pp. 912–27.

24. Joseph E. Stiglitz and Andrew Weiss, "Incentive Effects of Terminations,"p. 394. Stiglitz and Weiss have a very narrow definition of credit rationing. They reserve the term for instances in which only one of two potential borrowers is funded even though the rejected potential borrower was prepared to pay a higher interest rate, or for instances in which credit is denied to one group irrespective of the interest rate it offers while it is available when the total pool of credit is enlarged.

25. Jeffrey Sachs and Daniel Cohen, "LDC Borrowing with Default Risk" Jeffrey Sachs, *Theoretical Issues in International Borrowing*, pp. 23–25; Richard N. Cooper and Jeffrey D. Sachs, "Borrowing Abroad: The Debtor's Perspective," pp. 21–60.

26. Jeffrey Sachs "Theoretical Issues in International Borrowing." pp. 30–37.

27. Group of Thirty, *Risks in International Bank Lending*.

28. Group of Thirty, *How Bankers See the World Financial Market* (New York: The Group of Thirty, 1982).

29. Quantitative approaches to CRA are surveyed in Krishan Saini and Philip S. Bates, "A Survey of the Quantitative Approaches to Country Risk Analysis," *Journal of Banking and Finance*, Vol. 8 (1984), pp. 341–56.

30. Group of Thirty, *Risks in International Bank Lending* p. 17.

5

The Influence of the External Environment

This chapter examines the influence of shocks in the external environment in the 1970s on the run-up of debt. It focuses on four specific shocks to the current account of the balance of payments and to real income. Drastic changes in oil prices, in nonoil terms of trade, slower OECD growth, and volatile interest rates all influenced the outcome of the interest-export growth race depicted in Chapter 2.

The decade preceding the mid-1982 Mexican debt crisis saw two large increases in the price of oil in 1973–74 and 1979. These contributed to the emergence of stagflation in developed countries, with double-digit inflation and real growth halved from the level of the 1960s. Several years of extraordinary high nominal and real interest rates sharply increased the interest payments of debtors who had relied on variable-rate financing. Slow OECD growth reduced the growth in demand for exports from developing countries, while changes in the terms of trade cut into the purchasing power of nonoil exporting countries and often produced declines in export earnings.

The influence of the external environment on a particular country's current account, and hence on its accumulation of additional debt, depends on a host of factors. Obviously, oil-exporting and oil-importing debtor countries felt quite different effects from the oil price shocks. The influence of changing levels of world interest rates depends on the size of a country's stock of debt and on whether it is held at fixed or variable rates. Countries that had preferred to borrow from commercial banks rather than international lending agencies were more badly affected by the high interest rates of the late 1970s and early 1980s, since international agency rates are often fixed at low levels for maturities up to 50 years. For some countries, rising OECD protectionism has also been important. Finally, the extent to which countries' indebtedness was influenced by changes in the terms of trade depended, among other factors, on their reliance on primary products rather than manufactured exports.

In seeking to measure the influence of external shocks, a variety of approaches have been used. A methodology introduced by Balassa has been favored by a large number of analysts.[1] An alternative approach has been developed by Cline.[2] Narrower aspects of the role of external developments have been examined by Diaz-Alejandro, Dornbusch, and Sachs.[3] The approach used in the following pages borrows heavily from that adopted by Cline. Each of the four external shocks mentioned above are examined in four separate sections in this chapter. Each section contains a general overview of the shock before presenting detailed estimates of the impact on each of the twenty-four countries in the sample of Major Borrowers and seventeen Heavily Indebted Countries.

THE OIL SHOCKS: OVERVIEW

To a considerable extent, much of the savage reductions in living standards that have occurred in oil-importing debtor countries may be laid at the doorstep of the oil producing nations of the Third World. The changes in the terms of trade produced by the 1973 and 1979 oil price shocks had a profound impact on international resource flows. Borrowing permitted the impact on oil-importing countries to be delayed until well after the initial 1973 shock. Although it postponed the reduction in living standards for a while, the ultimate effects of the oil shocks were inevitable.

The borrowing by oil-importing countries was related to widespread decisions within the developing world not to adjust dramatically to a suddenly energy-scarce world. The unwillingness to drastically curtail the volume of oil imports reflected more than the ease of borrowing funds to pay for oil. It also reflected a political attitude that poor countries should not stifle their own development through such policies unless absolutely necessary. Thus, some of the debt crisis of oil-importing debtor countries in the 1980s may be viewed as belated adjustment to energy conservation; an adjustment that was inevitable, but whose full extent was postponed until international financing sources dried up.[4] While net petroleum importing countries went more deeply into debt to pay for oil, the petroleum exporters borrowed against the expected future income stream to be generated by oil revenues in later years. For both groups, the later impact of sky-high OECD interest rates would not have been so severe had the stock of debt not been swollen in the interim by the effects of the first oil shock. Apart from drastically increasing the cost of imports and producing a decline in terms of trade and in the purchasing power of exports, the two oil shocks had another major impact on developing countries. Incipient OECD recessions were deepened, causing a slackening in the demand for developing country exports. Ripple effects included a slackening of demand from other developing countries—a factor that was of particular importance in Latin America in the early 1980s.

A look at the manner in which the oil trade balance of net oil importing developing countries grew is revealing. Table 5.1 shows that not until 1982 do oil trade deficits stop growing. Not until 1984 is there a nonoil trade surplus large enough to be a significant offset to oil imports. The price paid, in additional foreign exchange, for failing to control oil import volume through conservation programs was staggering. Table 5.1 contains estimates of the implied resource transfer paid by the group of net oil-importing developing countries to oil exporters. It amounts to $357 billion over the 1973–84 period. In the absence of offsetting items elsewhere in their balance of payments, this was the sum to be borrowed to finance the resource transfer implied by the change in the relative price of oil. The estimates are based on a comparison of actual net oil trade balances with those that would have been observed if the price of oil had changed at the same rate as the price of nonoil primary products.[5] For much of the period, these resource transfers were concealed. The ability to finance the transfers through reliance on borrowing hid the reduction in real income associated with the drastic change in the terms of trade. When borrowing was no longer possible this reality was laid bare.

In one sense, the world economy had experienced something like this before. As the ultimate unmasking of a delayed real resource transfer, the debt crisis produced an interesting wrinkle on the "transfer problem" as it dates back to German war reparations after World War I. It may be recalled that the harshness of the terms imposed on Germany after World War I led Keynes to argue that the required reduction in German living standards would be so great as to threaten the terms of the agreement.[6] In the recent crisis, the non-oil developing countries that relied on financing rather than adjustment may be seen to have used borrowing as a way of shielding the domestic economy from the disruptions associated with the resource transfer required by higher oil prices. Fraga estimates that the oil shocks to the Brazilian economy produced a transfer burden which was twice as large as that imposed on the German economy by the reparations payments of 1925–31.[7] By altering the timing and the apparent source of this disruption, an important political dimension was injected into the later discussions on debt. In a North-South context, resource transfers associated with the debt crisis involve very obvious and very open South to North transfers. These recent transfers mask the less obvious South-South post-1973 oil price transfers.

Table 5.1 Trade and Current Account Balances of Oil-Importing Developing Countries, 1973–86

($ billion)

	1973	1974	1975	1976	1977	1978	1979	1980	1981	1982	1983	1984	1985	1986
Current Account	-8.8	-31.9	-36.4	-24.9	-25.0	-34.2	-45.2	-65.1	-77.3	-61.1	-39.2	-24.6	-22.5	-6.4
Trade Balance	-9.0	-30.7	-34.2	-22.5	-22.5	-31.6	-51.6	-72.7	-77.9	-57.8	-37.0	-17.0	-19.5	-6.7
Non-Oil	-4.0	-13.8	-16.4	- 0.8	2.1	-5.0	-12.1	- 8.9	-11.7	1.5	15.5	30.2	23.1	21.5
Oil	-5.0	-16.9	-17.8	-21.7	-24.6	-26.6	-39.5	-63.8	-66.2	-59.3	-52.5	-47.2	-42.6	-28.2
Resource Transfer	0.0	-11.0	-13.2	-15.6	-17.0	-18.9	-30.0	-53.6	-58.3	-52.8	-45.7	-40.6	-37.5	-22.3

Sources:
Trade data: IMF, World Economic Outlook, various issues. Non-oil primary product price index: IMF, World Economic Outlook, various issues. Oil price index: IMF, International Financial Statistics Yearbook 1986, p. 171.

Note: Resource transfer from higher oil prices estimated as difference between actual oil trade balance and its value if oil prices rose at same rate as non-oil primary products.

CONSERVATION

The problems of engaging in energy conservation once the world moved to much higher energy prices after November 1973 were more difficult for developing than for developed countries. Arguments concerning the relative merits of conservation versus growth, which often involved mere debating points in developed countries, took on a unique poignancy in the Third World. Low living standards provide little cushion to permit conservation though slowing development. More rigid economic structures limit adaptability to the drastic shift in the relative price of energy. A political unwillingness to impose additional burdens on urban masses restricted the extent to which governments could pass higher world energy prices through to the domestic prices of petrol, electricity, mass transit, and so forth. Thus, while the balance of payments reflected the higher world price paid for oil in foreign exchange, domestic prices often failed to reflect world prices. It sometimes took an IMF adjustment program to set the price of domestic oil increases to a level reflecting the cost to the country on the world market.

The second oil shock produced a change in oil consumption growth of non-oil developing countries. It remained relatively stagnant from 1979 to 1985. For the net oil importing members of the non-oil developing world, oil consumption fell by a total of 6 percent between 1979 and 1982.[8] In volume terms, for the whole nonoil group, net oil imports fell 45 percent between 1979–82, largely because of rising Mexican exports. For the net oil importers, volume fell 12 percent during the three years. It had increased by more than 40 percent from 1973–79.[9]

The conservation pattern among the twelve Latin American and Caribbean countries included in the sample was decidedly mixed. Only four of them engaged in significant conservation after the first oil shock. They were Argentina, Chile, Jamaica, and Uruguay. At the time of the second oil shock all of the others were consuming petroleum and petroleum derivatives at levels well above 1973 levels.[10] Mexico and Ecuador were particularly profligate. Both had more than doubled their consumption levels. This extravagant behavior on the part of two oil producers ignored the real resource cost of consuming a nonrenewable resource whose international price called for conservation by both oil producers as well as oil consumers.

The response of the Latin American countries to the second oil shock was more pronounced, particularly in the case of Brazil. In some other instances, petroleum consumption did not begin to decline until after the emergence of the debt crisis. Even Mexico registered small declines in consumption in 1982 and 1983. However, by 1984, its consumption level had risen to treble the 1973 level. Latin American countries were not the only major debtors to fail to respond adequately to changing oil prices. Table 5.2 shows that Egypt, Indonesia, South Korea, and Nigeria were also countries with a high growth rate of energy consumption between 1973 and 1984. All but South Korea are oil producers.

IMPACT OF OIL SHOCKS

Because the debt crisis occurred *after* the second oil shock and *after* the global recession of 1975, the contribution of the first oil shock of 1973 to the ultimate crisis is both remote and not very dramatic. However, as we have seen, it had a major part to play in the dripping tap that fed the outstanding external debt of this group of countries inexorably. In the absence of large autonomous capital inflows, a string of large annual current account deficits produced a large stock of accumulated debt. The second oil shock had a more immediate impact, although the first country to run into trouble, Mexico in August 1982, was an oil exporter and another, Brazil, had made major efforts at energy conservation. Despite being an oil exporter, Mexico stands out among the five fuel exporters in the sample of debtor countries as being the only one not to report a trade surplus in any year between 1970 and 1981.

The two groupings of Major Borrower and of Heavily Indebted Countries include gainers and losers from the oil shocks of the 1970s. Five of the twenty-four countries in these two debtor categories are classified as fuel exporters by the IMF because fuel accounts for more than 50 percent of their total export earnings.[11] They are Ecuador, Indonesia, Mexico, Nigeria and Venezuela.[12] In the years after 1973 a number of countries, for example Argentina and Colombia, switched from being net petroleum exporters to become net importers. Others, such as Mexico, became net exporters. The two largest consumers among the group of oil-importing developing countries, India and Brazil, are included in the sample. The growing oil self-sufficiency of these two countries was an important factor in reducing the oil bill of oil-importing developing countries.

Table 5.3 contains estimates of the direct impact of oil prices on the indebtedness of these countries. Indirect effects, through influences on interest rates, income levels, and so forth, are not included. The table contains historical estimates as well as projections to 1992. Unlike Table 5.1, the individual country estimates for 1973–85 are found by subtracting observed values of net petroleum trade from values obtained by assuming the real dollar price of oil had remained constant at 1973 levels. The projections from 1986–92 attempt to measure

Table 5.2 Energy Consumption over Selected Years

	Energy Consumption Growth per annum (%)		Energy Imports as % of Merchandise Exports				
	1965-73	1973-84	1960	1965	1981	1984	1985
Major Borrowers							
Argentina	5.9	2.6	14.0	8.0	11.0	6.0	6.0
Brazil	11.6	4.7	21.0	14.0	52.0	30.0	37.0
Chile	7.2	0.8	10.0	5.0	20.0	14.0	16.0
Egypt	-0.7	11.2	12.0	11.0	10.0	10.0	10.0
India	5.1	6.5	11.0	8.0	81.0	59.0	30.0
Indonesia	6.6	8.0	3.0	3.0	8.0	20.0	12.0
Israel	6.1	2.2	17.0	13.0	36.0	25.0	21.0
S. Korea	15.3	8.4	70.0	18.0	37.0	25.0	24.0
Malaysia	8.5	7.0	2.0	10.0	18.0	12.0	9.0
Mexico	7.2	7.9	3.0	4.0	0.0	1.0	1.0
Turkey	10.0	4.5	16.0	12.0	83.0	53.0	53.0
Venezuela	4.3	4.5	1.0	0.0	0.0	0.0	1.0
17 Heavily Indebted Countries							
Bolivia	5.2	5.8	4.0	1.0	0.0	0.0	1.0
Colombia	6.6	5.3	3.0	1.0	25.0	14.0	14.0
Costa Rica	12.2	2.7	7.0	8.0	21.0	22.0	14.0
Côte d'Ivoire	10.9	4.1	5.0	5.0	21.0	16.0	14.0
Ecuador	9.3	14.8	2.0	11.0	1.0	1.0	1.0
Jamaica	10.2	-3.0	11.0	12.0	51.0	54.0	59.0
Morocco	8.9	5.0	9.0	5.0	50.0	47.0	50.0
Nigeria	7.1	12.2	7.0	7.0	0.0	3.0	3.0
Peru	5.2	3.6	4.0	3.0	1.0	3.0	4.0
Philippines	9.0	2.3	9.0	12.0	45.0	44.0	44.0
Uruguay	1.8	0.3	35.0	13.0	44.0	28.0	30.0
Yugoslavia	6.8	3.5	8.0	7.0	35.0	34.0	31.0

Source: World Bank, World Development Report, various years.

the gains and losses stemming from the "third oil shock"—the price collapse that began in late 1985. These projections assume no growth in net oil trade over 1985 levels, a future U.S. inflation rate of 3 percent in the producer price index, and a constant real dollar price of oil at early 1986 levels. The projections are obtained by applying 1985 net oil trade levels to the differential between precollapse 1985 oil prices and early 1986 prices with future prices assumed to grow in line with U.S. inflation. These estimates are not directly comparable with the

Table 5.3 The Impact of Three Oil Shocks   ($ billion)

	SHOCK I 1973-78	SHOCK II 1979-85	SHOCK III 1986-92
Major Borrowers	23.6	113.0	-75.6
Argentina	-1.4	-0.8	-1.9
Brazil	-11.8	-40.8	12.4
Chile	-1.2	-4.1	1.3
Egypt	1.0	12.2	-8.6
India	-4.8	-25.1	8.2
Indonesia	20.0	56.5	-26.7
Israel	-3.1	-10.0	3.7
S. Korea	-5.4	-30.3	16.1
Malaysia	1.1	13.7	-9.0
Mexico	1.9	71.6	-42.7
Turkey	-3.6	-16.1	9.2
Venezuela	30.8	86.1	-37.7
17 Heavily Indebted Countries	42.5	168.1	-91.2
Bolivia	0.3	0.1	0.0
Colombia	-0.1	-1.6	0.1
Costa Rica	-0.3	-0.9	0.5
Côte d'Ivoire	-0.5	-1.8	0.8
Ecuador	1.8	8.8	-5.0
Jamaica	-0.7	-2.2	1.0
Morocco	-0.9	-4.9	2.8
Nigeria	31.4	82.4	-35.2
Peru	-0.4	3.5	-1.2
Philippines	-2.6	-9.0	3.7
Uruguay	-0.6	-1.9	0.7
Yugoslavia	-3.3	-16.4	9.1

Sources: Interamerican Development Bank, Economic and Social Progress in Latin America, 1986, Table 69; IMF, International Financial Statistics Yearbook 1986. Shocks I and II measured post-1973 excess of oil prices over US WPI. Post-1985 estimates based on 1985 trade volume, constant real dollar oil price, US WPI increases of 2.5% for 1987-1992.

historical estimates because they do not include any growth in trade volume.

The estimates show that when the effects on both oil exporters and oil importers are aggregated, the first two oil shocks had a positive net impact in excess of $100 billion on the group of Major Borrowers, and in excess of $200 billion for the group of Heavily Indebted Countries. The gains to oil exporters outweighed the losses to oil importers. Brazil, India, and South Korea were the three countries most adversely affected by the first two shocks. For Brazil, the $52 billion cumulative effect of both shocks amounts to approximately 60 percent of the increase in long-term foreign indebtedness between 1970 and 1985.[13] In the cases of both India and South Korea, the negative shocks exceed the run-up in foreign debt.

Among the major oil exporters on the list, Mexico's run-up in external debt occurred despite its switch from an oil importer to an oil exporter and despite its earning more than an additional $74 billion from the two oil shocks. Similarly, Venezuela and Nigeria accumulated their debt while enjoying positive shocks of $117 billion and $114 billion respectively.

The projections of the direct effects of a continuation of low real oil prices until 1992 suggest that Mexico would be the biggest loser, experiencing a cumulative $43 billion revenue loss; it is followed by Venezuela, Nigeria, and Indonesia. If the cumulative gains to South Korea and Brazil were applied to reducing their stock of debt, the Korean debt could be eliminated while the Brazilian debt could be cut by 20 percent.

THE TERMS OF TRADE: OVERVIEW

The changes in the terms of trade that followed the two oil price increases of 1973 and 1979 were a further factor influencing debt accumulation. As with oil, this was not always obvious at the time. The 1970s was the decade of demands for a New International Economic Order (NIEO). Designed and forcefully articulated by Gamani Coryea, then Secretary General of UNCTAD, the proposals called for a more just distribution of control over the planet's resources and for a revolution in the relative bargaining powers of developed and developing nations. The intellectual origins of NIEO may be directly traced to the earlier writings of Singer and Prebisch that stressed the importance of the terms of trade in defining relations between developed and developing countries and argued that there were structural reasons that would produce a long-term decline in the terms of trade of developing countries.[14]

OPEC's oil actions seemed to provide the Group of 77 with the economic muscle to produce a NIEO. The ability of the oil-exporting nations to unilaterally treble the price of oil in November 1973 was seen as striking directly at the touchstone of economic relationships: the terms of trade. In a spirit of international solidarity, and in many instances of unconcealed delight at the discomfort so widely apparent throughout the OECD, there were few public expressions of reservation among oil-importing developing countries at the prospect of their own higher oil import bills. The trebling of posted oil prices in November 1973 coincided with a general, nonoil, primary product price boom that had begun in 1972. The stagnation and cyclical gyrations in developing country export prices that characterized the 1950s and 1960s were replaced by rapid growth in the 1970s. With minor dips along the way, nonoil primary product export unit values trebled over the decade. This growth was sharply reversed from 1981 onward.

Just as those oil-importing developing countries that relied on traditional primary product exports were beginning to benefit from the export price boom emerging after 1972, they received a double blow on the import side of their balance of payments. Prices of oil imports rose. So did prices of manufactured goods imported from the OECD countries. These latter had risen with oil-led inflation. Thus, even in periods in which their export prices rose, oil-importing developing countries were still fated to experience a deterioration in their terms of trade. It is ironic that this opportunity for a substantial break with the past was overwhelmed by the direct and indirect effects of the increases in the price of oil imposed by the other members of the Group of 77.

Table 5.4 shows the path followed by the terms of trade for a number of developing country groupings. The terms of trade of nonfuel exporting developing countries show continuous declines until 1983. The terms of trade for the other aggregate groupings conceal the experience of those that are not fuel exporters.

Changes in the terms of trade produce international resource transfers. For those countries experiencing a reduction in real income through a worsening of the terms of trade, international borrowing represented a way in which the implied reduction in living standards might be staved off for a while. For those economies experiencing an increase in real income through a rise in their terms of trade, the improvement in income and trade balances represented an improvement in creditworthiness. Rising credit ratings make international borrowing easier. While the short-term balance-of-trade financing needs of these countries were reduced, long-run financing demands were increased if the terms of trade gain was seen to be permanent and if countries sought to borrow against future income. Changes in

Table 5.4 Changes in the Terms of Trade and Nonoil Commodity Export Prices in the 1970s and 1980s (%)

	1970-79	1980	1981	1982	1983	1984	1985	1986	1987
Non-fuel Exporters									
Terms of trade	-1.1	-5.8	-4.0	-2.0	0.6	2.6	-2.3	-2.9	0.6
Capital Importers									
Terms of trade	1.3	3.8	-1.6	-2.0	-1.4	2.3	-2.9	-11.4	1.9
Non-oil export prices	10.5	6.3	-13.8	-10.8	6.7	4.1	-13.0	-1.1	3.0
Capital Importing Fuel Exporters									
Terms of trade	11.7	37.3	4.7	-2.2	-7.6	1.3	-5.6	-41.8	9.8
Non-oil export prices	12.4	3.2	-17.1	-8.5	6.9	5.5	-12.9	2.0	8.8
Countries with Recent Debt-servicing Problems									
Terms of trade	1.8	5.4	-2.4	-3.4	-2.4	2.2	-2.4	-16.1	0.6
Non-oil export prices	9.9	5.1	-14.3	-10.1	7.3	1.2	-10.3	0.6	1.2
Fifteen Heavily Indebted Countries									
Terms of trade	4.8	13.4	-2.9	-3.6	-3.7	2.6	-2.6	-18.4	1.9
Non-oil export prices	10.4	2.7	-14.1	-8.8	6.3	2.5	-10.8	1.5	-2.1

Source: IMF, World Economic Outlook, April 1988, pp. 138-142.

export prices had direct effects on two of the key ratios used to measure debt burdens—the debt-export and interest-export ratio.

IMPACT OF THE TERMS OF TRADE SHOCK

Good terms of trade data is not available for all of the countries in the sample. Table 5.5 uses IMF and UNCTAD sources to obtain estimates of the real income and trade balance effects of terms of trade movements since the first oil shock. Time periods have been arranged to coincide roughly with the timing of the 1973 and 1979 oil shocks since these were the biggest influences on terms of trade over the period.

The largest declines in terms of trade in the 1973–85 period were experienced by Argentina, Chile, Philippines, Turkey, and Uruguay. While the terms of trade of some borrowers worsened, those of oil exporters were improving. The largest gains were experienced by Nigeria, Venezuela, and Ecuador, three oil exporters whose terms of trade rose approximately 200 percent. Bolivia, Indonesia, and Mexico also had massive terms of trade gains.

The effects of changes in the terms of trade on merchandise trade balances were estimated by assuming that, in the absence of the terms of trade shocks, debtor country export and import prices would have kept pace with the world price of tradables. The estimates were produced by comparing the observed pattern of export and import unit values with what might have been observed had actual trade volumes been valued by unit-value indices growing at the same rate as the export unit value index of Industrial Countries. The results indicate that eight of the twelve Major Borrowers and nine of the seventeen Heavily Indebted Countries experienced deteriorations in their trade balances as a result of the combined effect of changes in export and import unit values over the 1973–85 period.

Changes in the terms of trade also have impacts on the real income of a country. The size of the impact depends on the relative importance of the foreign trade sector in the overall economy. With the exception of the Côte d'Ivoire, all the countries in the sample followed the worldwide pattern of an increasingly important foreign trade sector. In some instances, the foreign trade sector more than doubled as a share of GNP. Weighting the changes in the terms of trade by the relative importance of the foreign trade sector in the overall economy produces estimates of the real income effect of movements in the terms of trade. The change in the terms of trade between 1970–73 and 1974–78 produced a boost of 30 percent to Venezuelan real income and

Table 5.5   The Effects of Terms of Trade Shocks

	Changes in Terms of Trade (%)		Cumulative Impact on Trade Balance ($ billion)			Annual Real Income Effects (% of GNP)		Trade Balance Effects Minus Oil Price Effects ($ billion)		
	SHOCK I 1974-78	II 1979-85	SHOCK I	II	COMBINED SHOCKS 1974-85	SHOCK I	II	SHOCK I	II	COMBINED SHOCKS 1974-85
Major Borrowers	NA	NA	**13.3**	**60.8**	**74.1**	NA	NA	**-10.3**	**-52.1**	**-62.5**
Argentina	-14.1	-26.7	-2.9	-19.5	-22.4	-1.1	-4.2	-1.5	-18.7	-20.2
Brazil	-4.7	-29.8	-5.5	-36.4	-41.8	-0.3	-2.7	6.3	4.4	10.7
Chile	-35.5	-30.3	-4.2	-21.5	-25.8	-3.8	-5.8	-3.0	-17.5	-20.5
Egypt	9.0	5.8	-2.7	-5.7	-8.4	1.1	1.3	-3.7	-17.9	-21.7
India	-23.3	6.7	-5.3	-17.6	-22.9	-0.9	0.5	-0.5	7.5	7.0
Indonesia	125.7	45.9	21.8	81.6	103.4	19.0	11.4	1.7	25.1	26.8
Israel	-9.4	-1.0	-4.2	-10.6	-14.8	-2.4	-0.4	-1.1	-0.6	-1.8
S. Korea	-19.2	-1.6	-7.8	-31.7	-39.5	-3.7	-0.5	-2.4	-1.4	-3.8
Malaysia	1.7	10.2	2.0	9.9	11.9	0.7	5.7	0.9	-3.8	-2.9
Mexico	43.2	26.9	2.4	55.1	57.6	2.1	2.6	0.5	-16.4	-15.9
Turkey	-15.1	30.9	-5.4	-21.2	-26.6	-1.0	-2.8	-1.8	-5.1	-7.0
Venezuela	147.5	61.9	25.1	78.5	103.6	30.4	15.7	-5.7	-7.6	-13.3
17 Heavily Indebted Countries	NA	NA	**40.0**	**98.4**	**138.5**	NA	NA	**-2.5**	**-69.7**	**-72.1**
Bolivia	89.4	16.7	1.1	2.7	3.8	10.3	3.2	0.8	2.6	3.4
Colombia	40.3	-14.9	3.0	2.3	5.2	4.4	-1.9	3.1	3.8	6.9
Costa Rica	-6.0	-13.3	-0.3	-1.3	-1.6	-2.0	-4.3	-0.0	-0.3	-0.3
Côte d'Ivoire	11.4	-14.3	1.4	0.3	1.7	3.6	-4.0	1.9	2.1	4.0
Ecuador	48.7	50.9	3.1	10.7	13.8	26.0	10.9	1.3	1.9	3.2
Jamaica	24.8	-22.4	0.5	-0.8	-0.4	9.0	-11.6	1.1	1.4	2.5
Morocco	67.5	-24.1	1.0	-0.6	0.5	9.4	-4.1	1.9	4.4	6.2
Nigeria	53.8	66.6	27.6	68.7	96.3	20.7	15.6	-3.8	-13.7	-17.5
Peru	-7.6	-27.1	-1.3	-7.2	-8.5	-0.9	-5.1	-0.9	-10.6	-11.5
Philippines	22.4	-25.8	-4.8	-20.9	-25.7	-3.4	-4.9	-2.2	-11.9	-14.1
Uruguay	25.9	-14.8	-0.9	-2.8	-3.7	-2.3	-2.0	-0.3	-0.9	-1.2
Yugoslavia	-6.1	0.4	-5.2	-8.9	-14.1	-1.0	0.1	-1.9	7.5	5.5

Note: SHOCK I is change from 1970-73 average. SHOCK II is change from 1974-78 average. Trade effects estimated by revaluing trade volumes with unit value indices changing at industrial country export value index growth rate. Real income effects estimated by multiplying change in terms of trade by trade weights. Non-oil trade balance effects obtained by subtracting oil shock estimates of Table 5.3. For Sources see note 15.

increases of between 20–25 percent for Ecuador, Indonesia, and Nigeria.

For most developing countries, changes in the terms of trade were dominated by changes in the relative price of oil. The trade effects of the oil shocks have been discussed above. Subtracting the oil shock effects of Table 5.3 from the terms of trade effects provides a crude measure of the nonoil effects of changes in the terms of trade on the trade balances of the borrowers. The final columns of Table 5.5 show these net effects. This rough approach to netting out nonoil terms of trade effects on trade balances does not correct for the very considerable indirect influences of oil prices on many other export and import prices, nor for the fact that the import volume of oil exporters was heavily determined by the income effect of greater oil revenue. Accordingly, the estimates should be treated with considerable caution.

As the final columns of Table 5.5 show, a number of debtor countries that experienced cumulative trade balance deteriorations through terms of trade effects between 1973–85 would have experienced a trade balance improvement in the absence of oil price effects on their terms of trade. Brazil, India, Jamaica and Yugoslavia fall into this category. On the other hand, such oil exporters as Mexico, Venezuela, and Nigeria would have seen the terms of trade worsen their trade balances in the absence of an increase in the real dollar price of oil.

The results presented above may be compared with those produced by a number of other investigators. Cline estimated that nonoil developing countries lost $79 billion through the 1981–82 fall in their terms of trade.[16] Sachs' estimates of the effects from 1975–78 show a number of countries experiencing losses exceeding 2 percent of GDP per year while other countries gain significantly.[17]

INTEREST RATE SHOCKS: OVERVIEW

Three of the four external shocks discussed in this chapter involve shocks transmitted through commodity markets. Interest rate shocks bring us to asset market developments. One of the most obvious asset market developments of the mid-1970s was the redirection of liquidity from the depressed demand of OECD capital markets to the liquidity-hungry developing countries. In the United States, the extent of the depressed loan demand immediately after the first oil shock may be deduced from a comparison of interest rate and money supply trends. As Table 5.6 shows, 1974 and 1975 were years of negative real growth in the broadly defined money supply. Despite the reduction in real money supply, *ex post* real short-run interest rates went sharply negative and remained so until 1979.

Table 5.6 U.S. Monetary Policy in the 1970s and 1980s (%)

	Nominal M3 Growth	Nominal 3-Month T-Bill Yield	Nominal 10-Year Bond Yield	GNP Deflator Growth	Real M3 Growth	Real 3-Month T-Bill Yield	Real 10-Year Bond Yield
1970	10.2	6.5	7.4	5.5	4.7	1.0	1.9
1971	14.6	4.4	6.2	5.7	8.9	-1.3	0.5
1972	14.1	4.1	6.2	4.7	9.4	-0.6	1.5
1973	11.2	7.0	6.8	6.5	4.7	0.5	0.3
1974	8.7	7.9	7.6	9.1	-0.4	-1.2	-1.5
1975	9.5	5.8	8.0	9.8	-0.3	-4.0	-1.8
1976	11.9	5.0	7.6	6.4	5.5	-1.4	1.2
1977	12.3	5.3	7.4	6.7	5.6	-1.4	0.7
1978	11.8	7.2	8.4	7.3	4.5	-0.1	1.1
1979	9.7	10.0	9.4	8.9	0.6	1.1	0.5
1980	10.2	11.5	11.5	9.0	1.2	2.5	2.5
1981	12.3	14.0	13.9	9.7	2.6	4.3	4.2
1982	9.2	10.7	13.0	6.4	2.8	4.3	6.6
1983	10.2	8.6	11.1	3.9	6.3	4.7	7.2
1984	10.6	9.6	12.4	3.7	6.9	5.9	8.7
1985	7.3	7.5	10.6	3.0	4.3	4.5	7.6
1986	9.2	6.0	7.7	2.7	6.5	3.3	5.0
1987	5.0	5.8	8.4	3.3	1.7	2.5	5.1
1988	5.3	6.7	8.9	4.0	1.3	2.7	4.9

Source: The Economic Report of the President 1988. "Ex-post" real values expressed as nominal values minus annual growth in implicit GNP deflator.

With negative (or low) real rates of return being offered on assets within the United States in the mid-1970s, it was to be expected that asset markets would adjust through capital flows toward areas offering higher risk-adjusted expected real rates of return. Adjusted for risk, dollar-denominated assets that could be loaned abroad at higher interest rates than prevailed in the United States would earn a higher real rate of return. The ability of a number of developing countries to run up their external debt throughout the 1970s might have been considerably more curtailed had developed country asset markets not been so depressed. Only after the build-up in debt stock was well under way did interest rates rise sharply.

There have been a number of explanations of why real U.S. interest rates were so low during much of the 1970s.[18] Wilcox has shown how the pattern of the 1970s may be explained by a combination of rising rather than constant inflationary expectations coupled with negative supply shocks. The reduction in supply of intermediate inputs such as oil lowered the rate of return on capital. He concludes that by 1978 supply shocks alone had cut real pretax interest rates by a percentage point while rising expected inflation reduced them by a further one and a half points.

The years after the 1973 oil shock were not only years of negative short-term real interest rates, they were also, as Sachs describes them, years of limited investment opportunities in OECD economies with the maturation of the post World War II boom, a sharp squeeze on profits as labor's share of GNP rose and pretax rates of return on capital fell.[19] Simultaneously, there were expanding investment opportunities in LDCs for direct private investment. These included some shifts from import substitution to export orientation, capital liberalization, and an investment boom in primary products. For Sachs, the growing indebtedness of LDCs was attributable not to oil shocks but to such global shifts in direct private investment and was not a cause of concern. As long as the debt reflected financing of a savings-investment gap rather than efforts to maintain consumption at preoil price increase levels, Sachs saw limited ground for concern.[20] He did, however, warn of dangers if high real interest rates persisted.

While developed country real interest rates were going negative through much of the 1970s before bouncing back to steeply positive values in the early 1980s, real interest rates faced by the *borrowing* countries followed the same general pattern but with much greater amplitude. The IMF has estimated that real money market rates plunged sharply negative after 1973, reaching levels more negative than –25 percent in 1974.[21] This was a dramatic reversal of the long range pattern of positive rates that stretched back to at least 1955. In the years after 1973, real rates zigzagged between +5 percent and –10 percent until the strongly positive trend began in 1980 culminated in a peak around 20 percent in 1982.

Table 5.7 contains data on nominal and real interest rates for the period 1977–87. Three separate price indices have been used in the deflation of nominal interest rates in an effort to obtain real six-month interest rates facing borrowers in the United States, in developed countries and in heavily indebted developing countries. The U.S. GNP deflator was used to obtain real short-term interest rates inside the United States. The world export unit value index was chosen as the appropriate deflator of LIBOR to obtain a measure of real rates facing developed country borrowers. The real rate facing heavily indebted developing countries was obtained by deflating nominal LIBOR plus the non-OPEC country spread by the export unit value index of fifteen heavily indebted countries.

Real interest rates are highly sensitive to the choice of price deflator. The appropriate real interest rates are *own country* rates. Theoretically, as Dornbusch points out, real interest rates are world nominal interest rates adjusted for exchange rate changes and *domestic* rather than world inflation.[22] More accurately, the adjustment would be in terms of *expected* exchange rate and domestic inflation. Bacha and Diaz-Alejandro discussed the choice of appropriate deflators in their 1982 study and after referring to choices made by other authors, plump, on grounds of "practical considerations," for a weighted sum of dollar import and export prices. Their weights are the marginal shares of exports and imports in the adjustment process.[23] Sachs measures the real interest rate in dollar tradable goods prices, using an average of each country's dollar export and import unit values as the measure of dollar price of tradables.[24] In the absence of adequate import unit value indices, Sachs uses the export unit value index of developed countries. Cline, however, uses U.S. inflation as his measure of dollar tradable prices.[25] Table 5.7 may be used to crudely separate the forces at work on interest rates into those that developing country borrowers may be justified in considering to be exogenous shocks and those which might more properly be considered endogenous. Loans to developing countries are tied to LIBOR or U.S. Prime with a country spread reflecting the perceived risk of lending to a particular country. Dornbusch reminds us that there are two spreads, reflecting two separate risks of holding assets that are not "risk-free."[26] Neither LIBOR nor U.S. Prime are risk-free interest rates. LIBOR, in particular, reflects the risk of lending to a banking institution rather than to the presumably "risk-free" U.S. Treasury. The spread between six-month dollar-denominated LIBOR and the six-month U.S. Treasury bill rate reflects "bank risk." The spread between LIBOR and the rate on a country loan reflects "country risk."[27] Both are subject to changed

Table 5.7 Nominal and Real Interest Rates, 1977–87   (%)

	1977	1978	1979	1980	1981	1982	1983	1984	1985	1986	1987
NOMINAL:											
US 6 month T-Bill	5.5	7.6	10.0	11.4	13.8	11.1	8.8	9.8	7.7	6.0	6.1
6 month $ LIBOR	6.4	9.2	12.2	14.0	16.7	13.6	9.9	11.3	8.6	6.9	7.3
Bank Spread	0.9	1.6	2.2	2.6	2.9	2.5	1.1	1.5	0.9	0.8	1.2
Country Spreads											
OECD	1.0	0.8	0.6	0.6	0.6	0.6	0.7	0.6	0.5	0.4	0.3
Eastern Europe	1.1	0.8	0.7	0.9	0.6	1.0	1.2	0.9	0.6	0.3	0.2
OPEC	1.2	1.1	1.1	0.8	0.8	0.9	0.9	0.8	0.8	0.5	0.7
Other LDCs	1.6	1.2	0.9	0.9	1.0	1.1	1.7	1.4	1.0	0.7	0.7
LIBOR + LDC Spread	8.0	10.4	13.0	14.9	17.8	14.7	11.6	12.7	9.6	7.5	8.0
Average Terms of New Commitments	7.9	9.5	11.4	12.4	13.8	12.2	10.4	10.6	8.9	7.4	7.4
REAL:											
US 6 month T-Bill	-1.2	0.3	1.1	2.4	4.1	4.7	4.9	6.1	4.5	3.4	3.1
6 month $ LIBOR	-2.6	-0.8	-6.1	-5.7	17.8	17.2	15.5	13.3	10.5	1.8	1.8
LIBOR + LDC Spread	-3.2	10.6	-14.9	-19.2	16.6	21.1	18.2	11.0	15.4	23.9	-1.8
Average Terms of New Commitments	-3.4	9.7	-16.5	-21.9	12.6	18.6	17.0	8.9	14.7	23.8	-2.4

Sources: T-Bill rates and US GNP deflator in The Economic Report of the President 1988. Country spreads from OECD, Financial Market Trends, various years. LIBOR (IFS 60lde) from IMF, International Financial Statistics Yearbook 1987, p. 104, and deflated by world export unit value index (IFS 74d) in IMF, International Financial Statistics Yearbook 1987, p. 129 and IMF, International Financial Statistics May 1988, p. 76. Average terms of newcommitments from private creditors from World Bank, World Debt Tables 1988-89. Both LDC rates deflated by export unit value index of fifteen heavily indebted countries from IMF, World Economic Outlook, Oct. 1986, p. 65 and April 1988, p. 138.

perceptions. The decomposition of interest rates into a base rate and two separate spreads suggests that there were three primary factors influencing debt-servicing charges for the variable-rate component of developing countries' debt. The first was OECD monetary policy, particularly U.S. policy. The second was the deteriorating financial position of the world's banking system. The third was the risk attached to lending to a particular country. A case may be made for considering the country spreads to be an endogenous rather than an exogenous shock to developing countries since this spread reflects external perceptions of the internal policies of the debtor and these are perceptions over which the debtor has some control. External perceptions may be wrong; they may even be unfair in the eyes of the debtor, but they are controllable through changes in internal policies. To that extent, country spreads are endogenous.

The behavior of the six-month T-bill rate may be used as indicator of U.S. monetary policy. Changes in the T-bill rate are a purely exogenous shock to LDCs. United States inflation, banking deregulation, and the adoption of monetary targets caused nominal T-bill rates to double between 1977 and 1980 before peaking in 1981. LIBOR did not track the T-bill rate over this period, producing considerable variation in the "bank spread." A variety of forces altered perceptions about risk in international banking. These include the impact of U.S. deregulation, poor loan decisions in the areas of real estate, oil and gas, and, of course, developing countries. Bank spreads in 1979–82 were significantly above 1978 or post-1982 levels.[28] The bulk of the changes in bank spread may be seen as exogenous shocks to the rates that developing countries were asked to pay on their loans since the years of high bank spread precede the Mexican crisis of August 1982.

The table shows country spreads for four country groupings. Nominal non-OPEC LDC spreads peaked in 1983 and declined sharply thereafter, in part as a result of lower spreads on reschedulings.[29] Although the nominal rates facing LDCs peaked in 1981 as T-bill rates and bank spreads both peaked, the declines in U.S. interest rates and bank spreads from 1981 to 1983 were not fully passed on to LDCs because of rising country spreads.

The behavior of *ex post* real interest rates is also presented in Table 5.7.[30] United States domestic real rates (measured by deflating the T-bill rate by domestic U.S. inflation) were positive from 1978–86, rising to a 1984 peak. Internationally, real rates facing debtor countries followed a quite different pattern because of the different behavior of the dollar price of their tradables. In particular, the 1982–84 decline in real rates facing LDCs was very abruptly reversed in 1985 as a result of the sharp fall in export unit values. The collapse in oil prices in 1986 caused a further 16 percent decline in the export unit value index of the highly indebted countries, producing a spike in real rates. The rebound in export unit values in 1987 more than compensated for the slight rise in LIBOR, producing negative real rates for the first time since 1980.

The interest rate shock of 1981–83 was much more pronounced in real than in nominal terms. 1981 was a year of dramatic reversal from double-digit negative real rates to double-digit positive real rates. The reversal amounted to a more than 30 percentage point change in one year. Negative real interest rates had been a powerful inducement to borrow. The reversal to sharply positive rates produced an enormous real resource burden for countries attempting to service debt.

The years from 1981 through 1985 were years of extraordinary levels for real international rates on dollar-denominated assets. The reversal from negative or near negative *ex post* real interest rates was due much more to the collapse in the inflation rate of the dollar price of tradables, particularly export prices, of developing countries than it was to the behavior of nominal interest rates in the OECD countries. In 1979 and 1980 the inflation rate of the dollar prices of exports of the IMF's fifteen heavily indebted countries had been approximately 30 percent per annum. As mentioned earlier, the 1981–86 period saw a catastrophic decline in developing country nonoil export prices.

By 1986, real rates facing developing countries were even above the heights of the early 1980s. Nominal LIBOR had been halved since 1982. Country spreads had been negotiated downward. But the *negative* inflation rate for the dollar prices of tradables of Baker Plan countries in each year from 1982 to 1986 meant that real LIBOR facing these countries *exceeded* nominal LIBOR. It took a rebound in export prices in 1987 to lower the real interest burden significantly and produce negative real rates.

For many of the countries in the sample, the real interest rates contained in Table 5.7 were meaningless. With the shut-off of credit, these countries faced credit rationing through quantity rather than price. Moreover, with reschedulings, unilateral payments moratoria, and so forth, interest rates on original loan contracts were not being honored. Real effective interest rates on public and publicly guaranteed debt for the countries in the sample are shown in Table 5.8. They are *ex post* rates, obtained by using observed changes in the dollar price of tradables of each country as a deflator. While nominal effective interest rates provide an indication of the financing flows used to service debt, real effective rates show the resource transfer associated with the interest payment. The sharp reversal from double-digit negative real rates to double-digit positive rates in 1981 is all too apparent. Yugoslavia is the single sample country to avoid the sharp reversal from negative to positive real effective rates in 1981.

Table 5.8 Real Effective Interest Rates, 1975–86

	1975	1980	1981	1982	1983	1984	1985	1986
Major Borrowers								
Argentina	3.1	-8.7	13.1	16.9	11.6	3.7	12.8	10.0
Brazil	1.7	-6.6	8.9	16.5	13.7	8.7	13.3	13.5
Chile	11.8	-7.6	21.3	17.5	8.3	15.1	7.8	10.3
Egypt	2.3	-17.6	3.6	10.2	9.1	5.3	3.2	15.5
India	-12.5	-14.7	19.6	3.8	4.6	10.7	-7.3	8.4
Indonesia	-4.8	-30.7	4.8	8.7	13.2	7.7	9.4	23.1
Israel	-1.2	-11.2	9.9	15.3	10.8	7.0	9.8	6.9
S. Korea	7.3	-4.4	4.7	14.9	12.6	6.0	11.4	10.1
Malaysia	7.8	-12.7	6.1	11.6	9.6	8.0	19.4	28.8
Mexico	-0.5	-18.9	10.7	15.4	15.4	13.3	11.0	19.7
Turkey	0.3	-32.5	13.5	11.2	18.7	10.9	13.4	-3.5
Venezuela	0.8	-26.1	7.4	17.9	19.9	11.0	9.5	23.9
17 Heavily Indebted Countries	NA	-15.6	7.1	15.5	13.1	7.8	12.8	14.0
Bolivia	-0.2	-22.3	19.4	13.2	4.9	12.5	3.3	6.1
Colombia	2.1	-3.7	10.3	8.8	8.6	1.8	14.2	4.6
Costa Rica	-7.5	-17.2	16.3	7.2	18.4	3.2	10.2	1.8
Côte d'Ivoire	-6.8	-2.8	25.1	16.4	12.0	4.1	5.8	2.1
Ecuador	-3.4	-28.1	12.5	18.6	11.0	14.0	9.1	16.1
Jamaica	-32.6	-15.5	11.1	12.4	10.2	10.7	16.2	10.2
Morocco	-12.1	-14.5	5.6	14.6	10.6	6.6	2.0	5.7
Nigeria	-5.1	-30.5	8.3	13.8	16.1	12.1	10.3	17.9
Peru	3.7	-9.5	15.3	15.9	7.6	6.6	3.3	4.7
Philippines	13.2	-8.4	2.4	21.6	3.5	-5.0	15.2	18.4
Uruguay	17.2	-14.2	11.2	18.9	14.2	5.0	15.7	13.7
Yugoslavia	-1.3	-14.2	-0.8	4.7	7.0	9.7	7.5	6.8

Note: Effective rates from INT/XGS and DOD/XGS ratios in World Bank, World Debt Tables 1987-88, deflated by changes in country-specific dollar price of tradeables indices from IFS 74d, 75d or from UNCTAD, Handbook of International Trade and Development Statistics, 1988.

As with other measures of real rates, the extreme variability of real effective rates is largely due to the behavior of the dollar price of tradables, particularly the price of exportables as estimated by export unit value indices. Although debt restructuring helped to limit nominal interest payments after 1982, the real burden of interest payments was still heavily influenced by movements in the prices of tradables. Table 5.8 shows considerable variation by country in real effective rates. In 1981, Egypt faced a real effective rate as low as 2 percent, while that of Chile was 16.7 percent. There was also great variation by year. Whereas average real effective rates peaked in 1982, a number of countries (Colombia, Jamaica, Malaysia, and Yugoslavia) had higher real effective rates in 1985 than in earlier years. For oil exporting Venezuela and Mexico, the collapse of oil prices in 1986 produced extraordinary high real interest rates in that year.

IMPACT OF INTEREST RATE SHOCKS

It is possible to obtain crude estimates of the impact of the real interest rate shock for each country by first obtaining an estimate of the net debt that may be considered to be at variable interest rates, and then applying an estimated real interest rate shock to this base. Following Cline, the gains from the higher interest rates earned on interest-bearing foreign exchange reserves are netted out by assuming that all nongold foreign exchange reserves are held in variable rate assets.

For Cline, the real rate shock is calculated as the difference between historical and actual levels of real LIBOR where LIBOR is deflated by the growth in the U.S. producer price index. Cline provides a historical value of real LIBOR in the 1960s and 1970s of 1.66 percent.[31] Deflating LIBOR by changes in the U.S. wholesale price index would produce estimates of the average real LIBOR facing the United States from 1971–80 of 0.3 percent per annum. Between 1981 and 1984 it averaged 9.2 percent per annum.

Much larger interest rate shocks are obtained if LIBOR is deflated by indices representing the dollar prices of tradables of each country. The 1981–84 period saw a sharp reversal of trends in tradable goods prices for debtor countries. These had risen at annual rates in double digits in the 1971–80 period while U.S. wholesale prices rose at 9.4 percent per annum. In the 1981–84 period, however, all debtor countries in the sample experienced declines in tradable goods prices while U.S. wholesale prices continued to rise at 3.7 percent per annum. Thus, the use of country-specific indices for tradable goods prices adds a further component to the real interest rate shock.

As Table 5.9 shows, the difference produced by applying the two methodologies to the same estimates of the stock of variable debt is considerable. The estimates contained in Table 5.9 make no allowance for debt restructuring or other actions that have reduced real *effective* interest rates and contain no correction for the observed increases in country spreads. Further, the estimates do not include the impact of rising interest rates on the *additions* to the stock of fixed-rate debt. The estimates of the real interest rate shock contained in Table 5.9 are several orders of magnitude larger than those reported by Cline or Sachs. Although using Cline's approach to estimating the stock of variable debt, I depart from Cline's method of estimating real LIBOR and prefer to use country-specific price indices of tradables rather than to rely on a U.S. price index. While using Sachs' general approach to estimating price indices, I use LIBOR rather than an estimate of the implied interest rate. I stress that Table 5.9 does *not* show how much extra was actually paid because of higher real rates, but rather how much extra would have been paid had there been no accommodation to repayment difficulties.

As Table 5.9 shows, rising interest rates produced a cumulative interest rate burden in excess of $260 billion for the twelve Major Borrowers over the years 1981–85. The cumulative burden for the seventeen Heavily Indebted Countries over the same period amounted to $277 billion. The largest cumulative shock was felt by Mexico with a shock of $77 billion, which would have amounted to over half its total debt.

In recent years, India has relied less than other sample countries on variable rate loans. Some countries have a variable rate component of public and publicly guaranteed long-term debt amounting to 40–90 percent. India's has been in the 2–5 percent range. Its small variable rate debt is exceeded by its holdings of nongold foreign exchange reserves to produce a negative net variable debt. As a result, India stands alone among the sample countries as a net gainer from high real interest rates.

SLOW OECD GROWTH: OVERVIEW

The first oil shock marked the end of an era for developed economies. High rates of economic growth came to an end, to be superceded by years of low growth, rising levels of unemployment, and several recessions. The years after 1973 saw developed country growth rates halved from the levels of the 1960s. Between 1960 and 1974 the Industrial Countries averaged real GDP growth rates of 4.76 percent. From 1974 through 1985 growth averaged 2.37 percent. Of the

Table 5.9 Real Interest Rate Shocks

	Real LIBOR (%) Annual Average		Annual Change in Interest Payments ($ billion)					Cumulative Shock	Cline's Method
	1971-78	1981-85	1981	1982	1983	1984	1985	1981-85	1981-85
Major Borrowers	NA	NA	-36.5	-55.9	-59.1	-55.3	-53.6	-260.4	-90.9
Argentina	-3.9	15.3	-3.8	-7.4	-6.3	-4.1	-6.0	-27.6	-11.6
Brazil	-5.0	15.0	-9.4	-13.7	-14.5	-13.1	-13.8	-64.5	-24.4
Chile	-3.4	16.9	-2.0	-2.5	-1.9	-2.9	-1.8	-11.1	-4.5
Egypt	-7.6	14.8	-0.8	-0.9	-1.1	-0.9	-0.8	-4.5	-1.5
India	-4.2	15.7	2.0	0.4	0.1	0.1	-0.0	2.5	0.5
Indonesia	-15.5	14.5	-0.9	-1.5	-2.9	-2.5	-2.7	-10.5	-2.7
Israel	-6.1	15.3	-0.8	-1.2	-0.9	-1.0	-0.9	-4.6	-1.7
S. Korea	-3.5	13.4	-2.3	-3.9	-3.8	-3.0	-4.1	-17.1	-7.7
Malaysia	-7.6	15.9	0.4	-0.1	-0.9	-1.1	-1.9	-3.5	-1.2
Mexico	-9.1	14.4	-11.3	-16.6	-17.9	-17.6	-13.7	-77.2	-25.2
Turkey	-7.1	18.5	-1.7	-1.3	-1.4	-1.2	-1.5	-7.1	-2.1
Venezuela	-15.4	14.5	-5.9	-7.3	-7.6	-8.0	-6.4	-35.2	-8.9
17 Heavily Indebted Countries	NA	14.2	-39.7	-62.0	-61.2	-58.3	-56.0	-277.2	-97.1
Bolivia	-12.4	17.1	-0.4	-0.3	-0.2	-0.4	-0.3	-1.6	-0.4
Colombia	-4.2	12.7	0.1	-0.2	-0.5	-0.6	-1.2	-2.3	-1.1
Costa Rica	-4.9	15.1	-0.5	-0.4	-0.4	-0.3	-0.3	-1.9	-0.8
Côte d'Ivoire	-7.1	16.1	-1.3	-1.1	-1.0	-0.6	-0.7	-4.7	-1.6
Ecuador	-16.8	14.3	-1.2	-1.7	-1.7	-1.5	-1.4	-7.5	-1.9
Jamaica	-8.8	17.5	-0.1	-0.1	-0.1	-0.2	-0.2	-0.6	-0.2
Morocco	-10.1	14.2	-0.8	-1.2	-1.1	-1.0	-0.8	-4.9	-1.6
Nigeria	-17.8	15.2	0.9	-2.0	-2.4	-3.7	-2.9	-10.2	-2.5
Peru	-3.8	16.3	-0.8	-1.1	-0.9	-0.9	-0.6	-4.3	-1.7
Philippines	-4.7	13.2	-1.5	-4.2	-2.0	-0.7	-3.5	-12.0	-5.3
Uruguay	-8.8	15.4	-0.1	-0.3	-0.4	-0.3	-0.5	-1.5	-0.5
Yugoslavia	-5.0	9.9	-1.6	-2.0	-2.2	-2.5	-1.8	-10.2	-5.2

Source: Debt data from World Bank, World Debt Tables 1987-88. Non-gold reserves, LIBOR and deflator from IMF, International Financial Statistics Yearbook 1987 or from UNCTAD Handbook of International Trade and Development Statistics 1988 Supplement. Table 7.2 where IFS indices are not available.

Note: Shocks estimated by multiplying previous year's estimated net variable rate debt by the difference between country specific real LIBOR and 1971-80 average. Variable rate net debt defined as the sum of variable rate public DOD, private non-guaranteed debt and short run debt minus non-gold reserves. Country-specific real LIBOR obtained by deflating nominal six month Euro-$ LIBOR by average of export and import unit values. Cline's method uses difference between LIBOR deflated by the US WPI and its 1960s and 1970s average of 1.66.

major OECD economies, only France managed to escape negative growth rates at some point in the years between 1974 and 1984. The United States had negative GNP growth in 1974, 1975, 1980, and 1982.

There are a number of reasons why pre-1973 OECD growth rates might be expected to have slackened even in the absence of an oil crisis. Not least of these was the maturation of the post World War II recovery boom, which might be seen to have run its course by the late 1960s. The arrival of new dynamic economies such as the NICs may have heralded the end of the high growth record of many of the more mature OECD economies.

For any debtor country, the shortfall in export earnings produced by slow growth in developed country markets depends on the commodity composition and destination of its exports. Debtor nations with a large component of their export trade in cyclically sensitive commodities and with a heavy reliance on those countries suffering the most drastic slowdowns in GNP growth rates suffered the most. Rising OECD protectionism also hurt, particularly for debtor countries that export manufactures.

The impact of OECD growth on the debt mountain was felt through a reduction in export earnings of debtor countries. This depends on the size of the OECD income elasticity of demand for the volume of developing country exports and on the elasticity of developing country export prices with respect to OECD income. These two elasticities determine the sensitivity of developing country export earnings to developed country economic growth. Empirical estimates vary considerably.[32] Empirical estimates of nonoil commodity price elasticity with respect to developed country industrial production suggest values around two.[33]

The most comprehensive range of OECD income elasticity estimates is provided by Cline.[34] He reports a marginal elasticity of 3, and an average elasticity of 2, for nonoil developing country export volume. His estimates for export revenue range from a one-year elasticity of 3.5 to a five-year elasticity of 2.6.[35] These estimates are generally at the high end of the range of estimates available.[36] If so, they would overestimate the extent to which slow OECD growth contributed to the accumulation of debt and would also lead to optimism concerning the role of OECD growth in solving the problem.

THE IMPACT OF SLOW OECD GROWTH

Estimates of the impact of slow OECD growth on debtor country export earnings may be obtained by applying OECD income elasticities of demand for developing country exports to a base level of export earnings and to the differential between historical and actual OECD growth rates. A recent study of empirical estimates of income elasticities of export volume and export prices is found in Goldsbrough and Zaidi.[37] However, to remove terms of trade effects it was decided to apply a mean income elasticity of export volume of 2. By using 1973 nonoil export revenue as a base, two projections of post-1973 export revenues are obtained by applying the income elasticity for exports to the observed shortfall in industrial country GDP growth from the historical average of the 1960s. The results, contained in Table 5.10, do not reflect changes in market shares in the years after 1973. All losses are proportional to a country's share of the 1973 base. The losses of Argentina, Brazil, and South Korea are particularly large.

Table 5.10 Cumulative Shortfalls in Nonoil Export Volume Due to Slow OECD Growth   ($ billion)

	1974-78	1979-85
Major Borrowers	-32.6	-176.7
Argentina	-3.9	-20.9
Brazil	-7.3	-39.5
Chile	-1.4	-7.8
Egypt	-1.2	-6.2
India	-3.4	-18.6
Indonesia	-1.9	-10.2
Israel	-1.7	-9.2
S. Korea	-3.8	-20.6
Malaysia	-3.5	-18.7
Mexico	-2.6	-14.3
Turkey	-1.5	-8.4
Venezuela	-0.4	-2.2
17 Heavily Indebted Countries	-28.5	-154.5
Bolivia	-0.3	-1.7
Colombia	-1.4	-7.5
Costa Rica	-0.4	-2.2
Côte d'Ivoire	-1.0	-5.5
Ecuador	-0.3	-1.6
Jamaica	-0.5	-2.5
Morocco	-1.1	-5.8
Nigeria	-0.7	-3.7
Peru	-1.3	-7.1
Philippines	-2.2	-12.0
Uruguay	-0.4	-2.1
Yugoslavia	-3.4	-18.2

Sources: Exports and industrial growth from IMF, International Financial Statistics 1986 Yearbook, pp. 114-15, 154-55. Estimates based on post-1973 slowdown of industrial GDP growth from 1960s average of 4.9%, using an export income elasticity of 2.

CONCLUSION

The impact on debtor countries of the four exogenous shocks examined in this chapter was considerable. A summary table, organized around the timing of the first two oil shocks, is presented in Table 5.11. The gains from negative real interest rates in the 1970s have been suppressed. The arbitrarily assigned time periods to produce seven "shocks" and the absence of a technique to isolate effects fully calls for great caution in the interpretation of the results. With these *caveats* in mind, a number of general conclusions may be inferred from Table 5.11 by identifying, for each country, the least damaging and the most damaging shock.

With the exception of India, the combination of slow growth and high interest rates had negative impacts on all countries in the sample. While the oil shocks obviously benefited oil-exporting countries, a number of countries also gained from nonoil terms of trade effects. In no instance was the first oil shock the most damaging of the seven shocks. However, in four instances (India, Israel, South Korea, and Turkey) the second oil shock was the most damaging of all the shocks. For four other countries (Chile, Egypt, Nigeria, and Peru), the post-1979 terms of trade shock was the most damaging shock. Six countries (Brazil, Chile, Ecuador, Indonesia, Mexico, and Venezuela) suffered most from the real interest rate shock. Finally, slow OECD growth was featured as the most important factor in the largest number of cases (Bolivia, Colombia, Costa Rica, Côte d'Ivoire, Jamaica, Malaysia, Morocco, Uruguay, and Yugoslavia). This group includes most of the smaller economies in the sample and it contains only one major debtor country. The Philippines was equally affected by slow growth and interest rates.

It is not always possible to separate shocks that are likely to prove transitory from those that are likely to prove permanent. As a result, it is difficult for policymakers to choose between financing and adjusting to any particular shock. If a policy of adjustment is chosen, there will be alternative views of the optimal pace of adjustment. There is one matter on which there is likely to be little doubt. Political pressures will call for a slower rather than a faster pace of adjustment. Political pressures will also influence the manner in which the burden of adjustment is distributed.

The counterfactual approach used in this chapter should be treated with great caution. In his 1983 study of the Brazilian crisis, Diaz-Alejandro warned of the dangers in choosing unsuitable counterfactual scenarios.[38] Diaz-Alejandro used what he termed a prudent planner's counter factual projections – projections he would expect a prudent planner to make based on recent historical experience. The

Table 5.11 Summary of All Shocks, 1973–85 ($ billion)

	Oil Shocks		Non-Oil Terms of Trade		Real Interest Rates	Slow OECD Growth	
	1973-78	1979-85	1973-78	1979-85	1981-85	1974-78	1979-85
Major Borrowers	**23.6**	**113.0**	**-10.3**	**-52.1**	**-260.4**	**-32.6**	**-176.7**
Argentina	-1.4	-0.8	-1.5	-18.7	-27.6	-3.9	-20.9
Brazil	-11.8	-40.8	6.3	4.4	-64.5	-7.3	-39.5
Chile	-1.2	-4.1	-3.0	-17.5	-11.1	-1.4	-7.8
Egypt	1.0	12.2	-3.7	-17.9	-4.5	-1.2	-6.2
India	-4.8	-25.1	-0.5	7.5	2.5	-3.4	-18.6
Indonesia	20.0	56.5	1.7	25.1	-10.5	-1.9	-10.2
Israel	-3.1	-10.0	-1.1	-0.6	-4.6	-1.7	-9.2
S. Korea	-5.4	-30.3	-2.4	-1.4	-17.1	-3.8	-20.6
Malaysia	1.1	13.7	0.9	-3.8	-3.5	-3.5	-18.7
Mexico	1.9	71.6	0.5	-16.4	-77.2	-2.6	-14.3
Turkey	-3.6	-16.1	-1.8	-5.1	-7.1	-1.5	-8.4
Venezuela	30.8	86.1	-5.7	-7.6	-35.2	-0.4	-2.2
17 Heavily Indebted Countries	**42.5**	**168.1**	**-2.5**	**-69.7**	**-277.2**	**-28.5**	**-154.5**
Bolivia	0.3	0.1	0.8	2.6	-1.6	-0.3	-1.7
Colombia	-0.1	-1.6	3.1	3.8	-2.3	-1.4	-7.5
Costa Rica	-0.3	-0.9	0.0	-0.3	-1.9	-0.4	-2.2
Côte d'Ivoire	-0.5	-1.8	1.9	2.1	-4.7	-1.0	-5.5
Ecuador	1.8	8.8	1.3	1.9	-7.5	-0.3	-1.6
Jamaica	-0.7	-2.2	1.1	1.4	-0.6	-0.5	-2.5
Morocco	-0.9	-4.9	1.9	4.4	-4.9	-1.1	-5.8
Nigeria	31.4	82.4	-3.8	-13.7	-10.2	-0.7	-3.7
Peru	-0.4	3.5	-0.9	-10.6	-4.3	-1.3	-7.1
Philippines	-2.6	-9.0	-2.2	-11.9	-12.0	-2.2	-12.0
Uruguay	-0.6	-1.9	-0.3	-0.9	-1.5	-0.4	-2.1
Yugoslavia	-3.3	-16.4	-1.9	7.5	-10.2	-3.4	-18.2

Sources: Tables 5.2, 5.5, 5.9, 5.10.

results that have been obtained here are not likely to be those of a "prudent planner." In the first instance, it is unlikely that a prudent planner would expect OECD economic growth to bounce back to the levels experienced in the 1960s. Most of the results contained in this chapter are based on deviations from past trends with no implication that these would continue.

The analysis in this chapter suggests that external shocks were major sources of the debt problem. These are factors over which policymakers in debtor countries have no control. This does not mean that all factors were beyond their control. Debtor countries cannot be held blameless in causing their own difficulties. Even in the absence of appropriate policies to respond to the external environment, domestic policies also contributed to the debt difficulties of a number of countries.

NOTES

1. See Bela Balassa, "The Newly-Industrializing Developing Countries after the Oil Crisis," *Weltwirtschaftliches Archiv*, Vol. 117 (1981), pp. 142–94; Balassa, "Adjusting to External Shocks: The Newly-Industrializing Developing Economies in 1974–76 and 1979–81," *Weltwirtschaftliches Archiv*, Vol. 121 (1985), pp. 116–41; Balassa, "Policy Responses to Exogenous Shocks in Developing Countries," *American Economic Review*, Vol. 76, No. 2 (May 1986), pp. 75–78; Thomas Enders and Richard P. Mattione, *Latin America: The Crisis of Debt and Growth* (Washington, D.C: The Brookings Institution, 1984), p. 19.

2. William R. Cline, *International Debt and the Stability of the World Economy* (Washington D.C.: Institute for International Economics, 1983); Cline, *International Debt: Systemic Risk and Policy Response* (Washington D.C.: Institute for International Economics, 1984); Cline, "International Debt: From Crisis to Recovery," *American Economic Review*, Vol. 75, No. 2 (May 1985), pp. 185–90; Cline, "International Debt: Analysis, Experience and Prospects," *Journal of Development Planning*, No. 16 (1985), pp. 25–57.

3. Carlos Diaz-Alejandro, "Some Aspects of the 1982–83 Brazilian Payments Crisis," *Brookings Papers on Economic Activity*, No. 2 1983, pp. 515–42; Diaz-Alejandro, "Latin American Debt: I Don't Think We Are in Kansas Anymore," *Brookings Papers on Economic Activity*, No. 2 (1984), pp. 335–89; Rudiger Dornbusch, "Policy and Performance Links between LDC Debtors and Industrial Nations," *Brookings Papers on Economic Activity*, No. 2 (1985), pp. 303–56; Jeffrey D. Sachs, "External Debt and Macroeconomic Performance in Latin America and East Asia," *Brookings Papers on Economic Activity*, No. 2 (1985), pp. 523–64.

4. The collapse of oil prices after 1985 provides some support for the argument that developing countries were correct to view the oil shocks as temporary

phenomena that should be financed, rather than permanent shocks requiring adjustment.

5. A number of alternative measures might have been chosen. Cline, for example, bases his estimates on what would have happened if the real dollar price of oil had remained constant, that is, if oil prices had risen in line with U.S. inflation. His results suggest a resource transfer of $259.5 billion between 1974 and 82. Enders and Mattione use a similar approach to estimate 1979–82 effects on seven Latin American countries. See William R. Cline, *International Debt and the Stability of the World Economy* (Washington D.C: Institute for International Economics, 1983), p. 21; Thomas Enders and Richard P. Mattione, *Latin America: The Crisis of Debt and Growth* (Washington, D.C: The Brookings Institution, 1984), p. 19.

6. John Maynard Keynes, *The Economic Consequences of the Peace* (London: Macmillan, 1919); Keynes, "The German Transfer Problem," *Economic Journal,* March 1929.

7. Arminio Fraga, *German Reparations and Brazilian Debt: A Comparative Study,* International Finance Section Princeton, Essays in International Finance No. 163, July 1986, p. 20.

8. IMF, *World Economic Outlook 1983,* p. 147.

9. IMF, *World Economic Outlook 1983.*

10. Inter-American Development Bank, *Economic and Social Progress in Latin America, 1985 Report,* Table 69, p. 440.

11. IMF, *World Economic Outlook April 1986,* p. 172.

12. An additional four countries, Bolivia, Egypt, Malaysia, and Peru, were included as "net oil exporters" in an earlier classification in IMF, *World Economic Outlook 1984,* pp. 167–68.

13. *World Debt Tables 1986–87,* p. 286.

14. Hans Singer, "The Distribution of Gains between Investing and Borrowing Countries," *American Economic Review, Papers and Proceedings,* May 1950, pp. 473–85; Raul Prebisch, "Commercial Policy in the Underdeveloped Countries, *American Economic Review, Papers and Proceedings,* May 1959, pp. 251–73.

15. Terms of trade from export and import unit values, IFS 74d, 75d *IFS Yearbook 1987,* pp. 128–31, IFS May 1988, pp. 76–77 and from UNCTAD *Handbook of International Trade and Development Statistics, 1988 Supplement,* Table 7.2. Merchandise trade values from IFS 77aad, 77abd, in *IFS Yearbook 1986* country pages. Trade weights from GNP data, World Bank, *World Debt Tables 1986–87* and average of IFS 77aad and 77abd, *IFS Yearbook 1986.*

16. William R. Cline, *International Debt and the Stability of the World Economy,* p. 25.

17. Jeffrey D. Sachs, "External Debt and Macroeconomic Performance in Latin America and East Asia," p. 529.

18. James A. Wilcox, "Why Real Interest Rates Were So Low in the 1970s," *American Economic Review,* Vol. 73 No. 1 (March 1983), pp. 44–53; Frederic Mishkin, "The Real Rate of Interest: An Empirical Investigation," *Carnegie-Rochester Conference Series on Public Policy: Supply Shocks, Incentives and National Wealth,* Spring, 14, pp. 151–200.

19. See Jeffrey D. Sachs, "The Current Account and Macroeconomic Adjustments in the 1970s," *Brookings Papers on Economic Activity*, No. 1 (1981), p. 225.

20. Jeffrey Sachs, "The Current Account and Macroeconomic Adjustments in the 1970s," pp. 243–44.

21. IMF, *World Economic Outlook 1985*, Chart 9–1, p. 188.

22. Rudiger Dornbusch, "External Debt, Budget Deficits and Disequilibrium Exchange Rates," mimeo, April 1984, p. 7.

23. Edmar Lisboa Bacha and Carlos F. Diaz-Alejandro, *International Financial Intermediation: A Long and Tropical View* International Finance Section, Princeton Essays in International Finance No. 147, May 1982, p. 12.

24. Jeffrey D. Sachs, "External Debt and Macroeconomic Performance in Latin America and East Asia," *Brookings Papers on Economic Activity*, No. 2 (1985), p. 531.

25. William R. Cline, *International Debt and the Stability of the World Economy* (Washington D.C.: Institute for International Economics, 1983), p. 22.

26. Rudiger Dornbusch, "Policy and Performance Links between LDC Debtors and Industrial Nations," *Brookings Papers on Economic Activity*, No. 2 (1985), p. 340.

27. This spread will of course be influenced by the manner in which the mix of country debt is divided between private and public sectors, by the extent to which it is guaranteed, and by its maturity structure.

28. Bank spread averaged 21–23 percent of U.S. T-bill rate from 1978 to 1982, but only 13–15 percent from 1983 to 1985.

29. Spread data need to be interpreted with great caution because of difficulties in incorporating loan management fees, rescheduling fees, etc.

30. Alternative (and more sophisticated) treatments of real interest rates may be found in Rudiger Dornbusch and Stanley Fischer, "The World Debt Problem: Origins and Prospects," *Journal of Development Planning*, No. 16 (1985), p. 59; Dornbusch, "Policy and Performance Links between LDC Debtors and Industrial Countries, p. 341; William R. Cline, "Comments on Dornbusch," *Brookings Papers on Economic Activity*, No. 2 (1985), p. 362; Jeffrey D. Sachs, "External Debt and Macroeconomic Performance in Latin America and East Asia, p. 528.

31. William R. Cline, *International Debt and the Stability of the World Economy* (Washington: Institute for International Economics, 1983), p. 23.

32. Rudiger Dornbusch, "Policy and Performance Links between LDC Debtors and Industrial Nations," p. 337.

33. See David Goldsbrough and Iqbal M. Zaidi, "Transmission of Economic Influences from Industrial to Developing Countries" in IMF, *Staff Studies for the World Economic Outlook*, July 1986, p. 159, for a survey of recent estimates.

34. William R. Cline, *International Debt and the Stability of the World Economy*.

35. William R. Cline, "International Debt: Analysis, Experience and Prospects," *Journal of Development Planning*, No. 16 (1985), p. 53.

36. David Goldsbrough and Iqbal Zaidi, "Transmission of Economic Influences from Industrial to Developing Countries," p. 166.

37. David Goldsbrough and Iqbal Zaidi, "Transmission of Economic Influences from Industrial to Developing Countries," p. 166.

38. Carlos Diaz-Alejandro, "Some Aspects of the 1982–83 Brazilian Payments Crisis," pp. 515–42.

6

Governments and the IMF

This chapter concentrates on the manner in which the debt crisis was influenced by profound structural changes in developing country political institutions, in the organization of the international financial system, and specifically in the roles of the Bank and the Fund. The political complexion of many debtor countries has changed dramatically from the years when the build-up of debt occurred. Similarly, the international financial system has evolved quite sharply from what had been created in Bretton Woods in 1944 as the financial component of the postwar multilateral political and economic structures.

These two sets of structural changes have complicated life for both the Fund and governments in their dealings with each other. In a number of instances, a debt build-up by military governments was inherited by fledgling democratic governments. Besides dealing with domestic political tensions produced by debt crisis austerity, these fragile governments have had to operate in a changed international environment. In the years before the eruption of the debt crisis a number of countries had studiously avoided borrowing from the Fund, preferring to pay the higher interest rates charged by commercial banks rather than tolerate Fund impingement on their choice of domestic economic policies. Among Latin American debtors, Brazil made no use of Fund credit during the period 1968–81, Argentina avoided the Fund from 1978–82, and Colombia managed to stay away from 1972–85.[1]

The decision to avoid the Fund implied, at the height of LIBOR rates in 1981, a willingness to borrow at 16.72 percent plus a country spread by turning down IMF loans offered at 6.6 percent. While this is a high price for citizens to pay in order that their governments might have complete freedom to pursue their own economic policies, it is an even higher price if paid to permit the adoption of unsuccessful policies. The arrival of the debt crisis permitted the Fund to reassert itself in its ultimate role of lender of last resort in the international system. Fund participation was a vital element in commercial bank debt restructurings. By 1985 use of Fund credit had quadrupled over 1980 levels. By 1989 the Fund and the Bank were financing debt reduction.

The first section of this chapter examines the changing political complexion of a number of countries in the sample of debtor countries, the internal political constraints on austerity programs, and how these influence relations with the Fund. This is followed by a broad overview of changes in the international financial system and the resulting change in the role of the IMF. The lending facilities of the Fund are described in detail in the chapter's final section. The controversial issue of Fund conditionality is reserved for separate treatment in Chapter 7.

DOMESTIC POLITICS AND BALANCE OF PAYMENTS ADJUSTMENT

In the years of debt run-up, the political institutions of the Major Borrowers and of the Heavily Indebted Countries mirrored those found elsewhere in developing countries. There was a preponderance of governments dominated by military officers. Opposition political parties were banned in a number of instances, there were few cases of a free press, torture was widespread and trade union rights were often severely restricted. Although there have been some improvements in the interim and while generalizations are both difficult and dangerous, it is safe to say that throughout the sample, the powers of the state are less controlled than in the democracies of the OECD. In a number of the countries in the sample, civilian governments rule under permanent states of siege or similar emergencies.

Like most developing countries, the majority of the countries in the sample possess weak or nonexistent democratic political systems. The pattern has changed with the democratization revolution that swept Latin America in the past decade. Of the twelve Major Debtor countries, Chile and Indonesia entered the 1980s ruled by dictators; Argentina, Brazil, and Turkey were ruled by military juntas while a government of ex-generals ruled South Korea. Only Egypt, India, Israel, Malaysia, Mexico, and Venezuela were ruled by civilian governments. In Mexico, the same party had been in power since 1929. In India, the Congress party had ruled since 1947 with only a short break in opposition. In two others, Egypt and Israel, ex-military officers were important forces in governments.

Although half of the Major Borrowers entered the debt crisis without popularly elected civilian governments, by the end of 1985 three of this six had transferred to the civilian column. A military government in Turkey was replaced by a civilian government. One of the most remarkable political events within the group has been the return to civilian governments in Argentina and Brazil as part of a wider Latin American phenomenon. By 1989, Chile was the sole Latin American military dictatorship in the sample. Civilian government was to return in December 1989. A month earlier, Brazil was to hold its first direct elections in 29 years.

In a number of instances, Ecuador (1979) and Peru (1980), the transfer to civilian government occurred before the crisis. Bolivia installed a civilian government in October 1982. Argentina returned to civilian government with elections in October 1983 after the Malvinas War, followed shortly thereafter by the election of the Sanginetti government in Uruguay in 1984 and the Sarney government in Brazil in 1985. Colombia, Costa Rica, Mexico, and Venezuela have had civilian governments for longer periods of time. In 1989, the number of military governments in the sample of Major Borrowers had been reduced to two (Chile and Nigeria), while the group of Heavily Indebted Countries contained two one-party states (Côte d'Ivoire and Yugoslavia). The governments of such multiparty states as South Korea and Turkey were either dominated or heavily influenced by the military.

Military governments were responsible for much of the enormous run-up in Latin American external debt during the late 1970s. Their willingness to go deeper into debt may be seen as, in part, a way of buying popularity. The general populace enjoyed increases in living standards that were financed abroad, rather than produced from domestic resources. Some civilian governments used foreign borrowing to finance the purchase of military hardware to keep the armed forces happy and forestall military coups. A military government in Argentina used foreign borrowing to pay for the Malvinas campaign. In Brazil, a military government used borrowing to finance grandiose investment projects and its own military-industrial complex.

With the onset of the crisis, these policies ground to a halt as financing evaporated. The experience in Chile has shown that a military dictatorship is capable of surviving prolonged periods of economic austerity. Civilian governments face a more delicate balancing act when required to introduce austerity measures. The Peronist-inflicted election reversals suffered by Alfonsin's Radical Party government in Argentina in September 1987 were attributed to the austerity measures introduced with a July IMF agreement after the failure of the Austral Plan.[2] The Sarney government of Brazil encountered similar difficulties as it sought to introduce a new constitution. The July 1988 Mexican Presidential election witnessed an unprecedented struggle between the PRI's candidate, Salinas, an ex-PRI member and son of the President who nationalized the oil industry in 1938, Cuauhtemoc Cardenas, and the PAN candidate,

Manuel Clouthier. The two opponents of the PRI attacked the austerity policies of the PRI and called for a reduction in Mexico's debt service.[3] General elections in Argentina and Brazil in 1989 ousted unpopular incumbent governments and produced second-generation democratic governments.

The austerity measures synonymous with Fund-supported adjustment programs produce deep social divisions. Opposition parties will automatically seek to hold incumbent governments responsible for the implied loss of national sovereignty. Governments will seek to avoid being held responsible for the effects of policies by attempting to shift the blame on to the IMF. Trade unions will usually find themselves embroiled in bitter disputes with employers and with governments. The success of a Fund stabilization program often depends on how these disputes are mediated. In the words of previous IMF Managing Director Jacques de Larosiere, "political commitment and support for a program are indispensable to successful adjustment. This means not only that the authorities believe in what they are doing and are determined to implement the program, but also that the rationale of the program is effectively communicated to the public at large so that the measures—the immediate impact of which is often hard to bear—are well understood and supported."[4]

The existence in the 1970s of private bank financing as an alternative source of financing to multilateral lending agencies or the limited bond market, reduced the short-term political costs of borrowing. Commercial bank loans provided borrowing governments with the ability to borrow without the strings attached by multilateral agencies. These agencies were often viewed as promoting development strategies either too in tune with the interests of Western countries, too oblivious to the political aspirations of developing country masses, or too insensitive to the plights of precarious governments facing daunting economic and political demands. The balancing acts performed by developing country finance ministers faced with outside demands for devaluations and internal demands for their resignations if they succumbed had been studied by Cooper in 1971.[5] More than political careers are at stake. The death toll in riots protesting austerity introduce a new measure of the human cost attached to acceptance of outside demands for austerity and stiffened developing country resistance to acceptance of IMF-supported adjustment programs.

In 1984, austerity-induced riots in the Dominican Republic left 55 dead and over 200 wounded; over 60 were reported killed in food price riots in Morocco; Tunisian bread riots left 89 dead and 938 wounded.[6] In 1985, bus fare increases provoked riots that left at least two dead in Guatemala.[7] At least 15 were reported to have died in riots protesting maize price increases in Zambia in December 1986 following the ending of subsidies.[8] In 1988, six people died in riots in April demonstrating against increases in Nigerian gasoline prices while the death toll from riots protesting Algerian austerity measures exceeded 245, with over 1,000 reported injured.[9] In 1989, up to 375 were reported killed and 1,000 wounded in Venezuela in riots protesting increases in public transportation fares and gasoline price increases (from 16 cents per gallon to 26 cents) introduced as Venezuela signed an IMF letter of intent; eight deaths and 87 injured were reported following riots in Jordan sparked off by price increases in cigarettes and gasoline as part of an IMF program; 3 deaths and 30 wounded were reported in austerity riots in Nigeria[10] The list of other countries that have suffered loss of life in austerity-induced riots, not all IMF-related, include Egypt in January 1977 (65 dead, hundreds wounded), Chile, Haiti, Jamaica (seven killed in fuel-price riots in January 1985), Poland (44 dead in December 1970), and Sudan. Recent years have also seen instances in which austerity measures in a number of countries have been revoked within hours of announcement because of the violent reaction. As the image of the Fund was vilified in internal political debates, Fund staff lost the aura of elite VIP travelers and began to travel without luggage tags identifying them as Fund employees.

The social divisions exacerbated by Fund-supported programs arise in part because of changes in pricing policies toward commodities and services such as food, energy, and transportation. In many countries, price controls or subsidies are used to defuse the political tensions produced by the great inequality of income distribution. For the urban poor, food, electricity, and transportation consume a huge share of household income when priced at their real cost to the society. In much of the Third World, food price ceilings are used to buy political support from urban masses at the expense of the more geographically scattered and politically weaker rural peasantry. The resulting decline in agricultural production for domestic consumption is inevitable, making technological innovations in agriculture and investment in irrigation infrastructure and so forth irrelevant so long as producers cannot obtain prices that cover their costs.[11] When coupled with overvalued exchange rates, the end result is the depletion of foreign exchange reserves to pay for imported food. All of this may be self-evident to the detached economist. The political costs of adopting the economist's recommendations for policy changes are just as obvious to the engaged politician.

The challenges facing developing country governments are ones to which many sophisticated developed country governments might find themselves lacking. In addition to the challenge of raising per capita incomes to the aspiration levels of its citizens while having meager resources with which to accomplish the task, developing country governments face the added challenge of making good on their own egalitarian rhetoric. Rather than remove the underlying income inequalities, many developing countries settled for arrangements in which social peace is bought through price controls and subsidies. As Fund-supported adjustment programs remove these controls, the underlying social tensions due to income maldistribution are exposed. The countries most vehemently opposed to IMF-style adjustment programs have often been the Latin American countries, which have done least to reduce income maldistribution and which have fought hardest to maintain existing arrangements.

As is typical of most developing countries, the income distributions of debtor countries is considerably less equal than found within the OECD. Typically, highly developed economies report that the richest 10 percent of households earn between 22 percent and 30 percent of the total income of the country.[12] In developing countries, the figure is more likely to lie between 30 percent and 45 percent. Eight of the twenty-four countries in the sample do not provide income distribution data. The available data for the others show, with some notable exceptions, extremely inequitable income distributions quite at variance with socialist or egalitarian ideals often espoused by ruling elites. While some countries such as Argentina, Israel, and South Korea have income distributions not dissimilar from those of OECD countries, others show much higher percentages of total incomes in the hands of the richest 10 percent of their populations. In the case of Brazil, for example, the top 10 percent of the population control 51 percent of total income (based on 1972 data) while Costa Rica, Malaysia, Mexico, Peru, and Turkey show percentages equal to, or in excess of, 40 percent.[13]

For all debtor country governments, civilian or otherwise, the onset of austerity narrowed their options. Their ability to buy popular support and legitimize themselves was reduced. Efforts to emulate Western living standards have been delayed as living standards have been cut back to a level closer to the output of the economy rather than being raised temporarily by foreign borrowing. In many instances trade unions have been an important source of support for fledgling civilian governments. In Mexico, the trade union movement is an integral component of the ruling party, the PRI. In Argentina, trade unions long dominated the Peronist movement and were a major force in the return to democracy and later in Menem's 1989 victory. However, trade unions are also the natural organizations to lead campaigns against reductions in real wages or in social programs. Street demonstrations against austerity programs introduced with or without IMF adjustment programs are invariably led by organized labor. Because of the large number of state-owned or semistate enterprises, the influence of unions on government policy is more pervasive than is the case where a unionized manufacturing or service sector is entirely in private hands.

An additional factor that limited policy options was the often vitriolic rhetoric aimed at the IMF, which had become the *bête noire* of the Third World. Past attacks on the Fund, past promises not to deal with the Fund, past denunciations of predecessor governments that adopted Fund-supported adjustment programs all returned to narrow the maneuvering room open to governments when the drying up of credit sources precluded all options but the adoption of adjustment programs. For a while, past rhetoric held a number of governments hostage, forcing them to adopt their own adjustment programs without the amelioration of austerity that is produced by IMF credits. The absence of these credits would suggest that non-IMF-supported adjustment programs are even more harsh than IMF-supported ones. Brazil, which fell out of compliance with the terms of a 1983 $6 billion Fund agreement and found disbursements suspended, was among the most vehement critics of the Fund in the mid-1980s. Its boycott of the Fund, begun in August 1985, ended in early 1988 when the fourth Finance Minister to hold office in less than three years of civilian government sought to normalize relations with all of Brazil's creditors.[14]

Like its civilian counterparts in Brazil and elsewhere, the Nigerian government of Major General Ibrahim Babangida sought to avoid accepting IMF medicine while seeking a solution to its debt problems. Shortly after coming to power in September 1985 the military government of Babangida organized a national debate on whether or not the country should submit to IMF discipline. An interesting exercise in domestic politics produced the inevitable outcome of such a debate. However, by mid-1988, Nigeria was in the midst of an austerity program, complete with an end to some subsidies and the sale of nationalized industries.[15] Without it, the IMF arrangement necessary to permit debt rescheduling would have been impossible.

Indirect Fund participation through the "enhanced surveillance" component of a number of commercial bank reschedulings provided a subtle opening for improved relations between governments and the Fund.[16] It was first used for a 1985 Mexican commercial bank MYRA and a 1985 Paris Club MYRA for Ecuador.[17] Politicians who have fiercely denounced the Fund and insisted that they would never accept an IMF-supported adjustment program have agreed to creditor demands that they accept "enhanced surveillance" by the Fund as a condition of debt renegotiations. This provides a political opportunity for governments not only to adopt the type of measures commonly found in an IMF-supported program while simultaneously proclaiming that national sovereignty has been safeguarded, but also to hope to garner Fund plaudits for the home-grown policies. The Brazilian acceptance of a Paris Club demand for "enhanced surveillance" in January 1987 is an example. Within months of suspending payments on commercial bank debt in February 1987, Brazil had installed a new economic team and, for a while, embarked on the road to austerity. Brazilian politicians rationalized the *volte face* as needed not only to deal with inflation in excess of 100 percent but as also reflecting a change in IMF attitude, now headed by a French Socialist, Michel Camdessus.

Under "enhanced surveillance," the Fund gives its *imprimatur* to the debtor country adjustment program required by commercial banks as a condition for loan restructuring and the provision of new money. "Enhanced surveillance" does not involve an IMF loan. The size and maturity of the new commercial bank loans made possible when a country accepts "enhanced surveillance" exceed that of typical IMF extended arrangements or Structural Adjustment Facility loans. As a result, the required balance of payments adjustment is not compressed into so short a period of time. However, even with declining spreads, interest rates on commercial loans still greatly exceed IMF rates.

As "enhanced surveillance" shows, the debt crisis provided an opportunity for organizations such as the IMF to become more sensitive to developing country realities without encouraging the adoption of poor economic policies. The manner in which countries such as Brazil, Mexico, and Argentina handled their relationships with the Fund in the aftermath to the crisis may prove to have been an important influence on the future orientation of the Fund. With extremely few exceptions, member governments have gone to great pains to avoid being overdue on repayments of loans from the Fund. Among competing creditors, the Fund is the most preferred. Becoming overdue on arrears to the Fund is a sure way of ensuring that all sources of private credit disappear. However, it does not cause an end to credit from other official sources. In particular, World Bank loans may still be available to a country that is overdue on arrears to the sister Bretton Woods institution.

Not all members warded off disaster. By 1989, nine members were ineligible for further IMF assistance because they were over six months in arrears on previous Fund loans. These were Guyana, Liberia, Panama, Peru, Sierra Leone, Somalia, Sudan, Vietnam, and Zambia.[18] Liberia was also ineligible for Bank loans. One other country, Cambodia, was effectively barred from IMF lending because it no longer maintained relations with the Fund although remaining a member. The World Bank also found a number of countries slipping into arrears, causing it to increase its loan-loss reserves from $100 million to $500 million in the fiscal year ended June 1988.[19] In July 1988 eight members, Guyana, Liberia, Nicaragua, Panama, Peru, Sierra Leone, Syria, and Zambia, were in arrears on loans totaling $3.24 billion.

THE IMF AND THE CHANGING INTERNATIONAL SYSTEM

Some of the roots of the debt crisis may be found in the manner in which the international financial system has evolved over the years. By the late 1970s, the IMF was an institution that had lost one of its two central missions, that of policing an exchange-rate regime, and was being supplanted by commercial banks in its second mission, that of providing short-run balance-of-payments financing. The growing incoherence in the international financial system was also partly attributable to the much greater number of players than were found at the system's creation in the 1940s. Creation had occurred in an age prior to the successful decolonization of much of the planet. From being a cozy organization dominated by the United States and Britain, and always headed by a continental European, the Fund has had to adapt to demands from its new developing country clients, to shifting political and economic power among the bloc of developed countries as the United States moved to debtor nation status and as Germany and Japan, excluded from Bretton Woods, reassumed leadership roles.

For debtor countries, structural change in the international financial system produced a widening range of borrowing sources available to governments in search of loans.[20] This wider availability has caused developed country governments to all but disappear from the client lists of the multilateral lending institutions set up after World War II. A variety of Euro-bond and Euro-currency financial instruments are now available to them. Developing country governments, too, have come to rely less on official creditors and more on private banks.

Between 1970 and 1986, the percentage of developing country disbursed public or publicly guaranteed long-term debt that had been provided at concessional rates fell from 56 percent to 22 percent.[21] The share provided by official creditors fell from 68 percent to 44 percent. With the slowdown of commercial bank lending since the emergence of the debt crisis, the relative financing roles of private banks and international lending agencies have tilted back toward the traditional pattern. According to the Fund, only about 30 percent of the 1984 combined current account deficits of developing countries was financed through commercial lending. In 1981, the private share had exceeded 50 percent.[22] For many developing country governments, the growth in private bank lending represented a temporary relaxation of the constraints faced by policymakers. However, although these flows produced a relaxation in the economic constraints on social and other policies, those who saw a permanent relaxation saw a mirage. This became evident in the adjustment years after 1982.

It is unclear to what extent private bank lending was a substitute for official flows and to what extent it represented a net addition to the supply of funds available to developing countries. In so far as private bank flows provided net additions to available financing flows, they represented an unambiguous relaxation of the short-term balance of payments and intertemporal budget constraints. To the extent that they were substitutes, there was a relaxation of constraints if the additional interest payments charged by commercial banks were less than the increased income produced by an economy not bound by the conditions often attached to multilateral agency lending. In many cases, this appears to be a dubious proposition.

THE CHANGING ROLE OF THE IMF

The membership of the Fund has grown from 44 nations at the Bretton Woods conference to 151 members in 1989. All but a handful of UN members belong to the Fund. Among the nonmembers are Switzerland, the Soviet Union, East Germany, Albania, and Czechoslovakia. Communist members include China, Hungary, Rumania, Yugoslavia, and Poland.[23] Voting and borrowing rights, as well as members' contributions to the Fund, are determined by the size of a member's quota. Over the years there have been eight general increases in quotas, providing the Fund with additional liquidity. Quota increases have occasionally been accompanied by modifications in their distribution, to permit voting strength to reflect shifts in global economic power. As the dominant position of the United States has been eroded, its share of Fund quotas and of Fund votes has fallen from 30 percent in 1949 to just under 20 percent.[24] Although most decisions are taken by consensus, the Fund's Articles of Agreement provide for an 85 percent majority rule on fundamental decisions concerning quotas, Special Drawing Rights (SDR) allocations, and (SDR) valuations. The United States has veto power in matters governed by the 85 percent majority rule. No other country has veto power, but a number of coalitions are capable of vetos. Developing countries and the European Community are but two examples.

The political character of its government cannot disqualify a country from borrowing from an international agency of which it is a member. However, it may lead other member states to instruct their representatives on the executive board to vote against approval of loan applications. Because of the greater transparency of its policies, this is most obvious in the case of the United States.[25] The Fund's relationship with LDCs is significantly different from that which it had with developed countries during the era when developed countries constituted the bulk of the Fund's clients. Its changed clientele has altered Fund politics by bringing a North-South dimension to a Fund acting as financial intermediary between developed and developing nations.

The borrowing of developed economies from the Fund has been very limited in recent years. As late as 1978, developed countries accounted for 40 percent of outstanding Fund loans with the United Kingdom and Italy taking more than half of the developed country total.[26] In the years after 1982 developed country outstanding use of Fund credit was wound down as the sole developed country user of Fund credit, Iceland, repaid a Compensatory Financing Facility (CFF) loan. The only recent West European users of Fund standby arrangements have been Turkey and Portugal. However, East European use has grown with borrowing by Hungary, Rumania, and Yugoslavia. European countries which might have been expected to borrow from the Fund in recent years have instead used international capital markets or have borrowed from each other using a variety of lending schemes of the EC.[27]

As the predominant borrowers from the Fund, developing countries have been particularly hostile to Fund conditionality. Nevertheless, despite complaints and threats to avoid the Fund, many developing countries have been continuous users of Fund credit for lengthy periods of time.[28] By end-1986, two countries, Chile and Egypt, had made use of Fund credit continuously for almost thirty years, since 1958. Four other countries, Sri Lanka, Mali, Sudan, and Pakistan had at least twenty years of continuous use. In all, over forty members had used Fund credit continuously for the previous ten years.[29]

In the year after the emergence of the debt crisis the Fund more than doubled its lending to the countries in the sample. In the two years 1980–81 prior to the emergence of the debt crisis, nine sample countries were not making use of Fund credit. As the crisis deepened, most of them chose to borrow from the Fund. The use of Fund credit by the sample of debtor countries in the years since the first oil shock is found in Table 6.1.

Eleven countries made use of Fund credit every year between 1980 and 1988. Jamaica maintained standby, Extended Financing Facility (EFF) or Structural Adjustment Facility (SAF) arrangements in each year from 1979–87. On the other hand, three countries, Colombia, Nigeria, and Venezuela, made no use whatever of Fund credit during these years while three others, Indonesia, Israel, and Malaysia, also maintained no Fund standby, EEF, or SAF arrangement during these years. Brazil did not manage to hold out quite as long, finally going

Table 6.1 Debtor Country Relations with the IMF, 1980–88

	Years of Standby, EEF SAF or ESAF Arrangements	Use of Fund Credit (% of Quota)								Dec.
		1980	1981	1982	1983	1984	1985	1986	1987	1988
Major Borrowers										
Argentina	1983-88	0	0	0	101	101	189	201	244	246
Brazil	1983-86	0	0	50	173	292	288	252	192	170
Chile	1983-88	30	13	2	131	181	225	247	234	223
Egypt	1979-81;1987-88	41	25	15	11	11	8	5	28	25
India	1981-84	16	33	120	160	181	173	158	129	94
Indonesia		0	0	0	42	42	4	4	50	46
Israel		51	29	9	0	0	0	0	0	0
S. Korea	1980-87	209	418	446	279	346	297	274	80	0
Malaysia		0	50	65	57	48	20	0	0	0
Mexico	1979;1983-88	0	0	25	103	207	232	285	312	306
Turkey	1979-85	276	379	440	349	339	281	207	127	52
Venezuela		0	0	0	0	0	0	0	0	0
17 Heavily Indebted Countries										
Bolivia	1986-88	93	91	116	94	72	52	130	109	119
Colombia		0	0	0	0	0	0	0	0	0
Costa Rica	1980-83;1985-88	73	143	137	218	189	204	168	111	63
Côte d'Ivoire	1981-88	0	280	381	356	365	342	308	246	200
Ecuador	1983-87	0	0	0	135	161	217	264	229	223
Jamaica	1979-88	219	364	476	540	441	434	381	329	247
Morocco	1980-88	110	172	350	287	330	353	274	246	227
Nigeria	1987-88	0	0	0	0	0	0	0	0	0
Peru	1979-80;1982-85	151	135	239	271	208	193	180	180	180
Philippines	1979;1983-88	212	261	240	204	175	214	218	191	180
Uruguay	1979-87	0	0	69	139	139	195	197	169	140
Yugoslavia	1979-86	144	259	383	322	324	313	276	213	159

Sources: IFS 2cz in IMF, International Financial Statistics Yearbook 1987, and IFS, February 1989. Standby arrangements, etc. from IMF, Annual Report, various years.

to the Fund in 1982. Indonesia also had a long string of years with no use of Fund credit. Only three countries, Korea, Jamaica, and Turkey, appeared ever to come close to borrowing up to their limits at the Fund at any time since the first oil shock. All others avoided accepting the conditions likely to be imposed in the Fund's highest conditionality tranches, preferring to opt for the higher interest rates of commercial bank loans.

The Fund has long been a lightning rod for criticism. Usually this involves disagreement with the lending policies of the Fund, specifically with the terms of the adjustment programs required by the Fund as a precondition to receipt of Fund resources. Attacks on the Fund became more prevalent as its list of borrowers altered.[30] When its loans were to developed countries there was a much greater acceptance of its terms, and it was the legitimacy of government policies rather than that of the IMF policies that tended to be attacked.

In the past, there have been other criticisms, relating to the decision-making machinery of the Fund. The Fund's voting rules use a weighted voting system rather than UN General Assembly-type one country, one vote arrangement.[31] After 1973, the increased influence of OPEC countries caused a reallocation of quotas to take account of its increased share of international reserves. The absence of UN-style one country, one vote decisionmaking in an institution that obtains most of its resources from developed countries while lending them to developing countries has avoided developed country resentment of the type found with respect to the General Assembly. It has been replaced by developing country resentment.

Perhaps the most common claim from Third World politicians has been the charge that IMF programs do not take sufficient account of differences among countries, but seek to put all countries through the same straitjacket. Implicit in these charges is the premise that the IMF could still get its money back if the country were allowed to adopt policies of its own choosing. Implicit in IMF refusals to accept this premise are a number of competing premises. One is a belief that the country would be back borrowing again shortly thereafter—that is, that, left to themselves, countries will adopt policies that are unsustainable. A good example may be found in Brazil's much publicized Cruzado Plan, introduced in February 1986, but abandoned in June 1987 as inflation soared. An alternative hypothesis is the notion that repayment would be protracted in the absence of Fund conditionality, thus denying funds to other countries until the Fund is replenished through repayment.

In the academic literature also, there is a well-established tradition pointing to the weaknesses of the IMF approach. Helleiner summarized these criticisms as attacks on "its overemphasis on demand management, blunt monetary-policy instruments, and 'shock' treatment to reduce or eliminate inflation or balance of payments disequilibria; its relative neglect of supply-side policies, longer-term development, and income distribution; and its traditional aversion to controls, selective policy instruments, and 'gradualist' approaches".[32] These will be discussed in much more detail in the next chapter.

Under Michel Camdessus, the Fund undertook a number of measures to make its lending policies more flexible to the needs of developing country borrowers.[33] The introduction of a "contingency financing facility" provided some insurance that adjustment programs would not be disrupted by external shocks such as changes in interest rates, oil prices, and so forth. The notion of contingent conditionality was found in a $6 billion package for Mexico in 1987 which was contingent on no sharp fall in oil prices. In the event of an oil price collapse, Mexico would be eligible for further credits. The principle of contingency financing was institutionalized in 1988 when the existing Compensatory Financing Facility (CFF) was folded into a joint facility with the new External Contingency Mechanism (ECM) to produce the Compensatory and Contingency Financing Facility (CCFF), which provides financing for a wide range of external shocks including interest rate shocks.[34] The use of the ECM component of the joint CFF/ECM was made contingent on establishment of standby or EFF arrangements.

In January 1989, Trinidad and Tobago became the first country to use the external contingency mechanism of the CCFF introduced in August 1988. Camdessus had also proposed that monitoring of compliance with letters of intent be relaxed by cutting the frequency of progress assessments from quarterly to semiannual assessments. The number of performance indicators was also to be reduced.

In recent years, the Fund has responded to the need for a more medium-term approach to balance-of-payments adjustment. The Structural Adjustment Facility (SAF) provides concessional medium-term lending to low income countries with protracted balance of payments problems. Established in 1986, this facility is financed with SDR 2.7 billion in 1985–91 repayments of loans from the Fund's Trust Funds and is available to countries which qualify for IDA assistance. SAF loans carry an interest rate of 0.5 percent, a ten-year maturity with a five-year grace period. By end-April 1988, twenty-five countries had SAF arrangements.[35] In December 1987 the Fund's structural approach for low income members was bolstered by the introduction of the SDR 6 billion ESAF, financed from loans and grants from members and Switzerland. ESAF loans are repayable over ten years with 5.5 years of grace, and an interest rate of 0.5 per cent. Six ESAF loans were made in 1988, to Bolivia and five African countries.[36]

The main development agency, the World Bank, had already stepped into the medium-term gap with its loans for "structural adjustment." These medium-term loans aimed at financing structural adjustment to permanent shocks. They are similar to IMF loans in carrying conditionality, but are of longer maturity (though of shorter maturity than traditional Bank lending). Structural Adjustment Lending (SAL) was proposed by the Bank at its Annual Meetings in 1979 and was first used in 1981. SAL provides a middle ground between IMF lending and traditional Bank project lending by providing concessional nonproject lending for the general purpose of supporting policy reforms over time horizons longer than those used by the Fund.

In addition to losing its role as predominant supplier of credit to governments, there has also been a change in the nature of the public goods supplied by the IMF. The original purpose of the Fund of eliminating competitive devaluations, providing a pool of reserves, and disseminating confidential information could all be seen as public goods. A further public good is provided, if the Fund approach is "correct" (a matter of some controversy), when the Fund forces "sensible" policies on governments which might prefer to act differently and without sufficient regard to the resource costs on other countries. Of these four public goods, the first disappeared with the fixed exchange-rate system, and there remains much uncertainty about the manner in which it was replaced by the Fund's new "surveillance" role.

The second of the listed putative public goods has been greatly reduced by the private market, raising questions as to its ever having been a public good in the first place. The third has continued, though with a subtle widening of the pool receiving the confidential information, as debtor governments have begun to ask the Fund to release confidential information about their economies to private banks. The Fund's Executive Board has accommodated these requests by releasing Fund staff reports if the members concerned have entered into "enhanced surveillance" arrangements with the Fund. Otherwise, the Fund has guarded its confidentiality jealously, forbidding member governments to release Fund staff reports about their countries unless with the express approval of the Fund's executive board. The Fund's role in providing a public good such as "sensible policies" may have been eroded for a while but has been reestablished as bank loan syndicates required debtor countries to seek Fund standby programs before banks agreed to reschedulings, as governments steadfastly announce their independence from the Fund while pursuing Fund-type stabilization programs, or as Paris Club or bank loan restructurings require "enhanced surveillance" by the Fund.

With the debt crisis came the opportunity to provide a new public good as the Fund inserted itself into two areas requiring collective action. These were the need to ward off either cartelization of international financial markets or financial panics. The need for collective action to avoid financial panics had been stressed by Sachs while Diaz-Alejandro had warned of possible lender credit cartels.[37] Eaton and Gersovitz had claimed that default avoidance through governmental or paragovernmental action was preferable to doing it through lender cartelization because of the danger that the cartel would act as a monopolist, raising interest rates and restricting capital flows.[38] Thus, a Fund that encourages the collective action needed to reduce the free-rider problem and reestablish credit flows to debtor countries, is providing an anticartelization public good if it is able to do so in a way in which lenders do not charge monopoly interest rates.

The "concerted lending" approach to debt restructuring was the Fund's main early contribution to collective action during the debt crisis. This was an effort to link commercial bank debt restructurings to IMF adjustment programs by making approval of IMF financing contingent on additional financing by commercial banks. According to Watson et al., thirty Fund arrangements between 1982 and 87 were approved as part of concerted lending efforts involving additional commercial bank financing.[39] Fund staffers were also used by member countries in negotiations with commercial banks to explain how domestic policies would be changed under Fund-supported adjustment programs. In Paris Club restructurings, creditor countries have usually required debtor countries to maintain an upper credit tranche Fund arrangement or a SAF arrangement. A new debt-crisis role for the Fund emerged with the Miyazawa-Brady proposals for voluntary debt reduction on a case-by-case basis. In May 1989, the IMF's executive board decided that up to 25 percent of a country's borrowing limit under extended and standby arrangements could be used for debt reduction and that countries could qualify for further loans of up to 40 percent of quota for support of interest payments. The World Bank announced that 25 percent of its overall lending program to a country might be devoted to debt reduction.

FUND LENDING FACILITIES

Most countries borrow from the IMF by making use of its overdraft facilities. These are commonly called Standby Arrangements. Longer-maturity arrangements include the Extended Financing Facility (EFF), the Structural Adjustment Facility (SAF), and the Enhanced Structural Adjustment Facility (ESAF). There are a number of other more specialized lending programs, including some automatic unconditional withdrawals of sums provided to the Fund as part of a country's membership fee but still considered part of a country's foreign exchange reserves.

Standby arrangements have a limited life, and if not used within a specified period, they expire. Before being granted overdraft facilities, a member country must commit itself to a Fund-approved economic policy. Disbursement from the overdraft is conditional on the country meeting a number of the policy targets to which it has committed itself. Failure to meet some targets may lead to suspension of disbursements.

Technically, the lending of the Fund is accomplished by member states purchasing foreign exchange or SDRs from the Fund, paying for it with their national currency.[40] Loans are repaid by unwinding the position to restore the integrity of the fund as a mixed pool of key currencies and many almost worthless currencies. The size of the pool depends on the size of the quotas of members. Two broad sources are tapped by the Fund when it makes loans—its own resources and borrowed resources. Own resources are obtained through quota subscriptions. After the first oil crisis, the Fund began to borrow for the purpose of on-lending to members.

The Fund's reliance on borrowed resources grew sharply in the 1970s and early 1980s as a series of *ad hoc* arrangements with groups of member governments provided the Fund with additional liquidity for on-lending. The reliance on borrowing reflected a short-term solution in the absence of political agreement on the size of a general quota increase prior to the 1983 47.5 percent increase under the Eight General Review of Quotas. It also reflected the emergency measures put in place to cope with the oil shocks of the 1970s. Approximately a third of the credit tranche purchases made by members in 1986–87 were enlarged access drawings financed from borrowed rather than own resources.[41] Kenen points out that in the ten-year period 1975–84, borrowed resources provided one third of all Fund drawings and a little over half of total conditional drawings.[42]

Apart from the General Arrangements to Borrow (GAB), under which the Fund can borrow from a number of its members, borrowed resources have been used to finance two Oil Facilities, the Extended Fund Facility, the 1979 Supplementary Financing Facility, and its replacement, the 1981 Enlarged Access Facility. The latter raised the ceilings on the amounts that might be borrowed to a cumulative limit currently set at 440 percent of quota.[43]

The interest rate on member use of the Fund's borrowed resources is marked up from the Fund's cost of funds by a small margin, currently two tenths of a percentage point for loans up to 3.5 years.[44]

There is no spread to reflect differences in country risk. These rates are obviously well below the rates charged by commercial banks. When six-month Eurodollar LIBOR rates peaked in 1981, at an annual average of 16.72 percent, IMF interest rates were at 5.3 percent on own resources and averaged 6.92 percent on drawings from all Fund resources. The Structural Adjustment Facility, established in 1986, provides ten-year loans, at interest rates of 0.5 percent, to low income countries eligible to borrow from IDA. Goode has calculated that the grant component in recent Fund lending from own resources varies between 9.6 percent and 40.8 percent, depending on the length of the loan and the rate of discount used.[45]

While all Fund loans involve a subsidy because they are at interest rates below the market rates facing borrowers, there are additional subsidies to the poorest members. A trust fund, financed through the sale of 25 million ounces of gold from the Fund's holdings obtained under the gold tranche, provided loans on concessional terms between 1976 and 1981 to members with per capita income under SDR 300 in 1973 and SDR 520 in 1975.[46]

A new facility, the Structural Adjustment Facility, was established in 1986 to make further loans on similar terms to the 60 countries qualifying for International Development Association (IDA) loans with the proceeds of the SDR 2.7 billion in repayments from Trust Fund loans.[47] The SAF was reinforced by the ESAF in 1987, financed from member loans and grants. SAF loans finance medium-term adjustment in collaboration with World Bank loans, representing a convergence of missions of the two agencies.

Tables 6.2 and 6.3 provide further details of recent Fund lending. The sharp run-up in lending after 1982, both in value and in number of borrowers, is immediately obvious in Table 6.2. In 1984 and 1985 all credit tranche lending was subject to severe conditionality. As Table 6.3 shows, standby arrangements outstanding peaked in 1983 while undrawn balances as a share of Fund standby commitments fell continuously through 1985.

The maturity of Fund lending varies, depending on which lending facility is used by the borrowing member. In the case of credit tranche borrowing, the maturity is 3–5 years. A similar loan maturity is available under the CFF and the Buffer Stock Financing Facility (BSFF). Loans under the ordinary Extended Facility have 4.5- to 10-year maturities whereas enlarged access loans carry maturities of 3.5 to 7 years. In addition to the Fund's own resources, it manages two trust funds—the Trust Fund established in 1976 to provide concessional loans to developing countries largely through the sale of 25 million ounces of gold, and the SFF subsidy account.

Table 6.2 International Monetary Fund Lending (SDR billion)

	1978	1979	1980	1981	1982	1983	1984	1985	1986	1987	1988
Credit Outstanding	**12.10**	**8.80**	**8.30**	**9.60**	**14.80**	**23.60**	**31.70**	**34.90**	**34.60**	**31.60**	**27.80**
No. of Countries	72	73	74	78	79	85	84	83	79	80	76
Gross Lending	**2.64**	**1.90**	**3.16**	**5.44**	**6.96**	**10.26**	**10.16**	**6.06**	**3.94**	**3.17**	**4.12**
General Reserve	2.37	1.23	2.20	4.38	6.96	10.26	10.16	6.06	3.94	3.17	4.12
Trust Fund	0.27	0.67	0.96	1.06	—	—	—	—	—	—	—
Tranche Lending	**2.05**	**0.72**	**1.31**	**3.60**	**5.33**	**6.17**	**8.88**	**4.81**	**3.34**	**2.58**	**2.58**
First Tranche	0.09	0.13	0.16	0.78	0.02	0.03	—	—	0.29	0.02	0.04
Upper Tranches	1.85	0.35	0.93	1.90	2.73	3.68	4.16	2.77	2.55	2.31	2.28
Extended Fund	0.11	0.24	0.22	0.92	2.58	2.46	4.72	2.04	0.50	0.25	0.26
Special Facilities	**0.32**	**0.51**	**0.89**	**0.78**	**1.63**	**4.09**	**1.28**	**1.25**	**0.60**	**0.59**	**1.54**
Compensatory	0.32	0.46	0.86	0.78	1.63	3.74	1.18	1.25	0.60	0.59	1.54
Buffer	—	0.05	0.03	—	—	0.35	0.10	—	—	—	—
SDR Allocations	—	4.03	4.03	4.05	—	—	—	—	—	—	—

Source: IMF, Annual Report 1984, Tables 17 and 18, Annual Report 1986, Tables 15, II.2, and Annual Report 1987, Annual Report 1988, Tables 12 and II.2. Data is for financial years ending April 30. General Reserve lending excludes member purchases from gold tranche and consists of tranche policy lending and special facility lending.

Table 6.3 Standby, Extended, and Structural Adjustment Facility Arrangements, 1978–88

	1977	1978	1979	1980	1981	1982	1983	1984	1985	1986	1987	1988
					Standbys and Extended Arrangements							
Number	20	22	20	29	37	35	39	35	30	26	24	20
SDR billion	5.2	5.8	1.6	3.1	9.5	16.2	25.0	18.6	11.7	4.9	5.1	3.2
Undrawn balances as % of Commitments	68.9	63.2	86.1	89.1	85.2	68.8	65.6	49.9	47.5	48.5	58.9	41.2
						SAFs						
Number											10	25
SDR billion											0.3	1.4
Undrawn balances as % of commitments											57.5	57.0

Sources: IMF, Annual Report 1984, Table 17, p. 73; Annual Report 1987, Table 12, p. 50 and IMF, IMF Survey June 1 1987, p. 173 and May 30 1988, p. 175. All data are as of April 30th.

The choice between Fund reliance on quota increases and on borrowing for on-lending embroil the members in disputes over the need for greater liquidity in the international financial system and over the relative roles of private and multilateral lending. The Ninth General Review of Quotas in 1989 was conducted against the backdrop of the Fund's new role in financing the Miyazawa-Brady debt-reduction proposals. Prior to the Eight General Increase in Quotas, the Fund was forced to rely on borrowed funds to supplement its capital subscriptions from members. The Reagan administration had led developed country opposition to a large quota increase at the September 1982 Annual Meeting of the Fund.[48]

Williamson has pointed to a connection between the tougher conditionality faced by borrowing governments and the Fund's reliance on borrowing for on-lending to members.[49] When the Fund obtains its funds from a general increase in member quotas, the size of each tranche is increased proportionately to the general quota increase. As a result, the upper ceilings on each tranche are raised. Fund reliance on borrowing rather than a quota increase causes borrowing countries to bump up against credit tranche ceilings sooner. Amounts that would have been available in lower credit tranches had tranche ceilings been raised through a quota increase are now only available at the higher conditionality found in the upper tranches. In supporting calls for "extra liquidity," governments likely to borrow from the Fund seek to avoid higher conditionality.

While the borrowing strategy contributed to an increase in conditionality in the early 1980s, it also provided the Fund with greater operational flexibility. It was capable of being more responsive to sudden global needs for funds rather than waiting for the time-consuming and very political process by which members agree upon a general quota increase. The borrowing strategy placed the Fund in the role of a financial intermediary, borrowing from one source for on-lending elsewhere. This is a role quite different from the credit union, revolving fund one previously played by the Fund. Moreover, as Kenen argues, the borrowing strategy of the 1970s and 1980s was also a further erosion of the Fund's credit union mutuality under which member contributions through quota subscriptions determined drawing rights.[50]

CONCLUSION

International financial relations involving sovereign borrowers are intensely political relations whether lenders are private, official, or multilateral creditors. Both borrowers and creditors must respond to domestic political conditions in debtor countries. The run-up of commercial bank debt occurred in part because borrowers sought to avoid the political difficulties normally associated with IMF adjustment programs. Commercial banks represented a collective of lenders who had not yet come to ask too many questions.

The years of run-up in debt were years when the role of the IMF in a changing international financial system was undergoing some revision. In the aftermath to the crisis, the Fund has reasserted its influence. The most immediate reassertion occurred through "concerted lending" and the need to avoid financial panic in lending consortia. By 1989, the Fund was engaged in financing debt reduction.

While conditionality remains an essential part of the lending policies of both the Fund and the Bank, differences in their approaches to conditionality have, on occasion, caused relations between the two institutions to deteriorate sharply. In 1988, Argentina was able to obtain Bank approval of a structural adjustment loan under less stringent macroeconomic conditionality than had been sought by the Fund several weeks earlier. The sight of the Bank providing medium-term financing at a time when the Fund was unwilling to endorse Argentinean economic policies by providing an IMF package, was an embarrassing moment for both institutions and reinforced the need for the 1989 reexamination of the 1966 memorandum that governs relations between the Bank and the Fund. The next chapter examines some of the specific controversies that surround the question of conditionality.

NOTES

1. IMF, *International Financial Statistics 1986 Yearbook*, p. 39.

2. Alan Riding, "Alfonsin's New Drive on Debt," *New York Times*, September 11, 1987, p. D1.

3. It was also a reaction to the corruption, mismanagement, and arrogance of power as one political party enjoyed over fifty years of power and claimed to have permanently institutionalized a long-distant revolution.

4. J. de Larosiere, "Adjustment Programs Supported by the Fund," speech to the Centre d'etudes financieres, Brussels, February 6, 1984 (Washington, D.C: IMF, 1984), p. 11.

5. Richard N. Cooper, *Currency Devaluations in Developing Countries*, International Finance Section, Princeton Essays in International Finance No. 86, June 1971.

6. Clyde H. Farnsworth, "A Turbulent Rescue Role for the IMF," *New York Times*, May 4, 1984, p. D1; *New York Times*, January 25, 1984; *New York Times*, April 23, 1984.

7. Stephen Kinzer, "Guatemala Troops Leave University," *New York Times,* September 6, 1985, p. A3.

8. Clyde H. Farnsworth, "IMF Chief Challenges Criticism from Zambia," *New York Times,* May 7, 1987, p. D2.

9. James Brooke, "Nigerian Vows to End Military Rule," *New York Times,* October 22, 1988, p. 3; Paul Delaney, "Algeria to Lift State of Emergency as Unrest Ebbs in Riot-Torn Cities," *New York Times,* October 12, 1988, p. A12.

10. *New York Times,* March 1, 1989; Clyde H. Farnsworth, "Under Fire, as Usual, From the Third World," *New York Times,* March 8, 1989; Mark A. Uhlig, "Lines Form at Caracas Morgue to Identify Kin," *New York Times,* March 5, 1989; "Hussein Goes on TV and Vows an Election," *New York Times,* April 27, 1989.

11. For an analysis of the effects of developing country agricultural pricing policies, see World Bank, *World Development Report 1986,* pp. 61–109.

12. IBRD, *World Development Report 1988,* Table 26, pp. 272–73.

13. International comparisons of income distribution data are notoriously dangerous because of differences in collection methods and the age of many of the surveys. The data are collected at infrequent intervals and in some instances are almost twenty years old. In a number of cases, governments are too embarrassed to collect or publish any data.

14. Alan Riding, "Brazil Seeks to Mend Rift With Lenders," *New York Times,* February 12, 1988, p. D1.

15. James Brooke, "Ailing Nigeria Opens its Economy," *New York Times,* August 15, 1988, p. D4.

16. Enhanced surveillance consists of three key elements: the Fund agrees to provide a mid-year supplement to its annual Article IV consultations with a member; the member agrees to provide the Fund with an organized financial plan with numerical and internally consistent targets; the member agrees to provide the Fund's staff reports to the commercial banks with which it is renegotiating.

17. Maxwell Watson *et al., International Capital Markets: Developments and Prospects,* IMF Occasional Paper, No. 43, February 1986, p. 53.

18. IMF, *Annual Report 1988,* p. 57.

19. Clyde H. Farnsworth, "World Bank Sets Aside $500 Million for Loan Losses," *New York Times,* July 11, 1988, p. D1.

20. Eaton and Gersovitz offered four reasons why private lending to LDCs outstripped public lending—private lenders' need to on-lend OPEC deposits, the greater speed of decision making of private lenders, borrowers' perceptions of fewer restrictions on private loans, and, finally, developed country, especially U.S. disenchantment with foreign aid. See Jonathan Eaton and Mark Gersovitz, *Poor Country Borrowing in Private Financial Markets and the Repudiation Issue,* International Finance Section, Princeton Studies in International Finance No. 47, June 1981, p. 35.

21. The World Bank, *World Debt Tables 1987–88,* pp. 23; *World Debt Tables 1986–87,* pp. 2–3.

22. J. de Larosiere, "Perspectives on the World Economy and the Role of the IMF," speech to the Council on Foreign Relations, New York, November 29, 1984 (Washington, D.C.: IMF, 1984), pp. 9–10.

23. Some of these had been present at the Bretton Woods conference in 1944, but, with the exception of Yugoslavia, the communist parties that came to power in these countries after World War II did not maintain or apply for membership until recently. The Soviet Union had participated in the Bretton Woods conference but did not join. In a 1987 reversal, it sought to join.

24. IMF, *Annual Report 1987*, p. 124.

25. Congress had attempted in the late 1970s to have the U.S. Executive Director of the World Bank veto loans to Vietnam, to countries violating human rights and to countries seeking financing for projects that would compete with U.S. sugar, citrus, and soya-bean industries. Lobbyists for U.S. farmers have attempted to have U.S. executive directors at all multilateral development banks issued with instructions to vote against all agricultural development loans that might increase competition for U.S. farmers. Loans to China were suspended after the 1989 killings of students and workers.

26. This was largely attributable to the 1977 loans to Italy and the United Kingdom. In 1982 developed countries still making use of IMF credit were Australia, Finland, Iceland, Italy, Spain, the United Kingdom, and New Zealand.

27. EC arrangements include two short-term and two medium-term loan programs and a ECU 17 billion very short-term monetary support mechanism of mutual credit lines among European Monetary System (EMS) central banks. The latter provides funds for exchange-rate support operations to defend the parity grid in a manner reminiscent of pre-1973 IMF lending. EC medium-term loan facilities make disbursements based on conditionality determined by the EEC Council of Ministers. France obtained ECU 4 billion in 1983 and Greece obtained ECU 1.75 billion in 1985 in loans made conditional on macroeconomic adjustment programs of the kind familiar to developing countries that borrow from the IMF. See Horst Ungerer et al., *The European Monetary System: Recent Developments*, IMF Occasional Paper No. 48, December 1986, p. 6.

28. Richard Goode, *Economic Assistance to Developing Countries Through the IMF* (Washington, DC: The Brookings Institution, 1985), p. 20.

29. IMF, *International Financial Statistics Yearbook 1987*, pp. 36–41.

30. The Fund has also had its problems with developed country governments. In tracing the evolution of the Fund, Southard refers to angry sessions in which a U.S. and French effort to have the General Agreements to Borrow (GAB) organized outside the Fund was defeated. (Frank A. Southard, Jr., *The Evolution of the International Monetary Fund*, Princeton International Finance Section, Princeton Essays in International Finance No. 135, December 1979, p. 45.)

31. The weights or "quotas" assigned to each member were originally based on a formula that sought to measure a country's economic weight in the world economy. These weights determined not only a country's votes but also its contribution to the Fund and its borrowing rights.

32. G. K. Helleiner, *The IMF and Africa in the 1980s*, International Finance Section, Princeton Essays in International Finance No. 152, July 1983, p. 1.

33. Clyde H. Farnsworth, "IMF Trying to Be More Flexible," *New York Times*, February 1, 1987, p. D5.

34. IMF, *IMF Survey*, April 18, 1988, p. 118.

35. IMF, *IMF Survey*, May 30, 1988, p. 175.

36. IMF, *IMF Survey*, March 6, 1989, p. 79.

37. Jeffrey Sachs, *Theoretical Issues in International Borrowing*, Interrnatinal Finance Section, Princeton Studies in International Finance No. 54, July 1984, pp. 29–37; Carlos Diaz-Alejandro, "Latin American Debt: I Don't Think We Are in Kansas Anymore," *Brookings Papers on Economic Activity*, No. 2 (1984), pp. 335–89.

38. Jonathan Eaton and Mark Gersovitz, *Poor Country Borrowing in Private Financial Markets and the Repudiation Issue*, International Finance Section, Princeton Studies in International Finance No. 47, 1981, p. 26.

39. Maxwell Watson et al., "International Capital Markets; Developments and Prospects", *IMF World Economic and Financial Surveys*, January 1988, p. 51.

40. For details of the Fund's organization, see Anand G. Chandarvarkar, *The International Monetary Fund: Its Financial Organization and Activities*, IMF Pamphlet Series No. 42, 1984. See also IMF, *Annual Report 1987*, pp. 140–45.

41. IMF, *Annual Report 1987*, p. 63.

42. Peter B. Kenen, *Financing, Adjustment, and the International Monetary Fund* (Washington, D.C: The Brookings Institution, 1986), p. 15.

43. IMF, *Annual Report 1987*, p. 48.

44. IMF, *Annual Report 1987*, p. 71.

45. Richard Goode, *Economic Assistance to Developing Countries Through the IMF* p. 16.

46. Loans were for ten years at an interest rate of 0.5 percent. Gold was sold at market rather than official prices. The gold sale and the return of a further 25 million ounces to members were aimed at demonetization of gold as part of the efforts at international financial reform in the early 1970s.

47. IMF, *Annual Report 1987*, pp. 65–66.

48. Seamus O'Cleireacain, "Current U.S. Policies Toward International Financial Institutions," *CUNY Bildner Center for Western Hemisphere Studies Policy Paper*, No. 6, September 1983.

49. John Williamson, *The Lending Policies of the International Monetary Fund*, Institute for International Economics Policy Analyses in International Economics No. 1 (Washington, D.C.: Institute for International Economics, August 1982).

50. Peter B. Kenen, *Financing, Adjustment, and the International Monetary Fund* (Washington, D.C: The Brookings Institution, 1986), p. 9.

7

IMF and IBRD Conditionality

The debt build-up of the 1970s was partly the result of debtor country governments' aversion to loan conditions imposed by multilateral agencies and their preference for the fewer strings attached to commercial bank loans. The present chapter examines the lending policies of the two premier multilateral lending agencies, the International Monetary Fund and the World Bank. Fund lending policies provoke deep disputes. Theoreticians argue over the theoretical premises on which IMF recommendations are based. Policymakers argue over the feasibility of the recommendations. Of greatest importance, competing social strata of borrowing countries argue over how the costs of the recommendations are to be shared within society.

The first section of the chapter provides an overview of Fund conditionality. This is followed by a deeper examination of the theoretical paradigm that provides coherence to the Fund's lending policies, the monetary approach to the balance of payments. The third section of the chapter surveys the wide range of criticisms to which the Fund has been exposed. The particular issue of the effects of conditionality on income distribution is examined separately. An additional section surveys the empirical literature that attempts to measure the success of Fund-supported adjustment programs. The chapter concludes with a discussion of the growing importance of conditionality in the lending policies of the World Bank.

IMF CONDITIONALITY

Fund conditionality has evolved over the years with changes in the structural characteristics of Fund borrowers, with changes in intellectual fashions in economic theory, and with institutional changes in the international system.[1] Fund lending policies have always been controversial and were not formally included in the Articles of Agreement until 1969. At the Fund's inception, the issue of conditionality pitted the United States against European members. European representatives to the pre-Bretton Woods Conference Agenda Committee meeting in Atlantic City in June 1944, sought the right to borrow from the proposed fund without incursions on national sovereignty. In Dell's description of the rival positions taken by Keynes and the U.S. representative, Edward M. Bernstein, Keynes argued that countries had an unqualified right to make drawings.[2] The matter was not finally settled until a 1952 Fund decision in which the Europeans conceded the principle.[3]

There are a variety of reasons for requiring some degree of conditionality. Three cited by Kenen are the need to protect the revolving fund's liquidity, the possibility of using the Fund's superior information and experience to generate better designed policy, and the need to protect the collective interests of all members from possible attempts by some borrowers to improve their welfare at the expense of others.[4]

IMF conditionality remained important even as the Fund's share of sovereign debt shrank. Today, the influence exerted by the Fund extends well beyond the stabilization programs tied to its own loans. Even in instances in which it is not involved as a major lender, Fund views on appropriate adjustment policies wield great influence among both borrowers and lenders. These views shaped the financial system's response to the debt crisis. The Paris Club required that its debt restructurings of loans from official creditors be conditional on prior acceptance of a Fund program.[5] Commercial bank restructurings were made contingent on debtor country acceptance of either an IMF adjustment program or Fund "enhanced surveillance." A similar link exists with most of the World Bank's Structural Adjustment Lending (SAL). The Fund itself has also forced restructuring of commercial bank debt by insisting that private creditors be "bailed in" to provide fresh loans before the Fund would approve a standby agreement. According to the previous Managing Director of the Fund, Jacques de Larosiere, every dollar of Fund lending to Mexico and Brazil in 1983 and 1984 "unlocked about seven dollars of new loans and refinancing from commercial banks and governments."[6]

Fund conditionality encompasses policy preconditions that must be met prior to a member being granted access to a loan or Standby Arrangement, performance criteria contained in the member's Letter of Intent, and the less quantifiable policy understandings that are also included in the Letter of Intent. Devaluation is often a precondition for activation of a standby arrangement while supply-side policies of deregulation and a lessened reliance on subsidies have become common elements in policy understandings. Failure to meet performance criteria usually results in suspension of the phased disbursement of funds under the Standby Arrangement.

The conditions attached to the Fund's structural adjustment lending are developed in consultation with the World Bank. SAF and ESAF conditionality is based on a Policy Framework Paper prepared by the borrowing country. This contains a three-year adjustment program to overcome the macroeconomic and structural causes of a country's difficulties with its balance of payments and economic growth. It is the counterpart to the traditional Letter of Intent associated with Fund standby arrangements. Fund and Bank staff assist in the design of the policy framework position paper that is submitted to the Executive Boards of both the Fund and the Bank.

The general rules governing access to Fund loans and standby arrangements were set out in 1979 in a decision of the Executive Board.[7] Conditionality policies are reviewed periodically. Three comprehensive reviews were conducted in 1968, 1979, and 1988. In recent years the Fund has been moving toward a growth-oriented conditionality that would permit the introduction of some contingency provisions in its financing arrangements to allow for sudden shocks that disrupt adjustment programs. The 1988 review also addressed the need to design adjustment programs in ways ensuring that adjustment burdens do not fall excessively on the poorest sectors of society.

Article 4 of the 1979 Decision pays lip service to the sensibilities of borrowers by stating that: "In helping members to devise adjustment programs, the Fund will pay due regard to the domestic social and political objectives, the economic priorities, and the circumstances of members, including the causes of their balance of payments problems." Article 9 clearly limits the scope of the designers of a stabilization program by stating that "—performance criteria will normally be confined to (i) macroeconomic variables, and (ii) those necessary to implement specific provisions of the Articles or policies adopted under them. Performance criteria may relate to other variables only in exceptional cases when they are essential for the effectiveness of the member's program because of their macroeconomic impact."[8]

The 1979 review of lending policies had been the first review since 1968. The 1968 review had been demanded by developing countries who had argued that a 1967 United Kingdom standby arrangement did not contain the rigorous conditions demanded of developing country borrowers. Specifically, the conditions attached to the 1967 standby did not include the phasing of drawings ($1.4 billion was drawn in one draw-down that brought United Kingdom drawings to just under 200 percent of quota) nor did it include limits on credit expansion or government spending.[9] Since the 1967 U.K. episode, debates over Fund conditionality have centered not on whether some countries receive preferential treatment but on whether the Fund takes a doctrinaire approach to conditionality.

Although Fund critics often attack what they see as a rather doctrinaire, stringently "orthodox" approach to the design of stabilization programs, there is a lot less rigidity to these designs than is often believed. Indeed, the Fund insists that adjustment programs are not "IMF programs" but "IMF-supported programs" to emphasize that borrowing governments are actively engaged in the design of adjustment programs. A 1986 IMF staff study of the ninety four Fund-supported adjustment programs during the years 1980–84 showed the variation in the measures contained in individual country programs. It found that while all but eight of them involved restraint on government current expenditures, 55 percent of them included trade liberalization measures, 46 percent of them contained personal income tax measures. Wage and salary restraints were contained in 63 percent of the programs; transfer payment and subsidy restraints were found in 61 percent of them.[10] Only a very limited number of programs sought to restrict government current expenditures by specific functions. Defense spending was restricted in seven programs, educational spending in four, housing in one program, and official travel in five.

Fund standby and EFF loans exist for a relatively narrow purpose. They are most often provided for the purpose of assisting members in obtaining "sustainable" positions in their balance of payments, that is, to help *correct*, not *finance*, fundamental balance of payments disequilibria. Other objectives of stabilization programs that typically coincide with meeting this goal include doing something about a range of other indicators of internal disequilibrium such as inflation and unsustainable budget deficits.

Conceptually, a sustainable current account balance is one that might be expected to be financed by normal capital inflows. In some instances, prolonged current account deficits may be sustainable, for example, if a country is able to attract continuing direct foreign investment capital inflows to finance current account deficits. Empirically, the notion of a "sustainable" current account is a slippery concept. The "errors and omissions" category in the balance-of-payments statistics of many countries give reason to pause over the accuracy of capital flow data and hence over the size of "normal" capital inflows available to finance the "sustainable" current account deficit. Moreover, countries whose policies provoke net capital flight will find that no current account deficit is sustainable. Instead, a current account surplus must be produced to offset the net capital outflow.

If a current account deficit is not considered sustainable in the medium term at existing exchange rates, Fund conditionality will almost automatically require the adoption of a devaluation to a level deemed consistent with achievement of a sustainable balance of payments. Indeed, as mentioned already, devaluations are usually made a *precondition* for the granting of a standby arrangement. Although there are considerable difficulties in calculating it, the appropriate exchange rate to be adjusted is the real effective exchange rate, that is, the trade weighted exchange rate corrected for differences in inflation rates.

THE MONETARY APPROACH TO THE BALANCE OF PAYMENTS

The Fund's approach to analyzing the balance-of-payments difficulties of potential borrowers is often criticized as excessively "monetarist." This deserves some discussion. It is a generally accepted starting point among international economists that the balance of payments is a monetary phenomenon. That acceptance does not rule out the importance of real factors in determining the size and composition of the balance. It is merely a recognition that financial accounts are statements about the disposition of financial claims and liabilities.

Among the analytical pieces commonly cited as influential in developing the Fund's approach to adjustment is that of Polak (1957).[11] This early approach underwent considerable refinement with developments in monetary theory.[12] In his analysis of the monetary approach to the balance of payments, Williamson distinguishes carefully between the Fund's monetary approach as typified by Polak and what Williamson terms the Chicago monetarist approach of Dornbusch, Johnson, and Mundell.[13] Williamson reminds us that the monetarist approach of Polak was in part an effort to cope with the bad information usually available to policymakers in developing countries. Monetary data will be among the most timely and most reliable of all the macro data available even in the poorest countries and the Polak approach made use of that fact.[14]

The general approach adopted by the Fund in analyzing the adjustment needs of a country with persistent balance-of-payments difficulties is well within the mainstream of contemporary open-economy macroeconomic theory. It is premised on the absorption approach's notion that current account deficits represent the difference between a country's income and its absorption, that this difference is financed through foreign savings, and that these flows alter the stock of financial assets in the monetary sector.[15] The monetary approach to the balance of payments begins from the recognition that, by definition, the balance of payments is a monetary phenomenon and that national capital markets are integrated (if only imperfectly) with international capital markets. As a result, the balance of payments reflects the supply and demand for money and other assets both at home and abroad. With asset holders holding a mixed portfolio of domestic and foreign financial assets, the balance of payments becomes the mechanism through which equilibrium is achieved simultaneously in domestic and foreign asset markets. Any excess money supply leaks abroad through either a balance of payments deficit or through a decline in the international price of the domestic money, that is, a devaluation. Thus, in the presence of a stable demand for money function, balance-of-payments deficits are caused by excess money or credit creation. The operational use of the monetary approach involves the integration of national accounting, balance of payments, and flow of funds statistics.[16]

The Fund uses domestic credit expansion as one of the performance criteria in its conditionality. Given the underdeveloped credit markets and extensive role of the state in developing countries, reductions in credit creation would usually mean reductions in credit extended to the public sector. Some observers detect a bias toward privatization when a performance criterion that might otherwise be expressed in terms of domestic credit creation is instead expressed in terms of the public sector deficit.[17] However, this may also be seen as an effective way of controlling fiscal policy.

Much of the debate between the Fund and its critics is concerned with the time frame over which results are sought, and with the appropriate mix of policies. The Fund has shown that there is considerable diversity in the design of individual adjustment programs and that it is not wedded to a simplistic monetarist view of how economies function. If the simulation model used by Khan and Knight to examine the impact of Fund programs is considered typical of a "Fund approach," the Fund approaches economic analysis with its mainstream macro theory lenses firmly in place.[18] However, as we shall see later in this chapter, open economy macroeconomic theory developed for industrial economies may not always capture important structural characteristics of developing country economies.

CRITICISMS OF THE FUND

Lending criteria usually reflect the theoretical orientation of the lenders as to the causes and possible solutions of the external imbalance that made borrowing necessary. The Fund's critics see its lending criteria as rooted in an excessively doctrinaire view of the causes of balance-of-payments disequilibria, with this dogmatism requiring excessive austerity. In its defence, the Fund's previous

Managing Director, Jacques de Larosiere, denied the charge that the Fund is antigrowth or that its policies are rooted in austerity, claiming that this misconception existed because countries wait too long, delaying their approaches to the Fund until their economies are in deep crisis.[19]

Criticisms of the Fund's policy of conditionality have been succinctly summarized by a Fund staff member, Bahram Nowzad.[20] In Nowzad's summary, critics see Fund conditionality as based on the notions that the difficulties stem from excess aggregate demand and that they should be corrected over a short-time interval by a "standard package" of monetarist-based policies without regard to structural differences between countries or the extent to which the difficulties are the result of exogenous shocks. The critics conclude that the benefits of stabilization programs may jeopardize development strategies and may contain excessively harsh and self-defeating, if not irrelevant, conditions.

Though found elsewhere, critics of the Fund are heavily concentrated in Latin America, the region most affected by the debt crisis. Latin America has a venerable tradition of critiques of the Fund's approach to balance-of-payments adjustment. The region's stabilization policies of the 1960s and 1970s had often produced severe economic depressions and massive income redistributions. It comes as no surprise that the intellectual attacks against IMF conditionality have been led by Latin American economists appalled at the costs of these programs and asking whether these costs are necessary.[21]

Many critics of Fund stabilization programs make references to Fund orthodoxy, suggesting that the Fund takes a common approach to stabilization regardless of the circumstances of the country or the causes of its difficulties. Buira, for example, points to "the universal appearance of certain performance criteria such as ceilings on credit and public sector deficits" as enough to warrant the view that there is such a thing as a "Fund approach." Cline and Buira are among those who have outlined the general monetarist approach underlying the Fund framework.[22]

In Buira's depiction, the IMF approach downplays the supply-side of the economy and stresses control of aggregate demand by concentrating on relationships between money and nominal income. Buira finds no coherent analytical framework underlying the Fund's approach, which he sees as conditioned by the Bretton Woods era, leaving the Fund ill-equipped for the 1980s.[23] He finds that, until relatively recently, decisions on devaluation were often taken on an *ad hoc* basis without a comprehensive theoretical framework that would determine the degree of overvaluation and the optimal rate at which the overvaluation should be reduced. Buira claims that the Fund's earlier role of maintaining the Bretton Woods fixed exchange-rate regime caused it to call for devaluations as preconditions for Fund acceptance of stabilization programs that were then designed to maintain the new fixed exchange rate by limiting the rate of monetary expansion. In recent years, floating rates have become a more integral part of stabilization programs.

As mentioned earlier, one of the criticisms of the Fund has been the charge that its open economy macroeconomic theoretical framework may still inadequately describe important structural characteristics of developing economies. Among the exponents of a new structuralist macro-theory critique of Fund-supported stabilization programs have been Diaz-Alejandro, Foxley, and Taylor. In the 1980s version of the old 1950s and 1960s monetarist-structuralist debate over Latin American stabilization policies, both sides pay attention to supply-side considerations and recognize the need to cut price distortions that slow development by providing disincentives to private sector activities.

Some of the macro models of the new macro-structuralists embody institutional characteristics of typical semi-industrialized economies that cause these models to produce unorthodox results. These results include the possibilities that devaluations will worsen rather than improve the trade balance and have contractionary effects on output and that reductions in money supply will cause inflation.[24] Such perverse results are possible in orthodox theory under particularly unlikely assumptions, but these assumptions take on somewhat greater credibility in the context of developing countries. However, perverse results such as the two listed above are usually possible only in the short run. In the medium and longer term, more traditional results may be expected to hold.[25] Meanwhile, however, these models show that there is a possibility that, in the short run, the costs of stabilization programs may be even higher than orthodox theory would suggest. They also suggest that there is a danger of "overkill" in the use of macroeconomic policies mistakenly used to dampen the supposedly expansionary effects of actually contractionary devaluations.

The contractionary devaluation models of Cooper, Krugman, and Taylor produce their results by having the expenditure-switching effects of devaluation overpowered by the expenditurer-eduction effects. Taylor, for example, produces his short-run effects by introducing a short-run macro model of an open semi-industrialized economy with limited financial institutions and in which the short run is defined as the time period over which nominal wages and the real capital stock remain fixed. He uses a cost-based production theory in which nominal interest rates influence costs and prices. Changes in nominal interest rates on business loans are an important feature in cost-induced inflation. Under suitable assumptions it is then possible to show that a contraction in the money supply will produce not only a reduction in output but also, through the influence of nominal interest rates on costs, a higher level of inflation.

The structuralists are not alone in being able to produce such effects. Monetarist models may be constructed in which devaluation is contractionary in small open economies because the domestic price level, determined by the world price level, rises with a devaluation to reduce the real money supply.[26] In his critique of the devaluation component of IMF programs, Buira argues that the boost to output of tradable goods produced by the devaluation's switch in relative prices is likely to be overpowered by the contractionary effects of the devaluation and of the accompanying stabilization program.[27] The expansion of production of tradables depends on how optimistically one views the relevant elasticities. The contractionary effect of the devaluation occurs as the inflation produced by the devaluation erodes real balances and hence aggregate demand. To this must be added the general contractionary effect of the other measures included in the stabilization program.

In his empirical analysis of devaluations in developing countries, Edwards summarizes the mechanisms through which neostructuralist theorists show that devaluations may have contractionary effects on real output.[28] Three channels producing devaluation-induced reductions in aggregate demand are real balance effects produced by inflation, income-distribution effects that shift income away from groups with a high marginal propensity to consume toward groups with a lower marginal propensity to consume, and the traditional elasticity-pessimism argument that the price elasticities of exports and imports are so low that a devaluation worsens the trade balance. On the supply side, devaluations may have contractionary effects on output through cost increases associated with higher prices for imported inputs.

In another review, Khan and Knight list the main instances of special assumptions used by each of the models that produce contractionary devaluations.[29] In their review of empirical studies of the effects of devaluation on growth they find that usually output growth would be higher after devaluation and that there is no strong empirical evidence to support the view that devaluation lowers growth even in the short run. A rather different conclusion is drawn by Edwards, who shows that devaluations produce contractionary effects in the short run which are then cancelled out by expansionary effects after one year.[30]

One of the implications of the contractionary devaluation literature is the likelihood that the pursuit of orthodox IMF deflationary policies will produce "overkill," because the reduction in aggregate demand produced by the devaluation may not require any further policy-induced reduction. At the very least, the possibility that devaluation may not produce much expansion in tradable production and, because of structural rigidities, may leave unemployed resources languishing in the nontradable sector, needs to be taken into account when designing the other measures of the stabilization program to avoid "overkill."

Because there is a danger that the structural conditions for devaluations to produce short-run contractionary effects exist in particular instances, there is a need to design adjustment programs for individual countries with some awareness of the dangers of "overkill." In his study of IMF conditionality, John Williamson lists five targets that the Fund should take into account in designing stabilization programs.[31] Four of these cover the traditional concepts of internal and external balance discussed in such classic treatments of the theory of policy in open economies as the works of Meade and Tinbergen.[32] These are the balance of payments, output, employment, and inflation. The fifth is a nontraditional target of macro policy and has been the subject of considerable controversy—income distribution. The effect of conditionality on income distribution will be treated separately below.

Trade-offs exist between these five targets, giving rise to the notion that stabilization programs have costs. These costs may appear excessive if the singleminded pursuit of one target has a large effect on other targets. For example, if policies designed to produce the balance-of-payments target are maintained after the target has been reached, some analysts, if not politicians, will call for relaxation of the policies in order to increase growth and eliminate some of the unemployment that has been generated. The time frame within which the balance of payments target is to be achieved also determines the size of the output and employment cost. A more severe contraction of output and employment will be required the shorter the time available to meet the balance-of-payments objective. A further trade-off exists between nominal exchange rate and inflation rates once a real exchange-rate level has been chosen to produce the balance-of-payments target.

The Fund has not been silent in the face of criticism. Senior Fund officials on occasion have been at pains to suggest that there is considerable variety in its approaches and that borrowing governments have considerable latitude to establish national priorities within a broad Fund framework.[33] Officials emphasize that the Fund seeks to limit its incursion into national sovereignty and to pursue a principle of political neutrality in the setting of national priorities. Pursuit of this principle of political neutrality causes the Fund to stress monetary aggregates rather than fiscal policy since the choice among cuts in specific subsidies, increases in specific taxes, and so forth, "...is essentially political, and the Fund has no right to prefer one action over another, provided that the final result is the required recovery of the balance of payments. Consequently, it was accepted as a general practice that access to Fund resources should be regulated in accordance with developments in the broadest of macroeconomic indicators, that is, global monetary aggregates—."[34] In response to another criticism, Finch emphasises, "a rather eclectic range of policy actions that have been accepted by the Fund as the basis for the extension of its financial assistance."[35]

As part of the Fund's counterattack on its critics, a study by two Fund senior staff members, Khan and Knight, addressed the criticisms of those who see the Fund as antigrowth.[36] Khan and Knight surveyed the existing empirical literature of cross-section studies as well as empirical studies of the effects of the types of policy measures typically found in a Fund stabilization program. As with other Fund staff members, they see great variety in the manner in which demand-management policies, supply-side policies and international competitiveness policies are combined in the design of individual stabilization programs and say that it is misleading to see the Fund approach as a mechanical application of the simple monetary approach to the balance of payments. Indeed, Khan and Knight argue that there is little difference between the Fund's approach and the guidelines proposed by Fund critics except for the critics' preference for the use of controls to correct the balance of payments.[37]

In their search of the empirical literature dealing with the effects of specific demand-management policies commonly used by the Fund, Khan and Knight find instances in which growth may be reduced in the short term. A prime example of this is the one-year impact of contractionary monetary policy. However, their search of the cross-country literature showed no clear pattern of a downward bias in economic growth for those countries that had experienced Fund programs. Khan and Knight reconcile these differences by arguing that the cross-country studies include supply-side effects ignored by the time-series studies of individual demand-management measures. Further, they point out, the time frame used in the two groups of studies differs; the time-series results they cite refer to policy effects after one year, whereas the bulk of the cross-section results refer to a one- to three-year period.

In response to the "overkill" charge, Khan and Knight argue that the empirical literature does not provide sufficient evidence to judge the merit of the attack. To test the hypothesis, they say, would require empirical studies comparing Fund programs with an alternative set of policies that were implemented subject to the same constraints as face an IMF program, namely the same international environment with its lack of alternative sources of financing, the same time frame for producing results, and the same need to be politically acceptable. They find no such studies in the literature.

One final study undercutting the "overkill" proposition deserves mention. Gylfason compared a sample of countries that entered into upper-tranche standby arrangements in 1977–79 with a reference group of nonoil developing countries that also experienced balance-of-payments difficulties but did not enter into standby arrangements with the Fund.[38] He showed that there were statistically significant differences between the two groups of countries for both reduction in credit expansion and improvement in the balance of payments but that intercountry differences in reductions in real output were not statistically significant. Gylfason interpreted his results as supporting the conclusion that the improvement in the external position of countries adopting IMF-supported adjustment programs was not coincidental while there was not a significant cost in terms of lost output and employment.

CONDITIONALITY AND INCOME DISTRIBUTION

The income redistribution effects of Fund stabilization programs have long been a target of critics of Fund conditionality. The official position of the Fund, as set out in the 1979 Executive Board decision that established present ground rules on conditionality, states that matters of income distribution are the sole concern of national governments.[39] However, as even a 1988 Fund study recognizes, discussions between countries and the Fund on the design of Fund-supported adjustment programs often include policies with important distributional effects such as tax policy, while the income distribution effects of more general measures such as devaluations and monetary and fiscal measures are receiving growing attention.[40] Reductions in real wages, increases in unemployment, and regressive income redistributions are often seen as the inevitable consequence of IMF-supported stabilization programs. As we shall see, both the theoretical and the empirical evidence suggest that falls in either real wages or real incomes are not always inevitable, though there must be a fall in the rate of growth of real consumption.

The Latin American stabilization programs of the 1970s often involved a blend of monetarist theory with an emphasis on structural reform of the supply side. The stress on structuralism introduced a longer time horizon which caused these programs to deemphasize the "shock treatment" previously associated with monetarist approaches. Foxley attributes the gradualism of some of these programs to the political conditions provided by authoritarian governments that could afford to ignore construction of the social consensus normally necessary when democratic countries are asked to endure prolonged austerity.[41]

The income distribution effects of IMF stabilization programs depend on the extent to which the improvement in the current account is to be obtained through deflation rather than devaluation. They also depend on changes in the mix of public and private output. Two factors are responsible for changes in this mix. First, drastic changes in relative prices in both the goods and factor markets will occur as inflation decelerates and as tax, subsidy, tariff, and exchange-rate policies are altered; secondly, the level of public services will be reduced as budget deficits are curtailed.[42] Changes in relative prices will often produce reductions in real wages and increases in short-term interest rates. The latter will lead to investment in financial rather than real assets, reducing long-term growth potential.

While stabilization programs are almost always accompanied if not preceded by exchange-rate changes, the relative emphasis that is to be placed on deflation rather than devaluation is subject to some variation. Any unanticipated inflation generated by devaluation has the usual distributional impact on asset owners of reducing the real value of wealth of those who hold their wealth in money and other financial assets rather than real form. Low income savers holding domestic currency financial assets such as cash or bank savings accounts will see their savings eroded to the extent that the inflationary pressures of devaluation are not countered by a tighter macro policy.

The distributional effects of exchange-rate changes depend on the extent to which the domestic currency relative prices of tradables and nontradables is switched. The switch will not occur without restrictive macro policy. Otherwise there would be a tendency for the general inflationary pressures resulting from higher import prices to erode any initial change in relative prices produced by a devaluation.

A successful devaluation *cum* macro policy package produces its effects on the current account by driving up the domestic currency prices of exports, imports, and import-competing products relative to the prices of the nontraded sector of the economy. The higher relative domestic currency price of exports and import-competing products makes these sectors more profitable, encouraging an expansion in the volume of production. In addition to the supply-side increases in the volume of exports and decreases in the volume of imports, the higher domestic currency relative prices of imports discourage the consumption of imports.

All of these relative price effects will only occur if the structure of the economy is flexible enough to permit the implied shifting of resources. No real economy is as frictionless as the theoretical models that predict these results and real economies vary widely in their structural characteristics. However, to the extent that they occur, and do so under conditions of diminishing returns, the expansion of output in the tradables sector and the contraction of output in the nontraded sector imply a decrease in marginal productivity in tradables and an increase in the nontraded sector. This requires the tradables sector to experience a fall in the nominal wage relative to the domestic currency price of tradables while the nontraded goods sector sees a rise in nominal wages relative to the price of nontraded goods.

These shifts in nominal wages relative to prices are consistent with rising nominal wages in both sectors. As Johnson and Salop point out, the more emphasis is placed on exchange-rate effects the more the shifts in the relative profitabilities of the two sectors may be achieved without the unemployment that would occur if nominal wages were rigid downward.[43] That much of the nontraded sector of the economy is comprised of the public sector, suggests that exchange-rate changes can reduce the potential unemployment burden that might otherwise fall on public employees *if* structural conditions make it possible to obtain the production increases in exports and import-competing goods. What happens to *real* wages in each sector, that is, nominal wages relative to the *general* price level of the economy, depends on the relative weights of traded and nontraded goods in the overall price level.

Stabilization programs are often accompanied by immediate acceleration in inflation. It may be caused by imported inflationary pressures generated by nominal devaluations and the surge in prices that follows the removal of price controls or subsidies that bottled up repressed inflation. The Latin American adjustment programs of the mid- and late 1980s were often accompanied by massive inflation. In his analysis of the earlier orthodox stabilization programs of Brazil (1964–67), Chile (1973–78), Argentina (1976–78), and Uruguay (1974–78), Foxley showed that inflation was extremely resistent to efforts to reduce it. Real wages fell by between 20 and 40 percent and family income distribution was altered in favor of the rich.[44] In three of the four cases it took over four years to bring the inflation rate down to 40 percent.

In a 1980 Fund study of the distributional effects of conditionality, Johnson and Salop examined the income distributional effects of the common features of Fund stabilization programs.[45] Credit ceilings, tighter fiscal policy, devaluations, and relaxation of foreign exchange controls produce functional redistributions of income between capital and labor, regional redistributions between urban and rural areas, sectoral redistributions, and redistribution between the public and private sectors and those who depend on each.

In the case of credit ceilings, Johnson and Salop argue that the introduction of ceilings tends to bias access to credit in favor of large and away from small firms, toward urban rather than rural areas, toward consumer goods industries and away from capital goods industries. These biases reflect the relative preprogram short-run profitability of bank loans to each of these sectors. A further important effect of Fund-imposed credit restrictions lies in the effects produced by the higher interest rates that will follow credit controls. Johnson and Salop point out that whenever excessive credit creation causes domestic real interest rates to fall below world levels, the public sector provides a subsidy to credit users. The subsidy is the amount of the reduction of foreign exchange reserves that occurs as a result of the balance of payment deficit associated with the excessive credit creation.[46] This subsidy is reduced by the rise in interest rates associated with the credit ceilings of the stabilization program.

In their analysis of the distributional effects of the tighter budgetary policies necessitated by Fund-imposed ceilings on credit extended to the public sector, Johnson and Salop see increases in taxes as producing declines in the disposable income of producers of exports, consumers of imports, large firm salary earners, and public employees relative to agricultural producers and the self-employed, because the former groups represent tax bases that are more easily taxed. On the expenditure side, cuts in public spending will tend to include reductions in food subsidies and in the real remuneration of public employees. Johnson and Salop see the bulk of government expenditure cuts as falling on public employees engaged in postponable capital-intensive infrastructure projects and on the private sector suppliers to these projects.

As part of the 1986 review of conditionality, the Fund produced a staff study of income distribution effects of the fiscal policy component in ninety-four Fund-supported adjustment programs undertaken from 1980–84.[47] After arguing that there was insufficient data to permit adequate empirical measurement of all income effects, this in-house study stated that, *a priori*, Fund-supported programs clearly lead to redistribution between different sectors of the economy, including gains to rural peasants at the expense of city dwellers. However, the study argued, there was little reason to expect Fund-supported programs to cause an overall worsening of income distribution, or, in particular, a cut in the living standards of the population's poorest quartile.

The IMF study recognizes that the general economic contraction commonly associated with Fund-supported programs may produce a decline in income for low income citizens, but argues that income distribution may not have been made more regressive because the incomes of the rich may have fallen even more.[48] Indeed, it claims, income distribution changes might be even more regressive in the absence of the Fund-supported program. One income distribution effect benefiting the wealthy was particularly noted by the Fund staff. This is the capital gain reaped by citizens who engage in capital flight and then benefit from the revaluation of their foreign assets denominated in local currency after the exchange-rate devaluation that usually accompanies Fund-supported programs.

The Fund has become more sensitive to the charge that adjustment programs may have undesirable income distribution effects. A 1988 Fund study of adjustment programs in seven countries attempted to disentangle which components of an adjustment program improve income distribution and which worsen it.[49] The effects vary with different types of poverty. The poor include landless rural poor, agricultural small holders, urban informal sector poor, and urban formal sector poor. If employed, they may also be employed in producing tradables or nontradables. Heller et al. examine the impact of various policy instruments on each of these groups and show how the effects depend on the structure of poverty and on the policy mix in a particular adjustment program. In some instances, the poor are helped; in others they are hurt. Devaluations, for example, hurt the urban poor who produce nontradables and the rural landless poor.

Although the Fund may not include income distribution among its performance criteria, even the Fund recognizes that its programs have considerable income distribution effects. As another Fund critic, Gerald Helleiner, has argued, providing borrowing governments with greater flexibility in the design of adjustment programs would permit of greater allowance for income distribution effects.[50]

HOW SUCCESSFUL IS CONDITIONALITY?

There are no noncontroversial measures of the "success" of Fund conditionality. In a 1982 Fund study of the countries that had undergone upper-tranche stabilization programs during the 1970s, Donovan compared the experiences of these countries with the aggregate performance of all nonoil developing countries.[51] He found that these countries experienced a greater adjustment in current account deficits than was reported by the nonoil group as a whole. Donovan also found that the immediate inflation experience of two thirds of the program countries consisted of an inflationary spurt after adoption of a stabilization program, and that almost half of the countries did not experience any reduction in their inflation rates relative to nonoil LDCs as a group during the period in which the stabilization program was in place. However, the longer-term inflation experience of program countries was below that of the control group once the short-term one-shot effects of the policies associated with the stabilization programs had been overpowered by the stabilization gains.

Finally, Donovan's results suggested that the real income growth of countries accepting Fund conditionality was not significantly different from that of all nonoil LDCs. There was no long-term sharp rise in real income relative to the control group. Neither did Fund medicine lead to a fall in real growth rates relative to this group. The impact of Fund conditionality on living standards may be measured by changes in real consumption per capita. Donovan claimed that real consumption fell in only approximately a quarter of program countries. Although the average real consumption growth rate fell for the group, it was still positive and, when corrected for population growth, would suggest some average increase in real living standards.

The "crash program" nature of Fund stand-by programs in the 1970s, prior to the creation of the EFF and the Bank's introduction of SAL is most evident in Donovan's findings that the improvement in the current account disequilibrium of program countries was achieved with a small increase in the savings rate and a larger decline in the investment rate. Donovan's central conclusion that Fund programs allowed countries to achieve "significant reductions in their external deficits while they exhibited only marginal changes in their growth rates of real GDP and consumption" leads him to infer that the costs associated with Fund stabilization programs may be less severe than critics of the Fund claim.[52]

In a related 1982 Fund study, Kelly examined the extent to which reduction in the external deficits of the program countries covered by Donovan's 1971–80 sample were associated with reductions in public sector deficits.[53] Kelly's results suggest that current account improvements depend to a large extent on reductions in public sector deficits. However, she also found that the percentage reductions in private sector deficits exceeded the reductions in public sector deficits.

The results of such studies by Fund staffers as Donovan and Kelly have led one Fund critic, John Spraos, to argue that the less-than-complete success achieved with the Fund's approach stems from a confusion of what should be appropriate policy targets and instruments.[54]

Spraos claims that the performance criteria typically found in a Fund program make targets of what should be instruments and that these criteria should be replaced by the single policy target that should matter, namely, improvement in the external accounts. He suggests that policy instruments should not be restricted as to how this target is to be achieved. Indeed, he points to the growing literature illustrating the limited success of IMF programs in meeting balance-of-payments targets and argues that success in meeting other targets is both irrelevant and perhaps counterproductive to meeting what should be the primary consideration.[55]

A compelling reason offered by Spraos for making a change from what he sees as ineffectual, inefficient, and mistargeted conditionality is the contentious nature of typical Fund programs which cause adjustment to be delayed longer than it would be if governments were perfectly free to determine for themselves the manner in which they would meet the current account target. These delays invariably reflect conflicts over the distribution of the costs to be associated with a stabilization program. Spraos argues that hostility to the Fund has become so pronounced that countries shy away from making use of even low-conditionality first-tranche drawings.[56] For Spraos, the relegation of the Fund to lender of last resort represents a failure of the Fund and is at sharp variance with its 1979 guidelines on conditionality in which the Fund stands ready to provide assistance not only at early stages of emerging difficulties but even as a precaution against potential difficulties.

Some targets of IMF stabilization programs are more easily achieved than others. As Diaz-Alejandro pointed out, stabilization programs have their quickest success with their balance of payments targets. According to Diaz-Alejandro, this success will be produced through changes in the capital account before it appears in the current account, and will reflect the fact that the stabilization program often produces domestic short-run real interest rates in excess of world levels, even after allowing for expected exchange-rate depreciation. Thus the net capital inflow. Liberalization of domestic capital markets and reductions in domestic credit expansion coupled with wage and price controls will all combine to drive up real interest rates.

Less success is likely to be achieved in bringing down the rate of inflation. The literature on the causes of Latin American inflation is voluminous. The persistence of inflation in the face of rising unemployment, lower budget deficits, reductions in the rate of money and credit creation produced by the typical stabilization program, all combine to permit some analysts to argue that the inflation is generated by structural characteristics influencing the supply side of Latin economies rather than by excessive aggregate demand.

Monetarists, however, are not persuaded that it is necessary to look beyond money supply growth and inflationary expectations to explain continuing inflation.[57]

The quick correction of the main objective, the balance of payments, provides ammunition to Fund critics who charge that as long as the external objective is being met, there is no need to continue with the pursuit of the internal targets. This leads to the charge that Fund programs contain an element of domestic "overkill." The Fund for its part will usually maintain that quick corrections to the balance of payments through the capital account do not produce sustainable improvements in the current account without continuing to squeeze the domestic economy.

Part of the traditional "overkill" of stabilization programs may be attributed to the manner in which the Fund had sought to pursue exchange-rate corrections in countries with high inflation rates. In the Bretton Woods era of fixed exchange rates, the Fund had a disposition to seek massive nominal devaluations and then had sought to peg the nominal rate. To obtain a sustainable real effective exchange rate in the face of high, though decelerating, inflation, the massive nominal devaluations were larger than necessary to produce the required real exchange rate. The real rate would fall as ongoing inflation further eroded the pegged nominal exchange.

This strategy produced wider fluctuations in the real exchange rate than would be produced if the nominal devaluation were limited to the amount of desired real devaluation and if the nominal rate were periodically adjusted thereafter by the rate of inflation to keep the real rate fixed.[58] In the present era of managed floating exchange rates, there is less systemic pressure on the Fund, as the organization charged with exchange-rate surveillance, to ensure that exchange- rate levels are pegged and defended once a realistic rate is adopted. Controlling inflation took on greater importance in IMF stabilization programs during the era of fixed exchange rates. According to Finch, the greater flexibility in the exchange-rate regime after 1973 has caused the Fund to give less urgency to the controlling of inflation.[59]

IBRD STRUCTURAL ADJUSTMENT LENDING CONDITIONALITY

The conditions attached to IBRD structural adjustment lending (SAL) programs are not yet as well defined as IMF conditionality. Though less precise, SAL conditionality may be characterized as supply-side conditionality in contrast to the Fund's demand-side conditionality.

The origins of SAL lie in the recognition that persistent balance-of-payments deficits require correction through permanent structural adjustment of economies. Deficits no longer financeable require correction. The extent to which this correction may be obtained without sacrificing the rate of economic growth depends not only on the size of the loans available but also on the amount of time available. The severity of IMF adjustment and its stress on demand management are byproducts of the relatively short time horizons available under IMF adjustment programs. The longer interval available under SAL allows for a greater reliance on structural, micro, or supply-side policies. More time also provides an opportunity to maintain the rate of economic growth while altering the composition of output through structural reform. Thus, as Yagci, Kamin, and Rosenbaum point out, SAL represented "an evolution of views about stabilization policy which had become increasingly skeptical that relatively narrow demand-based approaches to stabilization were by themselves sufficient".[60]

According to Stern, it was assumed from the beginning that SALs would normally be accompanied by an IMF stabilization program under either a stand by or an EFF arrangement.[61] SALs have a counterpart to the Letter of Intent provided by governments when borrowing from the Fund. This takes the form of a Letter of Development Policies. And as with a Letter of Intent, this letter may be seen as describing the conditionality applying to the SAL. And as with the Fund, conditionality is policed by providing SAL funds in tranches (usually two), with disbursement of the second tranche being conditional on satisfactory progress toward meeting the objectives established in the Letter of Development Policies.

The types of policy measures sought by the World Bank have been classified by Mosley under four categories: trade policy, resource mobilization, resource-use efficiency, and institutional reform.[62] Examples in each category include reductions in tariffs and quotas, tax and interest-rate reforms, energy and agricultural price reforms, and greater efficiency in public enterprises and public investment programs. Mosley argues that Bank conditionality is inherently loose because of the long delays, amounting to five years in some cases, between disbursement and the measurement of compliance. The wide range of possible interpretations on the extent to which some predisbursement promises are implemented represents a further difference from Fund conditionality with its stress on numerical targets.

The ultimate objective of structural adjustment lending is to obtain a medium-term strengthening of the balance of payments through policy reforms that adjust the structure of the economy. Reform of trade patterns to reflect more accurately a comparative advantage requires changes in price, tax, and subsidy policies as well as tariff rates if domestic production and consumption patterns are to be altered. Reform of exchange-rate policy is necessary so that foreign exchange is correctly priced. Too often it is set at a level which provides excessive import incentives to imports whose world price has risen, such as energy; or stimulates demand for importables, such as food, which could be produced at home with adequate incentives; or provides excessive export disincentives to nontraditional exports.

Three general areas of reforms are aimed at: macro policy, sectoral policy, and institutional arrangements. With an emphasis on structural reform in these general areas, the thrust of SAL programs is on deregulation and more rational pricing policies. Institutional policies are aimed at improving the management of government policies, encouraging deregulation, and reforming the operations of semistate bodies such as public enterprises.

In the case of macro policy, Stern cites such instances of typical SAL conditionality as reductions in budget deficits to increase funds available for productive investment, greater targeting of welfare programs toward the poor, a concern for nonproductive spending such as armaments and changes in the level, and sectoral orientation of public capital programs.[63] Sectoral policies are aimed at altering relative investment and production incentives in the economy through more rational exchange-rate, tariff, tax, and subsidy policies. Such alterations in relative prices seek to encourage energy conservation, increase domestic food supplies, remove disincentives to nontraditional exports, and reduce effective protection of inefficient industry. Privatization is a common objective of SALs. In general, the sectoral objectives of SALs may be seen as obtaining a more rational set of domestic incentives through reform of relative prices so that they more accurately reflect the changed international environment.

In their analysis of the design of SALs, Yagci, Kamin, and Rosenbaum point to the present absence of an overall analytical framework and the great reliance on partial equilibrium analysis in SALs. As a result, they claim, a number of inconsistencies between different objectives in SAL programs are usually not fully identified. Among the conflicts in objectives they list are those between trade liberalization and reduction in budget deficits (since revenue losses from tariff reductions increase budget deficits); between short-term stabilization and long-term economic growth; between privatization and goals to increase tax revenue and liberalize interest rates; and between stabilization and employment and income distribution goals.[64]

Although there may be areas in which the internal consistency of SALs may be improved, there is one notable area of SAL consistency. SALs mark a break in the previous inconsistency between earlier balance of payments and development financing. By providing a longer time horizon in which to make the structural adjustment, SALs increase the likelihood of obtaining balance of payments equilibrium in a manner consistent with economic growth. They also represent a narrowing of the gap between the approaches taken by the Fund and the multilateral development banks.

CONCLUSION

In the era of the 1970s, when bank debt was partly amassed as an end run around the restrictions imposed by the IMF, Fund conditionality could be both attacked and avoided. Developing country access to commercial bank balance of payments support helped strengthen the notion that the Fund should remain as lender of last resort with the stringent lending conditions appropriate for crisis situations in which all other financing options have been exhausted. The severity of Fund conditionality in the face of alternative sources of financing meant that its lending policies were making the Fund irrelevant to the needs of many developing countries, calling into question the appropriateness of its policies.

As debtor countries ran into commercial bank credit ceilings and as creditors insisted on Fund participation in rescheduling agreements, the Fund has been able to reassert its policy prescriptions on debtor countries. The 1980s' failure of unorthodox stabilization programs such as the Austral and Cruzado Plans contributed to this trend. As we have seen, there is considerable variation in Fund-supported adjustment programs within a general rubric of "realistic" real effective exchange rates, a limit to domestic price distortions, and greater monetary and fiscal discipline. There has been some convergence of views on the appropriate theoretical paradigm to be applied to balance-of-payments crises in developing countries. At the same time, the Fund's view of its role as a short-term lender has been altered to converge with those who have called for a more medium-term approach to Third World balance of payments financing. One result may be a lessening of the likelihood of "overkill."

NOTES

1. Excellent surveys of the historical development of conditionality may be found in Manuel Guitian, *Fund Conditionality: Evolution of Principles and Practices*, IMF Pamphlet No. 38 (Washington, D.C: IMF, 1981), and Sidney Dell, *On Being*

Grandmotherly, International Finance Section, Princeton Essays in International Finance No. 144, October 1981.

2. Sidney Dell, *On Being Grandmotherly*, p. 3.

3. Joseph Gold, *Conditionality*, IMF Pamphlet No. 39, pp. 24 (Washington, D.C.: IMF, 1979).

4. Peter B. Kenen, *Financing, Adjustment, and the International Monetary Fund* (Washington, D.C.: The Brookings Institution, 1986), p. 48.

5. There have been exceptions to this requirement. In 1986, Brazil had sought Paris Club acquiescence to a restructuring without reaching an IMF program. In January 1987, the creditor governments agreed to reschedule over six years $3.25 billion that had been owed in 1985 and 1986. In a pathbreaking deviation from past practice, the creditors did not make the rescheduling contingent on the prior acceptance of an IMF program, but settled for a Brazilian agreement to accept "enhanced surveillance" by the Fund (*New York Times*, January 22, 1987).

6. J. de Larosiere, "Perspectives on the World Economy and the Role of the IMF," speech to the Council on Foreign Relations, New York, November 29, 1984 (Washington, D.C.: IMF, 1984), p. 8.

7. Decision No. 6056-(79/38) of IMF Executive Board on Use of Fund's General Resources and Stand-by Arrangements, March 2, 1979.

8. The reference to specific articles of the Fund's Articles of Agreement is a reference to Fund strictures on trade barriers and capital controls as it seeks to maintain a relatively open international trading system.

9. Frank A. Southard, Jr., *The Evolution of the International Monetary Fund*, International Finance Section, Princeton Essays in International Finance No. 135, December 1979, pp. 31–32, and Margaret G. deVries, *The International Monetary Fund, 1966–1971*, Vol. I (Washington, D.C.: IMF 1976), pp. 343–48.

10. IMF, *Fund-Supported Programs, Fiscal Policy, and Income Distribution*, IMF Occasional Paper No. 46, September 1986, p. 2 and pp. 22–23. A similar policy content analysis of 1980 programs may be found in Morris Goldstein, *The Global Effects of Fund-Supported Adjustment Programs*, IMF Occasional Paper No. 42, March 1986, p. 9.

11. J. J. Polak, "Monetary Analysis of Income Formation and Payments Problems," *IMF Staff Papers*, Vol. 6 (November 1957), pp. 1–50.

12. Academic refinements include Jacob A. Frenkel and Harry G. Johnson (eds.), *The Monetary Approach to the Balance of Payments*, (London: George Allen and Unwin, 1976). Fund refinements include IMF, *The Monetary Approach to the Balance of Payments: A Collection of Research Papers of the Staff of the International Monetary Fund* (Washington, D.C.: IMF, 1977).

13. John Williamson, *The Open Economy and the World Economy* (New York: Basic Books, 1983), pp. 165–70.

14. For a simplified version of the Polak model see John Williamson, *The Open Economy and the World Economy* (New York: Basic Books, 1983), pp. 167–68. A simplified version of the general monetary approach of the Fund is found in Ariel Buira, "IMF Financial Programs and Conditionality," *Journal of Development Economics*, Vol. 12 (1983), pp. 119–22.

15. For a recent exposition of the Fund's approach see IMF, *Theoretical Aspects of the Design of Fund-Supported Adjustment Programs*, IMF Occasional Paper No. 55, September 1987.

16. See Poul Host-Madsen, *Macroeconomic Accounts: An Overview*, IMF Pamphlet Series No. 29 (Washington, D.C: IMF, 1979), Chart 4, p. 64, and Margaret R. Kelly, "Fiscal Adjustment and Fund-Supported Programs, 1971–80," *IMF Staff Papers*, Vol. 29, No. 4 (December 1982), pp. 564–66.

17. The role of privatization in Bank and Fund policies is examined by Don Babai, "The World Bank and the IMF: Rolling Back the State or Backing Its Role?" in Raymond Vernon (ed.), *The Promise of Privatization* (New York: Council on Foreign Relations, 1988), pp. 254–86.

18. Mohsin S. Khan and Malcolm D. Knight, *Fund-Supported Adjustment Programs and Economic Growth*, IMF Occasional Paper No. 41 (Washington, D.C: IMF, November 1985), pp. 26–30.

19. J. de Larosiere, "Adjustment Programs Supported by the Fund," remarks before the Centre d'etudes financieres, Brussels, February 6, 1984 (Washington, D.C.: IMF, 1984), p. 7.

20. Bahram Nowzad, *The IMF and Its Critics*, International Finance Section, Princeton Essays in International Finance No. 146, December 1981, pp. 9–10.

21. Carlos F. Diaz-Alejandro provided a useful stylization of IMF programs in his "Southern Cone Stabilization Programs," in William R. Cline and Sidney Weintraub, *Economic Stabilization in Developing Countries* (Washington, D.C.: The Brookings Institution, 1981), pp. 119–41.

22. William R. Cline, "Economic Stabilization in Developing Countries: Theory and Stylized Facts" in John Williamson (ed.), *IMF Conditionality* (Washington, D.C.: Institute for International Economics, 1983), p. 176, and Ariel Buira, "IMF Financial Programs and Conditionality," *Journal of Development Economics* Vol. 12 (1983), pp. 111–36.

23. Ariel Buira, "IMF Financial Programs and Conditionality," pp. 111–36.

24. Paul Krugman and Lance Taylor, "Contractionary Effects of Devaluation," *Journal of International Economics*, Vol. 8 (November 1978), pp. 445–56; Richard N. Cooper, *Currency Devaluation in Developing Countries*, International Finance Section, Princeton Essays in International Finance No. 86, 1971; Lance Taylor, "IS/LM in the Tropics: Diagrammatics of the New Structuralist Macro Critique" in William R. Cline and Sidney Weintraub (eds.), *Economic Stabilization in Developing Countries* (Washington, D.C.: The Brookings Institution, 1981), pp. 465–506.

25. A recent study of the effects of devaluation that confirms some traditional results is Steven B. Kamin, *Devaluation, External Balance, and Macroeconomic Performance: A Look at the Numbers*, Princeton Studies in International Finance No. 62, August 1988.

26. Rudiger Dornbusch, "Devaluation, Money, and Nontraded Goods," *American Economic Review*, Vol. 63 (December 1973), pp. 871–80.

27. Ariel Buira, "IMF Financial Programs and Conditionality," p. 125.

28. Sebastian Edwards, "Are Devaluations Contractionary?," *Review of Economics and Statistics*, Vol. LXVIII, No. 3 (August 1986), pp. 501–08.

29. Mohsin S. Khan and Malcolm D. Knight, *Fund-Supported Adjustment Programs and Economic Growth* p. 16.

30. Sebastian Edwards, "Are Devaluations Contractionary?"

31. John Williamson, *The Lending Policies of the International Monetary Fund*, Institute for International Economics Policy Analyses in International Economics No. 1 (Washington, D.C.: Institute for International Economics, August 1982), pp. 25–26.

32. James E. Meade, *The Theory of International Economic Policy*, Vol. I, *The Balance of Payments* (London: Oxford University Press, 1951); Jan Tinbergen, *On the Theory of Economic Policy* (Amsterdam: North-Holland, 1952).

33. C. David Finch, "Adjustment Policies and Conditionality," in John Williamson (ed.), *IMF Conditionality* (Washington, D.C.: Institute for International Economics, 1983), pp. 75–87, and Bahram Nowzad, *The IMF and its Critics*.

34. C. David Finch, "Adjustment Policies and Conditionality," p. 78.

35. C. David Finch, "Adjustment Policies and Conditionality," pp. 80–81.

36. Mohsin S. Khan and Malcolm D. Knight, *Fund-Supported Adjustment Programs and Economic Growth*.

37. Mohsin S. Khan and Malcolm D. Knight, *Fund-Supported Adjustment Programs and Economic Growth* p. 3.

38. Thorvaldur Gylfason, *Credit Policy and Economic Activity in Developing Countries with IMF Stabilization Programs*, International Finance Section, Princeton Studies in International Finance No. 60, August 1987.

39. IMF Executive Board Decision No. 6056-(79/38), March 2, 1979, in IMF, *Selected Decisions*, Twelfth Issue, 1986, p. 26.

40. Peter S. Heller et al., *The Implications of Fund-Supported Adjustment Programs for Poverty*, IMF Occasional Paper No. 58, May 1988.

41. Alejandro Foxley, "Stabilization Policies and Their Effects on Employment and Income Distribution: A Latin American Perspective," in William R. Cline and Sidney Weintraub (eds.), *Economic Stabilization in Developing Countries*, pp. 191–225.

42. See Albert Fishlow, "Comments" on papers by Ahluwalia and Lysy and by Foxley in William R. Cline and Sidney Weintraub, *Economic Stabilization in Developing Countries*, pp. 229–32.

43. Omotunde Johnson and Joanne Salop, "Distributional Aspects of Stabilization Programs in Developing Countries," *IMF Staff Papers*, Vol. 27, No. 1 (March 1980), pp. 1–23.

44. Alejandro Foxley, "Stabilization Policies and Their Effects on Employment and Income Distribution," p. 201.

45. Johnson and Salop, p. 13.

46. Johnson and Salop, p. 11.

47. IMF, *Fund Supported Programs, Fiscal Policy, and Income Distribution*, Occasional Paper No. 46, September 1986.

48. IMF, *Fund Supported Programs, Fiscal Policy, and Income Distribution* p. 3.

49. Peter S. Heller et al. *The Implications of Fund-Supported Adjustment Programs for Poverty*.

50. G. K. Helleiner, *The IMF and Africa in the 1980s*, Princeton Essays in International Finance No. 152 (July 1983), p. 18.

51. Donal J. Donovan, "Macroeconomic Performance and Adjustment under Fund-Supported Programs: The Experience of the Seventies," *IMF Staff Papers*, Vol. 29, No. 2 (June 1982), pp. 171–203.

52. Donald J. Donovan, "Macroeconomic Performance and Adjustment under Fund-Supported Programs," p. 197.

53. Margaret R. Kelly, "Fiscal Adjustment and Fund-Supported Programs, 1971–80," pp. 561–602.

54. John Spraos, "IMF Conditionality—A Better Way," *Banca Nazionale del Lavoro Quarterly Review*, December 1984, pp. 411–421.

55. John Spraos, *IMF Conditionality: Ineffectual, Inefficient, Mistargeted*, International Finance Section, Princeton Essays in International Finance No. 166, December 1986.

56. John Spraos, "IMF Conditionality: Ineffectual, Inefficient, Mistargeted," p. 6.

57. See Arnold C. Harberger, "Comments," in William R. Cline and Sidney Weintraub, pp. 226–29.

58. John Williamson, *The Lending Policies of the International Monetary Fund*, Policy Analyses in International Economics No. 1 (Washington, D.C.: Institute for International Economics, August 1982), p. 27.

59. C. David Finch, "Adjustment Policies and Conditionality," p. 81.

60. Fahrettin Yagci, Steven Kamin, and Vicki Rosenbaum, *Structural Adjustment Lending: An Evaluation of Program Design*, World Bank Staff Working Papers No. 735, p. 97.

61. Ernest Stern, "World Bank Financing of Structural Adjustment," in John Williamson (ed.), *IMF Conditionality*, p. 90.

62. Paul Mosely, *Conditionality as a Bargaining Process: Structural-Adjustment Lending, 1980–86*, International Finance Section, Princeton Essays in International Finance No. 168, October 1987, p. 5.

63. Ernest Stern, "World Bank Financing of Structural Adjustment," pp. 87–107.

64. Fahrettin Yagci, Stevin Kamin, and Vicki Rosenbaum, *Structural Adjustment Lending*, pp. 22–28.

8

Domestic Adjustment in Debtor Countries

The last chapter has shown that, within the Fund's general approach to adjustment, there are a variety of adjustment paths available. This chapter examines the pattern of adjustment displayed by Major Borrowers and Highly Indebted Countries in the years after the onset of the crisis in 1982. As financing flows vanished, severe adjustments became necessary in many, though not all, cases. For some debtor countries, these adjustments had been postponed in the earlier era of plentiful credit. The chapter begins with a short narrative of internal adjustment measures in three Latin American countries before turning to a wider examination of the twenty-four-country sample.

The domestic economic consequences of the debt crisis were traumatic for many countries. Economic disruptions have been widespread, particularly in Latin American debtor countries, where a succession of adjustment programs was introduced after 1982. Contrary to common perception, not all debtor countries experienced recessions and rising unemployment. As we shall see later, a number of governments managed either to maintain or to increase economic growth despite (or, because of) their external indebtedness. These governments were relatively successful in the short term in shielding their citizens from the full burden of adjustment. In some instances, a greater share of the burden may have been passed on to creditors or delayed for the future.

Despite hiccups, the crisis produced some dramatic changes in policies, including Mexico's accession to the GATT in August 1986. Accession overturned an article of nationalist and isolationist dogma in Mexican politics. Throughout Latin America there has been a general lessening of reliance on import substitution and protection, a reorientation toward export-led growth, and a retreat from state ownership or subsidization of enterprises. Shifts in budget priorities, and price increases to reflect more accurately the real social cost of goods and services, have reduced the ability of governments to rely on political patronage to shore up support.

The Latin American experience included some dramatic failures along the way to greater discipline. Some of the most highly touted Latin American efforts at domestic adjustment, most notably the Austral and Cruzado experiments in Argentina and Brazil, collapsed in a welter of inflation, devaluations, rising monetary growth, and public sector budget deficits. Some common characteristics are found in the domestic adjustment of many of the Latin American countries undergoing debt-induced restructuring. Inflation soared and real per capita GDP fell sharply below even 1980 levels. Real per capita GDP fell 15 percent in Argentina, 11 percent in Mexico, and 20 percent in Venezuela between 1980 and 1987, but rose 4 percent in Brazil.[1] In some, though not all countries, real wages fell too.[2] In Chile, Peru, and Uruguay, 1987 real wages were below 1980 levels, with the most pronounced decline being 20 percent in Peru. Internal economic crises have often been accompanied by trade surpluses and considerable foreign exchange reserves, but massive government budget deficits requiring internal financing as external sources disappeared. These crises produced some innovative domestic adjustment packages as well as a gradual return to reliance on the IMF.

ADJUSTMENT IN THREE LATIN AMERICAN DEBTORS

The adjustment policies of three major Latin American debtors, Argentina, Brazil, and Mexico—have been watched closely as the crisis has evolved. Adjustment policies in each of these countries underwent several rounds of revision between 1982 and 1989. In Argentina and Brazil, fledgling democratic governments have struggled with the legacies of military dictatorships. Mexico's economic policies are heavily influenced by the centerpiece of its political system: the single, nonrenewal six-year Presidential term. Policies are also often determined by the economic conditions inherited from the previous Presidency. The 1982–88 Presidential term of de la Madrid was a term of considerable austerity imposed by a party accustomed to weak political challenges.

Argentina's Austral Plan was introduced in June 1985 to cure threatened hyperinflation. The Plan produced a new currency to replace one made worthless by inflation which had reached 1900 percent per annum. A nine-month price and public sector wage freeze was introduced. The Plan also called for a fixed exchange rate and some tightening of fiscal policies through increases in tax revenues. Within months of relaxation of the Plan, inflation was again a major threat. In the following two years a variety of stop-go measures of surprise devaluations and new freezes were introduced against a background of triple-digit inflation, rising budget deficits, increased political uncertainty over constitutional changes, attempted military coups, and electoral defeats for the Alfonsin government. Structural measures included some privatization and a reduction in trade protection.

In October 1987 a new program of wage and price freezes was introduced.[3] It contained some relief for low-paid workers through a 75 percent increase in the minimum wage, a devaluation, and an increase in public sector transportation and electricity charges. The new program was aimed at reducing Argentina's budget deficit, which, at roughly 7 percent of GDP in 1987, was far from the 2.9 percent target in the country's Letter of Intent to the IMF.[4] President Alfonsin had initially attempted to manage without accepting an IMF package, but after the Austral Plan's failure he had finally been forced to go to the IMF. In a relaxation of earlier conditionality attitudes, IMF disbursements in 1987 and 1988 had continued despite Argentina's failure to meet several of the targets in the Letter of Intent governing a 1987 standby arrangement. Disbursements were eventually suspended as Argentina moved further from compliance. In August 1988 a new set of measures was introduced supported by a new IMF standby arrangement, World Bank loans, and a U.S. bridging loan. The new program sought to curtail the government budget deficit and reduce inflation from 600 percent annually.[5] It included a 12 percent devaluation, limits on price increases, increased energy and transportation charges, and a reduction in public sector employment.[6] When President Menem took office in July 1989, the program had collapsed into a welter of bankruptcies, inflation exceeding 100 per cent a month, growing hunger, and minimal foreign exchange reserves.

Brazil unveiled its Cruzado Plan in February 1986 as part of its continuing boycott of the IMF and as a way of coping with inflation, which had reached 227 percent in 1985. Relations with the IMF had ended when Brazil fell out of compliance with a 1983 standby arrangement. Like the Austral Plan, the Cruzado Plan introduced a new currency, a wage and price freeze, and a 33 percent increase in the minimum wage. It also eliminated indexation of short-term financial assets. However, in a sharp challenge to IMF orthodoxy, the Cruzado Plan did not contain major measures to slow monetary growth, reduce public sector deficits, or alter public sector prices, and it sought economic growth through export promotion and import substitution.

By early 1987 the Brazilian experiment had failed. The Cruzado Plan was abandoned and Brazil unilaterally suspended interest payments on its bank debt in February. An import boom had depleted foreign exchange reserves and inflation exceeded 500 percent with the removal of price controls. In June 1987 a new economic team introduced a shock stabilization program, including a new wage and price freeze after some adjustment of relative prices, and a new objective of reducing the public sector deficit from 6 percent to 3.5 percent of GDP.[7] Public investment projects were severely curtailed and some subsidies were eliminated. In December 1987, President Sarney, who opposed some of the proposed austerity measures, appointed Mailson da Nobrega to be his fourth Finance Minister in less than four years of civilian government. Nobrega ended the suspension of interest payments and a three-year boycott of the IMF by beginning negotiations with the Fund for a standby arrangement. In May 1988 Nobrega announced a two-month freeze on public sector wages. By August, inflation was running at 900 percent per annum. Between 1982 and 1988, inflation dipped below 100 percent in only one year (1986).

In Mexico, the public sector had been vastly expanded during President Echeverria's 1970–76 term. The ensuing public sector budget deficits were maintained by his successor, Lopez Portillo, who used oil revenues to borrow against the future. Difficulties began to emerge with the weakening of oil prices in 1981. As borrowing rose to finance the shortfall from oil revenues, an overvalued exchange rate produced a surge in both imports and capital flight. The next President, de la Madrid, took office within months of the August 1982 onset of the crisis. His term was one of economic austerity and erosion of the political power of the PRI. Some of the austerity measures were designed by de la Madrid's chosen successor, Carlos Salinas de Gortari, who served as his Planning and Budget Minister. Calling for reforms within the PRI, Salinas de Gortari was elected President in July 1988 by a historically thin margin amid widespread charges of electoral fraud and the emergence of a genuine multiparty political system.

Mexico tried a number of adjustment programs since the onset of the crisis in August 1982. These included the programs of late 1982, July 1985, mid-1986, and December 1987. The 1982 package was supported by an IMF-extended arrangement, whereas the 1986 package was backed by a Fund standby. Budget deficit reduction and import compression were augmented by structural reforms aimed at opening up the economy and stressing export competitiveness. A strategy of continuous real devaluation and trade liberalization measures announced in the mid-1985 package reoriented the Mexican economy away from import substitution toward export-led growth. Since the 1985 trade liberalization strategy was adopted, Mexico joined GATT in 1986, cut quantitative restrictions from 75 percent of imports in 1984 to 24 percent in 1987, reduced its top tariff rate from 100 percent in 1984 to 20 percent in 1987, and lowered its average tariff from 23 percent to 10 percent.

The collapse in oil prices in late 1985 required further major changes, and in July 1986 a comprehensive adjustment program was introduced. This was supported by a November 1986 IMF package that contained a novel contingency clause providing for additional financing if the per barrel price of oil fell below $9. Inflation in 1986 exceeded 100 percent as the 1985 package's real devaluation and reduced subsidies combined with rising nominal wages to feed inflationary expectations.

A "Pact for Economic Solidarity" was introduced in December 1987 as consumer price inflation soared to 160 percent for the year. The measures were announced less than a month after high inflation had caused a stock market crash, financial panic, and the collapse of the exchange rate. The Pact recognized the failures of the Austral and Cruzado Plans by including fiscal and monetary austerity; a 22 percent devaluation of the peso in the controlled market followed by a crawling peg exchange rate policy to devalue the currency in line with anticipated inflation; more trade liberalization measures; further increases in public sector fees and charges; and a wage and price freeze. Some privatization measures were announced in April 1988 and the freeze was extended in August.

The fiscal restraint promised in the Pact was not implemented as the PRI prepared for the 1988 Presidential election campaign. The Public Sector Borrowing Requirement (PSBR) rose from 10 percent in 1985 to 16.5 percent of GDP in 1987, although some of the increase was attributable to inflation-induced rises in interest payments on internal debt.[8]

ADJUSTMENT IN TWENTY-FOUR DEBTOR COUNTRIES

The manner in which individual countries in the twenty-four-country sample responded to their debt difficulties is examined in the rest of this chapter. A number of reasons may be advanced to explain the wide variety of response. Heterogeneity of the sample would make unlikely a common adjustment pattern among all sample countries in the years after 1982. Turkey's crisis predated the Mexican crisis of 1982; its adjustment had begun earlier. India's reliance on foreign aid rather than bank debt, and South Korea's reliance on export-led growth, limited the debt-servicing burden of these two countries. The debt difficulties of a number of other countries, not least the oil exporters, were compounded by falling export prices even as they struggled with the need to adjust to the shut-off of voluntary lending in the years after 1982.

Six broad indicators of policy instruments and policy targets have been chosen to examine individual country variation conditions and policies. Three policy instruments—monetary growth, budget balance, and the real exchange rate—are combined with the three policy targets of trade balance, inflation, and GDP per capita. Changes in these six indicators are measured by comparing four-year averages for the precrisis years of 1979–82 with those for the crisis period of 1983–86.

The most watched target of economic policy is per capita GDP. From the onset of the crisis, debtor country representatives spoke of the intolerable burden imposed by the crisis on debtor country citizens. The crisis produced a precipitous decline in living standards in a number of the debtor countries. Six of the twenty-four countries in the sample experienced negative average GDP growth rates in the four years after the emergence of the crisis in 1982. One country (Bolivia) had negative economic growth in each of the five years since 1982. Other countries with years of negative GDP growth in the 1982–86 period were Uruguay (four years) and Nigeria (three years). In terms of real per capita GDP, as late as 1986, half of the countries in the twenty-four debtor country sample had not regained their 1980 level.[9]

However, the decline in living standards was not so widespread as is commonly supposed. The sample contains some notable exceptions to falling debtor country living standards. Moreover, there are a number of problems with using a single year such as 1980 as yardstick, apart from the obvious one of choosing an appropriate base year. In particular, there is a need to avoid comparisons with years in which living standards might have been artificially inflated through unsustainable foreign borrowing. To ameliorate these problems, a precrisis 1979–82 period is compared with a 1983–86 crisis period.

In the 1983–86 crisis period, only half of the twenty-four debtor countries averaged negative real per capita GDP growth. Moreover, six of these (Argentina, Bolivia, Costa Rica, Jamaica, Nigeria, and Venezuela) had been among the seven countries averaging negative per capita growth even in the precrisis period. A majority of the sample, fourteen countries, suffered a decline in their 1983–86 average real per capita GDP growth rate compared to their 1979–82 period average. The most severe deteriorations were registered by Mexico (a 6.4 point swing from a 3.4 percent average growth rate to a –3 percent rate), the Philippines (from 1.6 percent to –4.5 percent), and Nigeria (from –2.4 percent to –7.1 percent).

Surprisingly, eight of the twenty-four Major Borrowers or Baker Plan countries had higher (or less negative) real per capita GDP growth rate averages in the crisis years than they experienced in the precrisis period. The largest gains were made by South Korea (from a

2.8 percent average growth rate to 7.5 percent), India (from –0.1 percent to 3.6 percent), and Turkey (from 0.4 percent to 3.5 percent). Two other countries (Colombia and Israel) registered unchanged per capita GDP growth rates between the precrisis and crisis eras.

These results suggest that, in ten of the twenty-four Major Borrower or Baker Plan countries, citizens were shielded from severe adjustment in the years immediately following the crisis precipitated by Mexico's mid-1982 difficulties. In at least one case, that of Turkey, the adjustment had come earlier. One of the strongest arguments advanced by those advocating comprehensive debt management schemes has been the need to allow debtor countries to grow again. The data on real per-capita GDP for the sample countries suggest that one group of countries was not growing even in the precrisis years, that another group managed to achieve growth despite its renegotiated debt burdens, while a third group managed to improve its negative growth rates even without a global debt plan.

An alternative measure of the adjustment that occurred in the 1983–86 crisis period may be obtained by comparing the precrisis and crisis levels of real GDP per capita that would have been obtained if economies has maintained the growth path observed in the years prior to the first oil shock in 1973. This comparison of deviations from longer-term trends in per capita GDP levels provides some further clues as to which countries have managed to use a heavily debt-financed development strategy to maintain a level of per capita income that, even with the adjustment produced by the crisis, is above the level that would have been obtained had growth continued along, for example, a 1965–73 trend line. Although the adjustment measures necessitated by the debt crisis have obviously been contractionary, it is worth bearing in mind that a large group of countries were not doing very well even prior to the crisis. Table 8.1 provides some comparisons of recent deviations from both pre- and post-oil shock growth paths.

As Table 8.1 shows, even in the era of heavy reliance on debt-financed development strategy from 1974 to 1982, twelve of the twenty-two countries for which data are available failed to maintain per capita GDP along a 1965–73 trend. The largest shortfalls were in Jamaica, Nigeria, and Israel. A number of countries that were hurt by the oil shocks were still able to rise above their earlier growth path. These included Brazil, South Korea, Uruguay, and Yugoslavia. When a longer perspective is taken by using the 1965–79 growth path, thirteen countries had a four-year average below trend even prior to the emergence of the crisis in 1982.

When the four-year averages around 1982 are compared, the last column of Table 8.1 suggests that debt crisis adjustment measures have knocked many countries even further off their longrun growth

Table 8.1 Cumulative Forecast Errors from Trend
(% of 1980 real per capita GDP)

	From Trend I		From Trend II	
	1974-82	1983-86	1979-82	1983-86
Major Borrowers				
Argentina	-1.0	-1.4	-0.4	-0.9
Brazil	+0.4	-0.5	-0.3	-1.0
Chile	-0.9	-0.6	+0.4	+0.2
Egypt	+1.7	+1.9	+0.4	+0.9
India	0.0	+0.2	0.0	+0.2
Indonesia	+1.0	+0.6	+0.2	0.0
Israel	-1.9	-2.0	-0.4	-0.9
S. Korea	+0.6	+0.7	-0.1	+0.2
Malaysia	NA	-0.1	+0.1	-0.1
Mexico	+0.2	-0.4	+0.2	-0.4
Turkey	-0.2	-0.5	-0.5	-0.6
Venezuela	-0.4	-1.3	-0.5	-1.3
17 Highly Indebted Countries				
Bolivia	-1.4	-2.6	-0.7	-2.1
Colombia	-0.2	-0.5	0.0	-0.4
Costa Rica	-0.4	-1.2	-0.4	-1.3
Côte d'Ivoire	NA	NA	NA	-0.4
Ecuador	+1.1	-0.1	-0.1	-0.9
Jamaica	-4.5	-3.8	-0.8	-1.1
Morocco	+0.9	+0.3	-0.1	-0.4
Nigeria	-2.7	-3.8	-1.0	-2.4
Peru	-0.6	-1.3	-0.3	-1.1
Philippines	+0.6	-0.3	+0.1	-0.7
Uruguay	+0.4	-0.3	+0.2	-0.6
Yugoslavia	+0.3	-0.3	0.0	-0.6

Notes: Two OLSQ trend lines ($Y = a + b$ time) were obtained for the 1965-73 and 1965-79 periods, using an index of real per capita GDP. These equations forecast per capita GDP in the four periods. Forecast values were compared with actual. Malaysia and Côte d'Ivoire forecasts based on 1970-79 and 1975-82 trends respectively.

paths. The deviations from the growth path were sometimes double or treble those registered in the four years when financing was still available. In four cases (Malaysia, Mexico, Philippines, and Uruguay), precrisis per capita incomes were above the long-run growth path and were moved below that path in the years after 1982. In only two instances, India and South Korea, were precrisis per capita income levels on or below the growth path replaced by levels above the growth path in 1983–86. In all, a total of four countries (Chile, Egypt, India, and South Korea) managed to remain above their growth path in the years of adjustment.

The two other indicators chosen to measure changes in policy targets are the trade balance and inflation. As late as 1986, ten of the twenty-four countries in the sample were running trade deficits. In 1982, the number had been thirteen. Those moving from deficits to surpluses were Colombia, South Korea, Malaysia, and Nigeria. Bolivia, after a run of surpluses, slipped into deficit in 1986. Comparing the precrisis average trade balances of 1979–82 with the postcrisis balances of 1983–86, the number of countries registering an average trade deficit fell from fourteen to eight. The largest trade balance improvements were made by Brazil, Ecuador, and Mexico. The cumulative trade surpluses run by a number of the debtor countries in the four years 1983–86 were considerable. Mexico's trade surpluses amounted to a cumulative $40 billion, Brazil's to $41 billion and Argentina's to $15 billion.

Improvement in the trade accounts of debtor countries was often achieved through savage "import compression." All but seven sample countries experienced declines in imports over the 1983–86 period compared to the 1979–82 average. Indeed, in only four countries (India, Israel, South Korea, and Turkey) did 1986 imports exceed 1981 levels. Jamaica, Nigeria, Peru, and the Philippines reported five successive years of falling imports from 1982 to 1986. Six other countries in the twenty-four-country sample had negative import growth in four of these five years. Export effort is more difficult to evaluate because of changing primary product prices. Only one sample country, South Korea, registered export increases in each of the five years after 1981. At the other end of the performance spectrum was Bolivia, whose exports experienced a free fall, declining year after year from 1982 to 1987.[10]

The three indicators chosen to reflect changes in the instruments of economic policy are the real exchange rate, monetary growth, and budget deficits. Domestic adjustment in many debtor countries has involved measures that produce one-shot sharp increases in price levels as subsidies are reduced or as currencies are devalued. In many instances, these adjustments have been allowed to produce lasting effects on inflation. Eighteen of the sample countries had double-digit inflation averages in the debt crisis 1982–86 period. Inflation was measured by changes in the wholesale price index where available. In other instances the consumer price index was used. There were no Latin American countries in the list of low inflation countries, which was composed of Asian debtors (India, Indonesia, South Korea, and Malaysia) together with the Côte d'Ivoire and Morocco.

Five countries, all Latin American (Argentina, Brazil, Bolivia, and Peru) except Israel, had inflation rates averaging over 100 percent annually in the four years after the onset of the crisis in 1982. Bolivia was at the top of the league with a four-year inflation average of 3,655 percent, followed by Argentina at 421 percent, Israel at 213 percent, and Brazil at 193 percent. Comparing the pre- and postcrisis period inflation averages, fifteen of the sample countries had higher inflation in the years after the crisis broke. Although the debtor countries that lowered their four-year inflation averages in the 1983–86 period were largely Asian (India, Indonesia, South Korea, and Malaysia), there were two Latin American countries on the list (Colombia and Costa Rica). The others were the Côte d'Ivoire, Morocco, and Turkey. There is no strong evidence to suggest that the inflation of the debt-crisis years is attributable to changes in the real effective exchange rate.[11] A simple correlation analysis of the link between inflation and the current or lagged REER for the eighteen countries with REER data since 1970 found only four instances of a significant negative correlation (Brazil, Egypt, Mexico, and Uruguay).

Exchange-rate devaluations are a classic response to balance-of-payments difficulties. Apart from their role as a switching device to alter relative prices, exchange rates have an important influence on capital flight. A misaligned exchange rate provokes expectations that a devaluation will ultimately occur. As governments have discovered, these expectations are a powerful force for capital flight, as asset-owners seek to avoid the foreign-currency denominated capital losses endured by those who hold domestic-currency denominated assets. This effect is not limited to financial assets. Misaligned exchange rates also give rise to the phenomenon of consumer flight into imported consumer durables, for example, cars, whose domestic currency prices may be expected to rise with both the expected devaluation and any new import or foreign exchange controls introduced with the eventual devaluation package.

Despite the widely accepted influences of devaluation on the balance of payments, not all of the sample countries had undergone real effective devaluations by the end of 1986. When exchange-rate levels are averaged over the four debt crisis years of 1983–86 and compared with the precrisis 1979–83 period, a surprising number of countries may be seen to have pursued exchange-rate policies that would worsen rather than improve any balance-of-payments disequilibrium. Real effective exchange rate (REER) data from Morgan Guaranty was available for eighteen of the twenty-four countries. Of these, six had higher average REERs in the crisis period than in the precrisis years, with Egypt and Nigeria averaging crisis period REERs over 40 percent above precrisis averages. However, in only three of the six cases of increasing REER average (Egypt, Israel, and Peru) were 1986 REER levels above 1980 levels.

Among the sample, the countries that relied most on REER adjustment (as measured by the fall in 1983–86 REER average over 1979–82 average) were Argentina (29 percent), Turkey (25 percent), and Uruguay (24 percent). Other major Latin American debtors, Brazil, Chile, and Mexico, relied much less on real devaluations. Their REER period averages declined by between 13 percent and 17 percent. Peru, on the other hand, pursued a policy of maintaining the level of its REER. Its 1983–86 REER average was just under 3 percent above its precrisis average.

Some of the motivations that may have led one third of the sample countries for which REER data are available to shun real devaluations have already been discussed in our earlier look at criticisms of IMF conditionality. In the case of small, open, primary-product exporting economies facing fixed foreign currency prices for their exports and imports, the expenditure-switching effects of devaluations on export earnings will be restricted to supply effects. These effects are likely to be low because of low price elasticities of supply. Most of the expenditure-switching gains must come through the discouragement of imports. As the earlier discussion on IMF conditionality showed, it is possible to construct theoretical models in which the expenditure-switching effects of devaluation are overpowered by the expenditure-reducing effects, causing such perverse effects as a worsening balance of trade and falling output. Other factors that may explain the reluctance to rely on devaluations include a political inability to introduce the macro measures needed to curb inflationary pressures likely to be generated as devaluations produce some import-led cost inflation.

While the income redistribution effects of devaluations are unclear, the relative inability of low income people to bear inflation-induced reductions in real income is not. Poor people are less able than rich people to afford any reduction in living standards. This is sometimes used as a reason to argue against devaluations, because nominal devaluations erode real income in the absence of complete indexation. However, the evidence would suggest that many governments have been unable to produce a medium- to long-term environment of limited inflation from any cause, devaluations or otherwise. Although inflation may have both structural and monetarist roots, even structurally rooted inflation cannot persist unless it is ratified by increases in the nominal money supply. The manner in which monetary policy has been conducted in debtor nations during the debt crisis is examined below.

As with the other indicators discussed so far, the pattern of monetary policy indicators is quite mixed. Data on *ex post* real money supply growth was available for all but three countries in the sample.[12] In the absence of adequate methods of measuring inflationary expectations, actual rates of inflation were used to deflate nominal M1 growth.[13] The twenty-one countries for which real money supply growth was available split almost evenly into those that adopted more restrictive monetary policy and those that did not. Using four-year averages of annual real monetary growth rates, eleven countries pursued more expansionary (or less restrictive) monetary policy in the debt crisis years than they had in the earlier period, while ten pursued less expansionary (or more contractionary) policies. In an astounding ten cases, negative growth in the four-year precrisis period of 1979–82 was replaced by positive growth in the crisis period, with the largest percentage point swings being registered by Israel (58 percentage points), Peru, Mexico, and Costa Rica (33–37 points each). As mentioned above, these results need to be treated with great caution. Alternative measures of nominal monetary growth and of inflation will produce different results.

International comparisons of measures of fiscal policy stance are also fraught with great methodological differences. National statistics vary enormously in their coverage of the economic role of the state. Data on the central government budget balance as a share of GDP were available on a roughly comparable basis for only thirteen of the twenty-four sample countries.[14] This series was used as a measure of shifts to a more expansionary or more contractionary fiscal policy by comparing the four-year precrisis and crisis averages. Fiscal policy became more expansionary in only five of the thirteen cases. Countries that relaxed their fiscal policy were Bolivia, Chile, India, Peru, and Uruguay. Some of the swings in fiscal rectitude were very impressive. The largest percentage change in budget balance share of GDP was reported by Brazil (164 percent), followed by Costa Rica (70 percent), Indonesia (60 percent), and South Korea (53 percent). Even in these instances, we should recognize that the transfer of programs from central government budgets to provincial or state enterprise budgets will reduce central government deficits without reducing the Public Sector Borrowing Requirement (PSBR).

The findings above are summarized in Table 8.2 by constructing two groupings of indicators and comparing the precrisis and crisis four-year averages of the indicators. One grouping of the three policy instruments—REER, real monetary growth, and fiscal policy—indicates the macroeconomic policy stance. A second grouping—consisting of per capita GDP, inflation, the trade balance—measures the impact of policy instruments on policy targets. Although complete data are available for all three policy targets, there are large gaps in data availability for the indicators of policy stance. The results contained in Table 8.2 make clear that there was no common response to the debt crisis. The manner in which the targets and instruments of

Table 8.2 Changes in Economic Policy from Precrisis to Crisis Years

	Policy Instruments			Policy Targets			1983-86 GDPP Growth
	Monetary	Fiscal	REER	BOT	INFL	GDPP	
Major Borrowers							
Argentina	+	NA	+	I	W	I	-0.1
Brazil	-	-	+	I	W	I	+2.2
Chile	NA	+	+	I	W	I	+0.7
Egypt	-	NA	-	W	W	W	+3.4
India	+	+	+	W	I	I	+3.6
Indonesia	-	-	+	W	I	W	+0.7
Israel	+	NA	-	I	W	0	+0.4
S. Korea	+	-	+	I	I	I	+7.5
Malaysia	-	-	-	I	I	W	+0.8
Mexico	-	NA	+	I	W	W	-3.0
Turkey	+	NA	+	I	I	I	+3.5
Venezuela	+	NA	+	I	W	W	-3.6
17 Highly Indebted Countries							
Bolivia	-	+	NA	W	W	W	-5.9
Colombia	+	NA	+	I	I	0	-5.9
Costa Rica	+	-	NA	I	I	I	-0.2
Côte d'Ivoire	+	NA	NA	I	W	W	-0.4
Ecuador	NA	-	+	I	W	W	-1.2
Jamaica	+	NA	NA	W	W	I	-1.4
Morocco	NA	NA	NA	I	I	W	+0.2
Nigeria	-	NA	-	W	W	W	-7.1
Peru	+	+	-	I	W	W	-1.8
Philippines	-	-	-	I	W	W	-4.5
Uruguay	-	+	+	I	W	W	-0.9
Yugoslavia	-	-	NA	I	W	W	-0.4

Notes: Changes are 1979-82 averages (1979-83 for GDPP) compared with 1983-86;
+ indicates a more expansionary monetary or fiscal policy or a real effective exchange
rate rise; I/W indicates an improvement/worsening. Monetary policy measured by real
M1 growth change; fiscal policy by change in central government budget balance's share
of GDP. REER is real effective exchange-rate; BOT is balance of trade; INFL is rate of
inflation; GDPP is real GDP per capita, last column shows actual growth.

open-economy macroeconomic policy were adjusted during the first four years of the crisis varied enormously from country to country.

The policy-instrument columns of Table 8.2 show that in only two instances (Brazil and Indonesia) do all three indicators suggest an unambiguous shift to a more contractionary macro policy stance in the 1983–86 period. Peru, on the other hand, is the only instance of an unambiguous shift to a more expansionary stance. By 1989, the Peruvian economy was in shambles after a 1988 inflation rate of 1,722 percent.[15] In the five other cases for which all three policy-instrument indicators are available, the signals are mixed. Four countries (South Korea, Malaysia, the Philippines, and Uruguay) reported contractionary stances for two of the three indicators, while in the case of India, two of the three suggest a shift to a more expansionary policy. The eleven cases containing both monetary and fiscal indicators may be grouped into five instances of unambiguous tightening of monetary and fiscal policy (Brazil, Indonesia, Malaysia, Philippines, and Yugoslavia), an unambiguous expansionary stance in India and Peru, and four cases (Bolivia, Costa Rica, South Korea, and Uruguay) where a shift to a more expansionary stance on one policy is balanced by a countervailing shift in the other policy.

CONCLUSION

The domestic adjustment experiences of the sample countries in the first four years after 1982 were extremely diverse. The sample includes some Major Borrowers, such as South Korea, which has not had a debt crisis at all. Among the others, individual countries differed in the timing of their difficulties and in the manner of their responses. In a very mixed picture, the clearest pattern emerges with the balance of payments and with inflation. With few exceptions, the trade balance improved between the two periods. With a few more exceptions, inflation generally worsened in the years of adjustment.

Domestic economic difficulties appeared to have been most pronounced among middle income Latin American countries. Low income debtor countries benefited from a range of special debt-relief programs without which greater internal adjustment might have been necessary. Middle income countries, on the other hand, found that the developed countries' case-by-case approach to the debt crisis differentiated between countries on the basis of percapita income. In the absence of general relief for middle income countries, the shortage of new money forced continuing adjustment.

Adjustment often unleashed considerable inflationary pressures as exchange-rate devaluations were combined with reductions in government subsidies and more accurate pricing policies. As late as 1989, seven years after the onset of the crisis, a number of Latin American countries were still attempting to bring inflation, monetary growth, and budget deficits under control. Import compression and greater export orientation had done much to restore external balance; the search for an internal equilibrium consistent with long-run growth and national aspirations continued.

NOTES

1. Cumulative percentage changes from UN, Economic Commission for Latin America and the Caribbean, *Preliminary Overview of the Latin American Economy 1987*, December 31, 1987, Table 3, p. 16.

2. UN Economic Commission for Latin America and the Caribbean, *Preliminary Overview of the Latin American Economy 1987*, December 31, 1987, Table 6, p. 17.

3. Alan Riding, "Argentina Reins in Economy," *New York Times*, October 15, 1987, p. D1.

4. *New York Times*, "Argentina Devaluation Renews Inflation Fight," October 10, 1987, p. 55; Shirley Christian, "Argentina Still Can't Carry Debts," *New York Times*, March 1988, p. D10.

5. Shirley Christian, "Argentina Prepares Plan to Try to Rescue Economy," *New York Times*, August 2, 1988, p. D1.

6. Clyde H. Farnsworth, "Treasury Working on $500 Million Loan to Aid Argentina," *New York Times*, August 5, 1988, p. D2.

7. UN Economic Commission for Latin America and the Caribbean, *Preliminary Overview of the Latin American Economy 1987*, December 31, 1987, p. 4.

8. The primary budget balance, which excludes interest payments and financial intermediation, showed a surplus of over 5 percent of GDP in 1987.

9. GDP data are not corrected for exchange-rate changes. Source: IMF, *International Financial Statistics*, IFS 99bpx and IFS 99z.

10. Bolivia's official trade statistics exclude its considerable cocaine exports.

11. Nominal devaluations undoubtedly add to inflationary pressures.

12. IFS 34x from IMF, *International Financial Statistics* deflated by wholesale price inflation (IFS 63x) where available, otherwise consumer price inflation (IFS 64x). Monetary data for Brazil were available to 1985.

13. The estimates of real monetary growth are sensitive to the choice of inflation measure. The use of wholesale price indices rather than the faster-rising consumer price indices produces higher estimates of real monetary growth.

14. IMF, *Government Finance Statistics Yearbook 1986*, supplemented in some instances by *International Financial Statistics*, IFS 80, adjusted to calendar year and expressed as a share of IFS 99b.

15. *New York Times*, "Peru's Inflation Put at 1722 percent," January 4, 1989, p. D7.

9

The Response of the United States

The debt crisis posed serious threats to the interests of developed countries, not least the United States. This chapter examines the manner in which U.S. institutions responded to these threats. The main economic threat, of collapse of the financial system through the bankruptcy of major commercial banks, was avoided. Secondary threats of lower income, reduced exports, lost employment, and higher government or tax expenditures, were not. In addition, the political threat remains. The nascent revival of democracy in a number of debtor countries is still threatened by austerity programs that increase the political pressure on struggling democratic governments.

The impact of the crisis on the U.S. economy has been considerable. The costs to the U.S. economy include capital losses on foreign assets, the reduction in income from delayed debt servicing and a considerable fall in export income and employment as debtor nations reduced imports. Some potential costs were avoided. In 1983, Data Resources Incorporated (DRI) had produced estimates of the likely impacts on the U.S. economy in the event of a payments moratorium by one or all Latin American countries.[1] DRI estimated that a general Latin American moratorium, extending from Spring 1984 to early 1985, would have produced a 2.25 percentage point increase in interest rates and a level of real GNP which, two years later, would be 2 percent lower than otherwise.[2] An accompanying 0.75 percentage point increase in unemployment would involve a job loss of a little over a million jobs. Although the costs of such a general moratorium have been avoided, there have been severe effects on U.S. exports and on the income and equity of bank shareholders.

Separate sections of the present chapter are devoted to the responses of Congress, the Administration and the Federal Reserve Board, and U.S. commercial banks. These are preceded by a short discussion of the impact of the crisis on the U.S. economy. The responses of the Administration and the Federal Reserve Board are treated in the same section because, despite the independence of the Fed, a number of regulatory measures required coordination between the two. The section on the response of U.S. commercial banks concentrates on their defensive response to the threat posed by poor loan decisions. Their participation in debt renegotiations is discussed in the next chapter.

THE RESPONSE OF CONGRESS

The early years of the debt crisis coincided with rising budget deficits, high unemployment, and a rampant Congressional mood of protectionism as U.S. industries suffered from an overvalued dollar. Congressional response was hostile. Its early concerns were concentrated on the burden-sharing problem of debt restructuring. Later, its appropriations for IMF quota increases, IBRD capital increases, and IDA replenishments, together with changes in trade policy, bank regulation, and the tax treatment of bank reserves, all helped to shape the ongoing crisis.

Throughout the crisis, Congress was largely concerned with avoiding any bailout of the commercial banks. Many of the proposed solutions to the crisis required developed country governments to provide guarantees to banks, insuring them against losses.[3] Congressional loan guarantees had been used in the 1970s to place financial safety nets under the creditors of New York City, Chrysler, Penn Central, and Lockheed. Opponents of a similar approach to the debt crisis were strenuous in their opposition to any "bailing out" of commercial banks through taxpayer assumption of the risks of default. Instead, banks were castigated for their poor commercial judgment in making loans.

The arrival of the debt crisis coincided with a Congressional debate over the 8th General Review of IMF quotas. Though technically not foreign aid, it is appropriated with foreign aid in the U.S. Congressional budget appropriation process and requires authorizing legislation from House and Senate Committees. There was considerable Congressional opposition to the $8.4 billion U.S. share of the increase.[4] In both the House and the Senate, the precrisis Reagan Administration position of contracting the role of the Fund in favor of reliance on private capital flows had already found some converts. Other members were concerned that the quota increase would be used to "bail out" the banks. Although finally passed, there were efforts to make passage of the quota increase contingent on greater regulatory control of the foreign lending of U.S. banks.[5]

Congressional concern with the previous lack of supervision of U.S. banks in the run-up of Third World debt led to the International Lending Supervision Act, passed in November 1983. The Act required

U.S. bank regulators to force banks to write off part of their loans or to set up specific reserves for these loans. The charging of loan restructuring fees in excess of administrative costs was also prohibited. There had been widespread complaints at the size of the rescheduling fees charged for the early reschedulings after mid-1982.

Perhaps the best-known Congressional proposal on debt reform was the Bradley Plan. Senator Bill Bradley (Democrat, New Jersey) proposed a three-year debt relief scheme for ten Latin American debtor countries under which $42 billion of relief would be provided by a three percentage point reduction in interest rates and a 3 percent per annum principal writeoff.[6] Like other proposals calling for write-offs of principal, the Bradley plan was attacked by some who argued that principal write-offs were tantamount to default, and would cut off future market access to the borrower. Supporters of write-off proposals responded that this was historically inaccurate and argued that, despite earlier losses, lenders had returned to Latin America after write-offs in the 1920s, to Europe in the 1950s, and to Indonesia in the early 1970s.[7]

A 1988 instance of the gulf between the Administration and Congressional approaches to the debt crisis was the 1988 Trade Bill proposal to create an International Debt Management Agency that would buy up debt at market discounts. Because of Administration objections, the clause was dropped from the 1988 Trade Act along with the more publicized plant closing clause.

THE ADMINISTRATION'S RESPONSE

The onset of the debt crisis precipitated an abrupt reversal of policy for the Reagan Administration. A further reversal was introduced in early 1989 by the Bush Administration's jettisoning of the Baker Plan in favor of the Miyazawa-Brady debt-reduction approach. The initial crisis caused the Reagan doctrinaire free market ideology to be tempered by a more pragmatic approach to international capital flows. The pragmatism included considerable U.S. state intervention to prop up the Mexican economy. Of particular importance in the longer term was the switch in attitudes toward the multilateral lending institutions. As the crisis developed, the Reagan Administration was drawn into taking a large number of measures to deal with the crisis. These included a reversal of its early stance of not increasing the lending capacities of the IMF and the Multilateral Development Banks (MDBs), regulatory actions to build up the defenses of U.S. commercial banks, the Baker Plan initiative, and participation in a number of *ad hoc* bridging loan arrangements to individual debtors.

These included Treasury Department cooperation with the Federal Reserve Board and other central banks in providing bridge loans, and cooperation with the IMF and the multilateral development banks (MDBs) in mounting rescues.

The immediate aftermath to the Mexican crisis taught some sharp lessons to a U.S. Administration widely seen at the time as inexperienced and short on top-flight talent in international finance. The secondary role played by Treasury Secretary Regan had left the Chairman of the Federal Reserve Board, Paul Volcker, with unusual responsibility in designing a response to the growing crisis. Volker is not only reported to have been more alert to the problems posed by the August Mexican crisis, he is also credited with an educational campaign in the months thereafter to counter the Treasury's doctrinaire attitudes toward the IMF. In particular, his views on the need to expand the lending capacity of the Fund had been at odds with positions adopted by the Treasury in the first years of the Reagan Administration.

The early Reagan Administration attitude toward lending policies of the established multilateral lending agencies matched the stress on privatization and deregulation found in its domestic policies. The policy sought a reduction in the growth of IMF lending, a tightening of Fund conditionality, and the encouraging of Fund borrowers to place greater reliance on international commercial bank credit. The further privatization of international capital flows that occurred in the 1970s as the world's commercial banks undertook the intermediation role of recycling petro-dollars was encouraged. As much as possible, the lending role of the Fund was to be restricted to that of genuine "lender of last resort," that is, to instances in which international commercial bank loans might not be expected to be forthcoming. Similar policies stressing a reliance on market forces were adopted with respect to MDBs such as the World Bank and the regional development banks.

From mid-1982 to Fall 1985 the changes were *ad hoc*. In 1985, the replacement of Treasury Secretary Regan by James Baker produced an abrupt about-face in U.S. international financial policy. Within a year, the G-5 Plaza Agreement on exchange rate intervention represented U.S. acceptance of European and Japanese views on the need for some exchange-rate management, while the Baker Plan, introduced at the Seoul IMF annual meetings in October 1985, recognized that there are limits to IMF austerity programs, that a solution to the debt crisis required adjustment with economic growth, and that there was a continued need for concerted lending on the part of private banks and the MDBs.

Policies Toward the IMF

Earlier chapters have shown that debtor country efforts to avoid IMF conditionality helped produce the crisis through a dependency on floating rate debt in an era of volatile interest rates. Once the crisis broke, it was apparent to all observers that there would be no solution without active IMF participation. In early 1982, the Treasury Department had opposed any expansion in the IMF's lending ability as part of the 8th General Review of the Fund's quotas. In the aftermath of the August Mexican rescue, the Administration sought to hold any increase to a 20–25 percent range with an additional permanent borrowing arrangement to be available to the Fund on a contingency basis. The contingency provision in the U.S. proposal was an effort to introduce a degree of conditionality into Fund *replenishment* as well as Fund *lending*. Rather than providing the Fund with a larger increase in quotas in the 8th General Review, the U.S. proposal would have left the Fund dependent on access to the Group of Ten's (G10) General Arrangements to Borrow (GAB). The GAB had been established as a system of lines of credit among developed country central banks that permitted the IMF to borrow for on-lending to a GAB member.

While discussions about the 8th General Review continued, the Fund made large commitments to Latin America in late 1982 and early 1983. Mexico entered into a SDR 4.2 billion extended arrangement in December 1982. Almost all of the Fund's lending in early 1983 went to Latin America. These included a SDR 0.5 billion standby to Chile, SDR 1.5 billion to Argentina, and SDR 0.4 billion and SDR 4.2 billion extended arrangements to the Dominican Republic and Brazil.[8] The heavy pace of IMF lending made it evident that the Reagan Administration's insistence on a small quota increase would place the Fund in difficulties. Accordingly, the participants in the GAB increased the Arrangements from the previous level of SDR 6.5 billion to SDR 17 billion and provided access to the IMF for on-lending to non-GAB members. In March 1983, Fund members concluded the 8th General Review by agreeing to a 47 percent increase in the Fund's lending capacity. Within a year of his own opposition to any Fund quota increase, Treasury Secretary Regan was placed in the rather undignified position of attempting to persuade a Senate banking subcommittee that U.S. participation in the quota increase was necessary because curtailment of Fund lending would cut U.S. GNP by half a percentage point with the loss of half a million jobs.[9]

The original opposition of the Administration to a Fund quota increase was consistent with its attitude that the Fund's entry into longer-term, development-oriented financing of structural adjustment should be ended and that this role should be confined to the specialist development banks. IMF extended arrangements began in 1974 as a way of financing adjustment to the first oil shock. The longer time span of extended arrangements allows its conditionality to avoid the "shock treatment" otherwise needed to correct balance of payments disequilibria in shorter time periods. The 1981 SDR 5.1 billion extended arrangement provided to India had been the largest extended arrangement loan provided by the Fund at the time, and was provided after strenuous objections from the United States, although the United States did not veto the loan. The United States had argued that India should have used commercial bank or World Bank credit.[10] Although the Reagan Administration was upset at India's use of the Extended Facility in 1981, it had few options with Brazil's and Mexico's use of it in December 1982 and March 1983.

In addition to its opposition to a quota increase, the Reagan Administration had also sought a tightening of Fund conditionality. A number of observers had already claimed to see an abrupt reversal in the Fund's stance on conditionality shortly after the installation of the Reagan Administration.[11] Williamson's analysis of the devaluations accompanying high conditionality loans had suggested that Fund conditionality was relaxed in mid-1979 and retightened in mid-1981. Further tightening of conditionality would have provided additional pressure for further privatization in international capital flows by restricting Fund lending to countries with no recourse to private bank lending. As tighter conditionality made the Fund a less attractive place from which to borrow, and as no quota increase limited future Fund lending, the role of the Fund as an international lending agency would have undergone a transformation as dramatic as that which overtook its exchange-rate role ten years earlier with the advent of flexible exchange rates. The Bush Administration's 1989 Brady Plan for voluntary, case-by-case debt-reduction represented a further shift in U.S. official attitudes toward the IMF. It was introduced after more than 300 had died in austerity riots in Venezuela. The proposals required active IMF and World Bank lending to allow debt or buy-backs of bank loans.

Policies Toward MDBs

The Reagan Administration's precrisis attitudes toward the Fund's sister institutions paralleled that adopted toward the IMF and is best exemplified by a 1982 Treasury Department study of the U.S. role in these agencies.[12] The report recommended that the United States seek "corrective action" in two areas of operations of multilateral development banks. It considered that there was an overemphasis on loan quantity rather than quality and it saw a need for a more effective graduation policy. The report also called for a greater reliance on private international capital flows, the more rapid graduation of countries from the easier terms of soft-window loans to hard-window loans, and a reduction in U.S. contributions to the agencies. By calling for a 12–16 percent reduction in U.S. contributions to soft-window replenishment, the IDA was particularly targeted. As the World Bank's soft-loan window for the poorest developing countries, the IDA does not lend to many of the countries in the sample of debtor countries as their per capita income exceeds IDA eligibility levels. Thus, U.S. policies toward IDA did not have a major impact on potential lending flows to Latin America, but the impact on Africa and Asia was considerable.

Under the Carter Administration, the United States had agreed to make three annual contributions of $1 billion each as its share of the Sixth Replenishment of IDA. The Reagan Administration altered the time table of U.S. contributions, providing $500 million in 1981, and $700 million in 1982. The delay in U.S. contributions caused other developed countries to threaten to withhold their contributions *pro rata*. During the 1983 negotiations for IDA VII, to cover the years 1985–87, the Reagan Administration limited U.S. participation to $750 million per annum. With the U.S. capital contribution set at 25 percent, the $2.5 billion contributed by the United States over the three years set the total size of IDA VII at $9 billion. To offset the impact of the reduction in U.S. IDA contributions, other developed economies established a special $1.2 billion IDA fund for Africa. The 1986 negotiations over IDA VIII to cover the years 1988–90 led to a total replenishment of $12.5 billion, with the U.S. share reduced to 23 percent. As voluntary commercial bank lending to developing countries dried up, the United States attitude toward MDBs changed in 1987, and the United States agreed to an increase in the capital of the Bank of $74.8 billion.[13] To maintain its veto share of the Bank's voting, the U.S. share of the capital increase was 18.75 percent. The 3 percent paid-in component of the capital increase required appropriations of $70.1 million annually for six years.[14]

Latin American debtors were more concerned with Reagan Administration attitudes to funding of the InterAmerican Development Bank. Congress had authorized U.S. participation in the Sixth General Increase in Resources for the IDB in December 1983. The U.S. contribution was to be made in four equal annual payments from 1983–86. By mid-1985 appropriations were running one year late, producing a $2 billion shortfall in IDB contributions. In 1987, plans for a further increase in IDB capitalization collapsed over Reagan Administration demands for a change in voting arrangements as part of an effort to alter the lending policies of the Bank. The IDB had traditionally differed from other multilateral agencies such as the Bank and Fund; lending policies were controlled by borrowing rather than lending countries. Latin American members preferred to forego the additional resources that would have been provided by an increase in IDB capital from $10 billion to $22.5 billion rather than accept the U.S. voting proposals, which would have given the United States and Canada a joint veto over IDB loans. The dispute was finally resolved in 1989 w' en the Bush Administration accepted a compromise, clearing the way for a $22.5 billion IDB capital increase.

One area in which there has been little reflection of U.S. policies toward the debt crisis has been the U.S. bilateral foreign aid program. The priorities that govern the distribution and overall level of U.S. foreign aid have been relatively unaffected by the crisis. As Table 9.1 shows, while five of the twelve Major Borrowers were among the top ten recipients of U.S. foreign aid in 1984, the number dropped to three in fiscal 1985 through 1988. These three, Israel, Egypt, and Turkey, ranked as the top three recipients of U.S. aid, receiving between 41 percent and 54 percent of all U.S. foreign aid in these years. Three other countries, Greece, Spain, and El Salvador, were a consistent second tier of aid recipients. None of the seventeen Heavily Indebted Countries was a major recipient of U.S. foreign aid in 1984, although the Philippines joined the list in 1985 through 1986.

The Baker Plan

Nothing so epitomizes the abrupt Reagan Administration *volte face* on international lending as the Baker Plan. Introduced at the Seoul Annual Meetings of the Bank and the Fund in 1985, the Baker Plan called for the mobilization of $29 billion of commercial bank and MDB loans over a three-year period to a group of fifteen Heavily Indebted Countries. The sum involved $9 billion to come from a 50 percent increase in disbursements by the World Bank and the IDB, and $20 billion to come from a 2.5 percent annual increase in exposure on the part of private banks. Of the $20 billion to be provided by private banks, $13 billion was to be provided by non-U.S. banks. The list of fifteen countries covered by the Baker Plan included all of the seventeen Highly Indebted Countries except Costa Rica and Jamaica and was dominated by Latin American countries. Five non-Latin countries were included: Côte d'Ivoire, Morocco, Nigeria, the Philippines, and Yugoslavia. The ten Latin American and Caribbean countries were Argentina, Bolivia, Brazil, Chile, Colombia, Ecuador, Mexico, Peru, Uruguay, and Venezuela.

Table 9.1 Top Ten Recipients of U.S. Economic and Military Aid, 1984–88 ($ billion; fiscal years)

1984		1985		1986		1987		1988	
Israel	2.61	Israel	3.35	Israel	3.62	Israel	3.00	Israel	3.00
Egypt	2.48	Egypt	2.48	Egypt	2.53	Egypt	2.30	Egypt	2.29
Turkey	.85	Turkey	.87	Turkey	.73	Turkey	.71	Turkey	.91
Pakistan	.57	Pakistan	.63	Pakistan	.67	Pakistan	.66	Pakistan	.68
Greece	.50	El Salvador	.56	Philippines	.48	El Salvador	.49	El Salvador	.43
Spain	.41	Greece	.50	El Salvador	.43	Philippines	.38	Greece	.43
El Salvador	.40	Spain	.41	Greece	.43	Greece	.34	Spain	.28
Sudan	.23	Honduras	.28	Spain	.39	Spain	.32	Philippines	.26
S. Korea	.23	Philippines	.26	Portugal	.18	Honduras	.27	Honduras	.24
India	.20	Sudan	.25	Honduras	.19	Guatemala	.16	Portugal	.21
TOTAL AID	11.99		13.73		12.72		14.80		15.24

Source: Agency for International Development, Fiscal Year 1988 Summary Tables revised February 1987.

Notes: 1987 data are estimates including supplemental. 1988 Administration request.

The Baker Plan represented an effort to move away from the short-term focus that makes IMF conditionality so deflationary. Relying on a longer time horizon than an IMF program permits, the Baker Plan stressed growth rather than deflation, emphasizing the structural adjustment loans of the Bank. By calling for the Bank to expand general-purpose lending at the expense of its more traditional project lending, the Plan reflected a balanced U.S. response to the hostility of developing countries toward IMF conditionality while still insisting that countries adopt market-oriented internal policies.

By 1987 the Baker Plan was in trouble. The Plan was introduced before the 1985–86 collapse in world oil prices. The fall in prices of almost 50 percent over 1985 levels altered the assumptions that had produced the Baker Plan's estimate that $29 billion would be needed over three years. Moreover, although the Baker Plan had outlined roles for private banks and for MDBs, it had left unclear the future role of developed country governments. Private banks sought a different division of burden sharing between private banks and governments, including easier regulatory treatment of foreign loans and expanded trade credits through export-credit guarantee facilities such as the U.S. EX-IM Bank.[15] Private bank reaction to the Baker plan was also cool in the absence of guarantees to insure additional exposure. As a result, while new money was provided by banks to barely meet Baker Plan targets, there was a wholesale reduction in total private bank exposure in most developing countries. The envisaged adjustment with growth did not occur. Per capital GDP often continued to fall. There were also difficulties with the MDB contribution to the plan. While the Baker Plan had not proposed any immediate increase in member-government capital contributions to the MDBs, the ability of the IDB to play a role was compromised by the 1987 dispute between the United States and the Latin American members of the IDB.

The Brady Plan

The key features of the Brady proposals of March 1989 resurrected the 1988 suggestions of Japan's Finance Minister Kiichi Miyazawa who met his political demise in the Recruit scandal. The proposals sought to separate a country's outstanding bank debt into a part that would be the subject of debt reduction, financed in part by loans from multilateral lending institutions, and a remaining part that would be the subject of interest reduction. IMF, World Bank, and bilateral (notably Japanese) flows were pledged to finance both debt reduction and interest payment guarantees. The proposals called for the use of three main mechanisms: swaps of bank debt for bonds at a discount from the face value of the bank debt; swaps of bank debt for bonds at no discount from face value but at lower interest rates; and debt-equity swaps. The Miyazawa-Brady proposals were first used in the Mexican debt reduction negotiations of 1989.

Direct U.S. Measures

In the years after the emergence of the Mexican crisis, the direct actions of the Reagan Administration and the Fed were largely concentrated on a mix of loan guarantees, swap facilities, and special short-term credit facilities, using the Treasury's Exchange Stabilization Fund and the Fed's reciprocal swap arrangements with the BIS and other central banks. Other measures have included trade credits and oil purchases.

The late Joe Kraft had chronicled the manner in which the Federal Reserve, the U.S. Administration and the IMF patched together the original Mexican rescue package over a frenzied weekend in August 1982.[16] Among the unusual steps taken by the United States were the Federal Reserve's contribution of half of the $1.85 billion loan from the world's central banks arranged by the Bank for International Settlements (BIS), a $1 billion Department of Agriculture Commodity Credit Corporation guarantee for private credit to pay for Mexican imports of U.S. basic foodstuffs, and a further $1 billion Department of Treasury loan facility with any facility drawings to be paid back through $1 billion of Energy Department advance payments for oil purchases for the U.S. Strategic Petroleum Reserve.

A number of later Administration *ad hoc* measures to assist specific countries were opposed by Congress. These included the 1983 Administration efforts to set aside $1.5 billion for Brazil and $0.5 billion for Mexico in the form of EX-IM financial guarantees and insurance. Congressional opponents objected that the Administration sought to use EX-IM subsidies for general balance-of-payments support of specific countries rather than provide loan subsidies for the export of specific U.S. products.[17]

Overall, between 1982 and end-March 1989, the U.S. Treasury and the Federal Reserve Board provided special assistance to ten debtor countries—Argentina, Bolivia, Brazil, Ecuador, Jamaica, Mexico, Nigeria, the Philippines, Venezuela, and Yugoslavia. Commitments to these countries totaled over $11 billion through end-1988, of which over $9 billion was drawn. The bulk of the combined Treasury-Fed support for indebted countries was provided from the resources of the Treasury's Exchange Stabilization Fund (ESF).[18] The Fed's direct contributions were limited to Mexico's use of its reciprocal Fed standby, under which $2.5 billion was drawn in August 1982, $272 million was drawn in August 1986, and $700 million in August 1988.[19] Details of Fed and Treasury support to debtor countries during the Reagan Administration are found in the Appendix.

Regulatory Response

The debt crisis occurred amid drastic deregulation and competitive changes in both international and U.S. banking. The rising riskiness of the industry was evident in the growing number of bank failures. From an average of four bank failures a year in the 1960s, the number had risen to an average of eight per annum in the 1970s, to 184 in 1987, and 221 in 1988. These failures were largely due to losses in the farm, energy, and real estate sectors rather than to loans to developing countries.

Although the great majority of U.S. bank failures involve very small banks, the system was particularly shaken by the 1984 near-failure of the Continental Illinois National Bank and Trust Company, the ninth largest U.S. bank holding company. In March 1988, the thirteenth largest bank holding company, First Republic, was rescued by a $1 billion FDIC loan in a rescue package that was estimated to cost $5 billion, exceeding the $4.5 billion cost of the Continental Illinois rescue.[20] In the same week, a second Texas bank, First City Bankcorporation, received a $970 million FDIC injection in another major bank rescue. The FDIC showed in the Continental Illinois, First Republic and First City rescues that, although it was prepared to let small institutions fail, it was not prepared to let this happen to a large institution. This difference in treatment is tantamount to providing an implicit guarantee to large depositors not covered by the FDIC's $100,000 limit on insured deposits. Shareholders, of course, are not protected. Large institutions pay a price for this implicit guarantee of large deposits through the closer scrutiny of regulatory agencies to which they have been subjected in recent years.

The volatility of the U.S. industry in the 1980s focused attention on the general inadequacy of bank reserves. The three regulatory agencies, the Federal Reserve Board, the FDIC, and the Comptroller of the Currency, responded with joint measures forcing banks to increase the capitalization of the banks under their respective supervision. In addition, there were measures to tighten accounting practices, require more frequent examination of banks, limit lending practices, and, in an unusual departure for regulators noted for their discretion, efforts publicly to embarrass individual banks by more public discussion of their difficulties. These changes became part of the international movement to harmonized risk-based capitalization standards in the late 1980s.

Even before the emergence of the debt crisis, the Comptroller of the Currency and the Federal Reserve Board had announced in December 1981 that they intended to raise the capital requirements of banks to 5 percent. At end-1981, the average ratio of primary capital to total assets of seventeen U.S. multinational banks stood at 4.63 percent. By mid-July 1983, shortly after the new capital requirements were introduced, the average primary capital ratio of the multinational banks had been raised to 5.35 percent.[21] In June 1985, the guidelines on capital adequacy were raised again, to a minimum ratio of primary capital to assets of 5.5 percent and a ratio of total capital to assets of 6 percent.[22] These increases in the primary capital ratio reduced bank profits and required the banking system to raise hundreds of millions of dollars of additional capital through retained earnings, new issues of stock or the sale of debt instruments. Within two years of the onset of the crisis, the reserve base of the U.S. banking system had been considerably strengthened.

In other regulatory moves to respond directly to the debt crisis, and to implement the International Lending Supervision Act passed by Congress in November 1983, the three supervisory agencies (the Federal Reserve Board, the FDIC, and the Comptroller of the Currency) introduced rules in February 1984 requiring banks to write off or to establish loan-loss reserves, Allocated Transfer Risk Reserves (ATRRs), for their loans to specific countries. ATRRs do not count toward meeting the capital-to-deposit ratio. A number of criteria are used by the Interagency Country Exposure Review Committee to determine if loans should be classified as "value impaired".[23] The criteria include a six-month lapse in full interest payments; lack of compliance with an IMF adjustment program and no immediate prospects of resumed compliance; a one-year failure to meet obligations on rescheduled debt; or no immediate prospects of resuming debt service payments. A loan is considered to be value impaired if two or more of these criteria are met. Banks are then given a choice between loan charge-offs or establishment of equivalent ATTRs. The amounts are determined by the committee and have varied from 10 percent to 100 percent. By July 1989, U.S. banks had established ATTRs for twelve countries. They included Argentina, Bolivia, Liberia, Nicaragua, Peru, Poland, Sudan, and Zaire.

Besides requiring more reserves, bank regulators also tightened up accounting practices for placing loans on a nonaccrual basis. When loan payments are more than 90 days late, banks must place the loans on a nonaccrual basis. In the case of loans that are less than 90 days late, banks may consider themselves as having earned interest on the loan and report this earning on their financial statements even if they have actually received no payment. This tends to inflate profits and share prices and avoids the need to set aside loan-loss reserves. Until regulators ended the practice in 1984, a number of banks had reported as nonaccruals only those loans that were more than 90 days late as of the date of the end of the quarter. In their joint battle against regulators, debtor countries had cooperated with banks by making just enough interest payments to keep their loans on an accrual basis on the critical reporting date even if they had fallen into nonaccrual earlier in the quarter. Under the tighter accounting regulations, any loan that had fallen into nonaccrual at any point during the quarter had to be reported as nonaccruing. The new rules eliminated the use of interim payments and made it necessary to make full payment of *all* of the overdue interest before a loan could be returned to accrual basis.[24] The change also had the effect of removing some of the crisis atmosphere which had surrounded bank negotiations with particular countries as end-of-quarter dates approached.

Although U.S. regulators had forced banks to raise capital ratios in 1983 and 1985, even more profound changes were to follow. In December 1987, twelve countries, including the United States and the United Kingdom, announced proposals for harmonized risk-based capitalization standards for banks. The Basle Agreement for a coordinated international approach to bank regulation contained a five-year timetable for raising bank capitalization ratios to 8 percent of assets by 1992.[25] The proposed increase represented a particularly large change for U.S. banks. FDIC officials estimated that U.S. banks and bankholding companies would be required to raise an additional $29.1 billion in capital while their German and Swiss counterparts were reported already to satisfy the new requirement.[26] Federal Reserve Board estimates were $12-$15 billion.[27]

The phased increased capitalization of U.S. banks between 1982 and 1992 has made it easier to absorb losses associated with debt equity swaps and other means of reducing developing country exposure.

In 1987 and 1988 U.S. bank regulators adopted two changes that improved the prospects for debt-equity swaps. The Fed's previous limit on the equity stake of bank-holding companies in foreign non-financial corporations was raised from 20 percent to 100 percent for thirty-three developing countries while Regulation K was amended to permit banks to hold up to 40 percent of foreign nonfinancial enterprises. These changes made it possible for banks themselves to participate in debt-equity schemes, widening the field of possible participants in the market for debt conversions.

The changes outlined above placed regulators in a stronger position not only *vis à vis* the banks they are supposed to supervise, but, indirectly, *vis à vis* sovereign debtor countries. By removing the discretion of private banks to determine the riskiness of individual countries, U.S. regulators (and their overseas counterparts in a less public manner) became even more involved in the debt renegotiation process, but without the major charges on taxpayers associated with global debt relief schemes.

PRIVATE BANK RESPONSE

The response of U.S. private banks may be subdivided into two general responses. The defensive response to the threats posed to them by the debt crisis are discussed in this section. Much of this response was prodded by the regulatory changes described in the last section. The joint debtor-creditor response through the debt renegotiation process is detailed in the following chapter.

Table 9.2 contains some of the details of the defensive response. A combination of greater capitalization, loan write-offs, exercise of loan guarantees and severe curtailment of lending, produced a rapid improvement in the loan-to-capital ratios of U.S. banks. The time that reschedulings purchased in the intervening years since 1982 permitted banks to consider debt reduction in 1989. The actions in the first half of 1987, when banks responded to Brazil's moratorium by drastically increasing their loan loss reserves to 30 percent of Latin American exposure, produced a particular improvement. Exposure-to-capital ratios were more than halved in the six years from 1982 to 1987. For the nine largest money center banks, nonoil LDC exposure did not fall below 100 percent of primary capital until 1988.

Throughout the crisis, U.S. banks reported a sharp increase in loans placed on a nonaccrual basis, as countries ran into repayment difficulties. Banks responded by writing off loans and by increasing loan-loss provisions. Terrell and Mills estimate that U.S. banks wrote off $1.2 billion in Latin American and $1.7 billion in all non-OPEC developing country loans over the years 1983 and 1984.[28] In 1987, U.S. banks added approximately $19 billion to loan-loss reserves for developing country debt.[29]

An abrupt change in bank policy occurred in 1987 when they made massive increases in loan-loss reserves and placed Brazilian loans on a nonaccrual basis. This was a response to a Brazilian suspension of commercial bank debt-service payments. Led by Citicorp, U.S. and foreign banks accepted large pretax losses as they increased their loan-loss provisions. By raising the primary capital of banks and lowering the foreign debt-to-bank capital ratio, the move strengthened the negotiating hand of the commercial banks in future debt

Table 9.2 Balance Sheet Response of U.S. Banks to the Debt Crisis

	1982	1983	1984	1985	1986	1987	1988
Exposure as % of Bank Capital:							
All Banks							
Non-OPEC LDCs	152.0	136.9	116.0	94.2	79.8	66.7	53.8
Latin America	118.8	106.0	93.5	77.3	68.0	57.8	47.3
Nine Money Center Banks							
Non-OPEC LDCs	228.9	209.1	180.3	147.5	126.6	110.0	91.1
Latin America	176.5	162.9	146.4	124.2	110.2	97.0	83.6
Next Largest 13 Banks							
Non-OPEC LDCs	159.6	153.2	123.2	91.2	79.1	65.2	50.7
Latin America	124.1	117.0	97.0	71.3	64.5	55.5	39.6
All Other US Banks							
Non-OPEC LDCs	69.0	60.2	49.3	42.6	34.0	25.9	17.7
Latin America	56.8	46.5	39.9	33.4	28.2	21.4	14.2
Foreign Loan Loss Provisions:							
$ billion	1.0	1.8	1.8	2.4	2.9	19.0	NA
% of all foreign loans	0.3	0.5	0.5	0.8	1.0	6.5	NA
Net Charge-off of Foreign Loans:							
$ billion	0.6	1.2	1.4	2.0	1.8	2.8	NA
% of all foreign loans	0.3	0.5	0.6	0.9	0.9	1.4	NA

Sources: Federal Reserve Board unpublished data; Deborah J. Danker and Mary M. McLaughlin, "Profitability of US-Chartered Insured Commercial Banks in 1985", Federal Reserve Bulletin September 1986, pp. 618-32; Martin H. Wolfson, "Financial Developments of Bank Holding Companies in 1984", Federal Reserve Bulletin, December 1985, pp. 924-32; Mary M. McLaughlin and Martin H. Wolfson, "The Profitability of Insured Commercial Banks in 1987", Federal Reserve Bulletin, July 1988, pp. 403-18; Federal Financial Institutions Examination Council, Country Exposure Lending Survey various issues. Notes: Charge-off and loan loss provision data not restricted to developing countries and only for banks with assets exceeding $300 millions and with foreign offices. 1982 and 1983 charge-off data not strictly comparable. Exposure data adjusted for guarantees and indirect borrowing.

renegotiations. This tactic will be more fully discussed in the next chapter.

Regional U.S. banks were the most aggressive in loan write-offs and reserve buildups. Not until the end of 1987, when Bank of Boston announced a $200 million charge-off of its $1 billion Latin American exposure, did a U.S. money-center bank announce that it had written off any of its Latin American debt.[30] Shortly afterward, American Express wrote off all of its $62 million private sector Latin American loans.[31] These write-offs did not add to bank losses already incurred when reserves were established, but produced tax savings for banks, adding to Treasury tax expenditures. In July 1988, the Mellon Bank Corporation used junk bonds to help finance the establishment of a separate entity to which it transferred roughly $1 billion in bad loans including developing country loans.[32] The transfer at less than face value caused a loss of about $200 million. The tactic was similar to that used earlier by Japanese banks.

The buildup in loan loss reserves allowed the fourteen largest U.S. banks to charge off an estimated $1.5 billion in developing country loans in 1987 and a further $3.8 billion in 1988.[33] These money-center banks varied considerably in the extent to which their outstanding developing country exposure was covered by loan-loss reserves. Prior to the implementation of the Brady Plan, the proportion of medium and long term developing country loans covered by reserves varied from under 30 percent for Bankers Trust, Chemical, and Manufacturers Hanover to 100 percent in the case of Bank of Boston.[34]

The exposure of U.S. banks in developing countries dropped sharply after 1983.[35] Some of the differing patterns in regional and country lending by U.S. banks of different sizes are discernable in Tables 9.3 and 9.4. Table 9.3 shows the regional variation in U.S. bank exposure while Table 9.4 contains details of U.S. bank exposure for the twenty-four countries in the sample.

Table 9.3 shows that in the six years since 1982, U.S. bank exposure in non-oil LDCs was cut by $34 billion. African exposure was more than halved; Asian exposure was halved. The smallest reduction in exposure occurred in Latin America. Whereas exposure in Asia and Africa peaked in 1983, the Latin American peak occurred in 1984. These reductions in exposure were produced by a combination of loan write-offs, loan repayments, the selling off of some loans, the calling in of official guarantees, the suspension of voluntary lending, and debt-equity swaps. Table 9.3 also shows that smaller U.S. banks reduced their Latin America exposure consistently since 1982, causing the nine money center banks' share of total U.S. bank exposure in Latin America to rise from 60 percent in 1982 to 73 percent in 1988.

Table 9.3 U.S. Bank Exposure in Non-Oil Exporting Developing Countries, by Region and Bank Size ($ billion)

	1982	1983	1984	1985	1986	1987	1988
Non-Oil Exporting LDCs	107.3	108.5	106.9	99.3	92.6	86.2	72.9
Latin America							
9 Money Center	42.4	42.7	45.3	44.4	44.0	43.2	40.3
Next 13 Biggest	14.3	15.0	15.3	12.8	12.4	11.6	8.1
All Other Banks	13.9	13.5	13.2	12.6	11.8	10.2	6.7
Total	70.7	71.2	73.7	69.7	68.2	64.9	55.1
Asia							
9 Money Center	20.7	20.0	18.1	15.7	13.4	12.1	9.4
Next 13 Biggest	6.8	7.2	6.6	5.7	4.8	3.9	4.0
All Other Banks	5.2	4.6	4.9	5.1	4.0	3.6	3.0
Total	32.7	3.2	29.6	26.5	22.2	19.5	16.4
Africa							
9 Money Center	3.7	3.3	2.8	2.3	1.7	1.5	1.2
Next 13 Biggest	0.5	0.6	0.5	0.4	0.2	0.2	0.1
All Other Banks	0.3	0.4	0.4	0.4	0.2	0.2	0.2
Total	4.1	4.2	3.7	3.2	2.2	1.8	1.5

Source: Federal Financial Institutions Examinations Council, Country Exposure Lending Survey, various issues. Adjusted for guarantees and indirect borrowing.

Table 9.4 Loan Exposure of U.S. Commercial Banks, 1982–88 ($ billion)

	All Banks							9 Money Center Banks						
	1982	1983	1984	1985	1986	1987	1988	1982	1983	1984	1985	1986	1987	1988
Non-Oil LDCs	107.3	108.5	106.9	99.3	92.6	86.2	72.9	66.4	65.9	66.2	62.4	59.1	56.7	50.9
Latin America	70.6	71.2	73.7	69.7	68.2	64.9	55.1	42.4	42.7	45.3	44.4	44.0	43.1	40.3
Asia	32.7	33.2	29.6	26.5	22.2	19.5	16.3	20.7	20.0	18.1	15.7	13.4	12.1	9.4
Africa	4.0	4.1	3.7	3.1	2.2	1.8	1.5	3.3	3.2	2.8	2.3	1.7	1.4	1.2
All Latin America	83.9	84.1	86.2	81.4	79.0	74.7	64.1	51.2	51.3	53.7	52.5	51.5	50.0	46.7
Major Borrowers	95.3	96.8	98.1	92.5	86.5	78.8	68.1	58.4	59.0	60.5	58.5	55.5	52.3	48.1
Argentina	8.6	8.8	8.4	8.7	9.0	9.2	8.0	5.6	5.8	5.5	6.2	6.4	6.7	6.2
Brazil	22.0	21.6	24.8	23.6	23.6	22.3	20.5	14.2	13.8	16.2	15.8	16.2	15.8	15.8
Chile	5.9	5.9	6.4	6.2	6.3	5.9	4.7	3.2	3.2	3.6	3.9	4.0	3.9	3.4
Egypt	1.2	1.4	1.0	0.7	0.3	0.2	0.1	0.9	0.9	0.7	0.4	0.2	0.1	0.0
India	1.4	1.2	1.2	1.4	1.4	1.2	1.3	0.9	0.9	0.7	0.9	0.8	0.7	0.7
Indonesia	2.7	3.2	3.1	2.5	1.9	1.2	0.9	2.2	2.7	2.5	2.0	1.5	0.9	0.6
Israel	2.7	2.3	2.2	2.1	1.9	1.2	1.0	1.3	1.2	1.2	1.0	0.9	0.6	0.5
S. Korea	12.4	12.4	10.9	9.9	7.1	5.1	5.0	7.5	6.7	5.8	5.2	3.9	3.1	2.7
Malaysia	1.7	2.0	1.9	1.3	0.9	0.5	0.4	1.2	1.4	1.2	1.0	0.7	0.4	0.3
Mexico	24.3	25.4	25.8	24.4	23.5	22.4	17.6	13.1	13.7	14.3	13.8	13.5	13.4	11.9
Turkey	1.4	1.6	1.8	1.9	1.7	1.6	1.1	0.9	1.1	1.2	1.4	1.1	1.1	0.7
Venezuela	11.2	10.9	10.6	9.8	8.7	8.1	7.6	7.6	7.5	7.3	6.9	6.3	5.7	5.4
17 Heavy Indebted	92.9	93.4	94.8	89.8	86.7	81.9	70.4	57.5	57.6	59.6	58.3	57.0	55.2	51.5
Bolivia	0.4	0.3	0.2	0.1	0.1	0.1	0.0	0.2	0.2	0.1	0.1	0.0	0.0	0.0
Colombia	3.7	3.6	3.0	2.5	2.2	2.1	2.1	2.6	2.4	2.2	1.8	1.5	1.4	1.4
Costa Rica	0.5	0.4	0.4	0.4	0.4	0.3	0.2	0.2	0.2	0.2	0.2	0.2	0.2	0.1
Côte d'Ivoire	0.6	0.5	0.5	0.4	0.4	0.4	0.3	0.5	0.4	0.3	0.3	0.3	0.3	0.3
Ecuador	2.1	2.0	1.9	2.0	2.0	1.8	1.3	1.2	1.1	1.1	1.2	1.2	1.1	1.0
Jamaica	0.2	0.2	0.2	0.2	0.1	0.1	0.2	0.2	0.2	0.1	0.1	0.1	0.1	0.1
Morocco	0.7	0.8	0.8	0.9	0.8	0.7	0.7	0.5	0.7	0.6	0.6	0.6	0.6	0.6
Nigeria	1.7	1.8	1.3	0.9	0.6	0.6	0.5	1.3	1.3	1.0	0.7	0.5	0.5	0.5
Peru	2.4	2.3	2.1	1.5	1.2	0.8	0.5	1.3	1.3	1.2	0.9	0.7	0.4	0.3
Philippines	5.5	5.5	5.1	5.1	4.9	4.4	3.6	3.8	3.6	3.5	3.6	3.6	3.2	2.7
Uruguay	0.9	1.0	1.0	0.9	0.9	0.9	0.9	0.6	0.8	0.8	0.7	0.7	0.7	0.6
Yugoslavia	2.2	2.3	2.2	2.2	2.0	1.8	1.8	1.4	1.4	1.4	1.4	1.3	1.2	1.2
Total Capital	71	79	92	105	116	129	136	29	32	37	42	47	52	56
Total Assets	1261	1336	1413	1529	1613	1633	1670	588	582	590	623	638	626	608
Capital Exposure Ratios:														
Non-oil LDC	1.52	1.37	1.16	0.94	0.80	0.67	53.8	2.29	2.09	1.80	1.48	1.27	1.10	.91
Latin America	1.19	1.06	0.93	0.77	0.68	0.58	47.3	1.77	1.63	1.46	1.24	1.10	0.97	0.84

Source: Federal Financial Institutions Examinations Council, Statistical Release E.16(126).
Notes: Total amounts owed US banks after adjustments for guarantees and external borrowing.

The changes in U.S. bank exposure to the twenty-four countries in the sample is displayed in Table 9.4. There were only four instances (Argentina, Brazil, Morocco, and Turkey) in which U.S. bank exposure rose over the 1982–87 period, but it fell back again in 1988. In the case of Argentina and Brazil, the increase had been confined to the nine biggest money center banks. There were also three instances (Chile, Mexico, and Uruguay) in which the nine biggest banks increased their exposure between 1982 and 1987, but not by enough to compensate for reduced exposure by other banks. As other banks reduced their exposure, the money center banks' share of total U.S. exposure rose. With the general reduction in exposure coinciding with the building up of bank capital, the ratios of exposure to capital were more than halved from those found at the beginning of the crisis in mid-1982. The write-offs of assets by the nine largest money center banks is reflected in the drop in the end-1988 value of their assets to $608 billion.

CONCLUSION

This chapter has analyzed the responses of several sectors of the U.S. economy. Over six years, the Reagan Administration's response moved from a doctrinaire, free-market approach hostile to existing policies of multilateral agencies to one that recognized the need for concerted government action supported by multilateral lending agencies. The Bush Administration's break from the Baker Plan, represented by the Japan-U.S. approach of the Miyazawa-Brady proposals, was a further recognition of the need to rely on multilateral agencies. The role of Congress was concentrated in banking legislation to bolster bank reserves while avoiding explicit charges against taxpayers. The myriad ingenious debt relief schemes requiring Federal guarantees or Federal subsidies received a hostile reception from a Congress that had spent the better part of the decade struggling with budget deficits and trade deficits, and that was suspicious of anything that smacked of "bailing out" big banks.

The reaction of U.S. commercial banks was twofold. Measures to increase capitalization through larger loan-loss reserves and new share issues were accompanied by a reduction in exposure in developing countries. The large reserve build-up of 1987 contributed to making it the worse year for large banks since the Depression of the 1930s. Eight of the fifteen largest bank holding companies reported losses for the year.[36] Plagued by the need to raise their equity ratios, U.S. money center banks were under severe competition from better capitalized superregional and foreign competitors, presaging major changes in the rankings of the top U.S. banks.

From its inception, the debt crisis posed a variety of threats to developed country institutions. This chapter has examined the defensive reactions of the institutions in the case of the United States. The next chapter examines the constructive reactions that occur through debt renegotiation proceedings.

NOTES

1. DRI, *US Review*, September 1983, pp. 1.24–1.28.

2. The DRI forecast assumed that the Federal Reserve would adopt an offsetting expansionary monetary policy and would manage to isolate the problem in the international sector of the banking market just as previously it had successfully isolated recent domestic financial problems such as Real Estate Investment Trusts (REITs), Penn Central, Franklin National, and Penn Square.

3. For a comprehensive survey of the many proposals see C. Fred Bergsten, William R. Cline, and John Williamson, *Bank Lending to Developing Countries: The Policy Alternatives* (Washington, D.C.: Institute for International Economics, 1985).

4. This is an off-budget item, and is not a charge against taxpayers. It does not add to the Federal budget deficit nor does it require an increase in U.S. taxes. The U.S. contribution to the Fund is offset by an equal increase in U.S. reserves at the Fund. In the case of capital contributions to MDBs such as the World Bank, there are small budget appropriations but these tend to be a very small percentage of the U.S. share of the capital increase because very little of the capital increase is called. Instead, it is common for less than 10 percent of any capital increase to be paid up, but the callable capital permits MDBs to borrow on international capital markets at extremely low interest rates. The bulk of the lending done by MDBs consists of on-lending of borrowed resources rather than lending of paid-up capital.

5. *Congressional Quarterly*, 1983, p. 370, p. 533.

6. Timothy B. Clarke, "Tackling the Debt Crisis," *National Journal*, September 8, 1986, pp. 1932–39.

7. Timothy B. Clarke, "Tackling the Debt Crisis," p. 1934.

8. *IMF Survey*, March 21, 1983, p. 89.

9. *New York Times*, February 15, 1983, p. D9.

10. Details of the India loan are described by Catherine Gwin in "Financing India's Structural Adjustment: The Role of the Fund," in John Williamson (ed.), *IMF Conditionality* (Washington, D.C.: Institute for International Economics, 1982).

11. Edmar Lisboa Bacha and Carlos F. Diaz-Alejandro, *International Financial Intermediation: A Long and Tropical View*, International Finance Section, Princeton Essays in International Finance No. 147, May 1982, p. 32; John Williamson, *The*

Lending Policies of the International Monetary Fund (Washington, D.C.: Institute for International Economics, 1982), p. 48.

12. U.S. Department of the Treasury, *U.S. Participation in the Multilateral Development Banks in the 1980s* (Washington, D.C.: Government Printing Office, February 1982).

13. Clyde H. Farnsworth, "World Bank Friends Talk of Bolting," *New York Times*, March 28, 1988, p. D1.

14. Hobart Rowen, "Baker Pushes for World Bank Funds," *Washington Post*, March 31, 1988, p. B3.

15. *New York Times*, October 22, 1985, p. D1, and October 30, 1985, p. D6.

16. Joseph Kraft, *The Mexican Rescue* (New York: The Group of Thirty, 1984).

17. U.S. House of Representatives, Subcommittee on International Trade, Investment and Monetary Policy of the Committee on Banking, Finance and Urban Affairs, *Hearings*, September 13, 1983.

18. The Exchange Stabilization Fund is a Treasury fund of dollars and foreign currencies used by the Fed and the Treasury to intervene in foreign exchange markets when they wish to influence the exchange rate for the dollar.

19. The Fed's reciprocal swap arrangements are the U.S. component of a web of standby arrangements among fifteen central banks and the BIS, which permit central banks to borrow foreign currency from each other when they wish to influence exchange rates. These ongoing standby arrangements date from the Bretton Woods era of fixed exchange rates when central banks often needed funds quickly and discretely. Mexico, with a standby line of credit of $700 millions, is the only developing country with which the U.S. has a reciprocal arrangement.

20. Kathleen Day and John M. Berry, "FDIC Rescues Texas Bank With $1 Billion Loan," *Washington Post*, March 18, 1988, p. B1.

21. *Federal Reserve Bulletin*, July 1983, p. 539.

22. *Federal Reserve Bulletin*, June 1985, p. 440.

23. Michael G. Martinson and James V. Houpt, "Transfer Risk in U.S. Banks," *Federal Reserve Bulletin*, April 1989, pp. 255–58.

24. *New York Times*, July 2, 1984, p. D1.

25. *New York Times*, December 11, 1987, p. A1.

26. Nathaniel C. Nash, "Capital Plan Feared as a Burden on Banks," *New York Times*, July 15, 1988, p. D1.

27. Nathaniel C. Nash, "Fed Approves Rules Requiring More Capital at All Banks," *New York Times*, August 4, 1988, p. D2.

28. Henry S. Terrell and Rodney H. Mills, "U.S. Bank Lending: How Big a Slow Down," *The Banker*, August 1985, pp. 64–69.

29. Mary M. McLaughlin and Martin H. Wolfson, "The Profitability of Insured Commercial Banks in 1987," *Federal Reserve Bulletin*, July 1988, pp. 403–18.

30. Eric N. Berg, "Bank of Boston in Big Write-Off of Latin Loans," *New York Times*, December 15, 1987, p. A1.

31. Robert A. Bennett, "American Express Bank Write-Off," *New York Times*, January 13, 1988, p. D1.

32. Sarah Bartlett, "Mellon Set To Shift Bad Loans," *New York Times*, July 28, 1988, p. D1.

33. Salomon Brothers estimates.

34. Salomon Brothers estimates.

35. Reductions in bank exposure do not imply reductions in LDC debt. The calling-in of guarantees, for example, merely shifts a country's liability from banks to the guaranteeing agency.

36. Robert A. Bennett, "Nation's Biggest Banks Had Worst Year in 1987 Since the Depression," *New York Times*, February 16, 1988, p. D5.

10

Debt Renegotiation and Rescheduling

Prior to the emergence of debt reduction in 1989, the crisis produced an ongoing series of restructurings and reschedulings of both official creditor and commercial bank debt. These agreements are the subject of the present chapter. The first section of the chapter is devoted to the evolution of terms of restructuring agreements. It is followed by two sections that describe the attitudes of debtor country governments and creditor banks to bank debt renegotiations. The final section describes the elements in the "menu approach" to debt restructuring and reduction. As its name implies, a variety of debt restructuring options have come to constitute the "menu approach." These options range from debt-equity and debt-bond swaps to debt commodity swaps and debt buy-backs.

According to the World Bank, between January 1980 and September 1988, fifty countries engaged in debt renegotiations involving $415 billions of commercial bank debt and $82 billions in official creditor debt.[1] Not all debtor countries rescheduled. Within the sample of twenty-four countries, six avoided any rescheduling of either public or private creditor debt through 1988. Avoiding rescheduling were Colombia, India, Indonesia, Israel, South Korea, and Malaysia. Two other members of the sample, Uruguay and Venezuela, had renegotiated private creditor but not public creditor debt.

Debt renegotiations are conducted in two loosely organized fora—the Paris Club and commercial bank advisory committees. Originally formed to deal with the debt difficulties of Argentina in 1956, the Paris Club handles renegotiations of official creditor debt, invariably foreign aid loans made by governments or private sector export-import loans guaranteed by governments. All of its official creditors usually attend Paris Club discussions with a particular debtor. Bank advisory committees consist of a group of 12 to 15 banks empowered to represent the several hundred members of a typical bank consortium. The main multilateral lending agencies, the IMF and the World Bank, have not allowed restructuring of their loans.

Table 10.1   Debt Restructuring Agreements, 1978–88

	The Paris Club		Commercial Banks	
	Debtors	Debt	Debtors	Debt
1978	3	1.8	2	0.3
1979	4	2.9	2	2.9
1980	3	3.1	3	1.5
1981	9	3.4	6	1.4
1982	6	0.6	6	9.2
1983	17	8.4	19	47.6
1984	14	4.3	21	91.3
1985	21	16.4	14	23.2
1986	18	11.3	13	72.2
1987	17	28.2	14	92.4
1988	7	7.0	7	76.8

Source: Maxwell Watson et al., International Capital Markets: Developments and Prospects, IMF, World Economic Outlook and Financial Surveys, December 1986, Table 49; World Bank, World Debt Tables 88-89 Vol. I, Table III-5; Peter M. Keller with Nissanke E. Weerasinghe, Multilateral Official Debt Rescheduling: Recent Experience, in IMF, World Economic and Financial Surveys, May 1988, Table 1.

Notes: 1988 data through September.   New money excluded.   Commercial bank data include deferments and are by date of signature of agreement in principle.   Paris Club data also include other official creditor agreements for Chile, Cuba, Poland, Turkey, Mexico and Yugoslavia.

Table 10.1 provides some of the details of the value of long-run debt covered by restructuring agreements, showing the relative role of the two fora. The Paris Club data are arranged by year in which an agreement was signed. The commercial bank data are dated by year of agreement in principle because this was often sufficient to release other funds.[2] In the years prior to 1982, Paris Club reschedulings tended to be larger than commercial bank reschedulings. The number of countries seeking restructuring rose sharply after 1982, peaking at twenty-one in 1985 in the case of official creditor reschedulings and in

1984 in the case of commercial bank debt. The value of official creditor reschedulings rose through 1987, whereas commercial bank long-run debt restructuring peaked in 1984 and 1987. The details of the pattern of London Club and Paris Club long-run debt restructuring agreements for the sample countries are found in Table 10.2.

THE EVOLUTION OF TERMS

Rescheduling of both official and private creditor debt went through four distinct phases from 1982 to 1989. In early agreements, the consolidation period covered debt on which the payments were in arrears or were due within two years. In the second phase, which began in 1984, multiyear restructuring agreements (MYRAs), which used much longer consolidation periods to remove humps in amortisation payments, were introduced. A third stage began in 1985 with the Baker Plan's proposals for new money to accompany rescheduling. In this phase, rescheduling terms became increasingly differentiated as the "menu approach" became widespread. A fourth phase, in which voluntary debt reduction became important, followed adoption of the Miyazawa-Brady proposals in 1989.

In the years after 1982, grace periods, maturities, and consolidation periods lengthened; and, in the case of bank debt, renegotiating fees and spreads over LIBOR fell. As it became obvious that the same countries would be returning annually to renegotiate debt not included in the previous consolidation period, serial reschedulings and multiyear restructuring became common. The large number of rescheduling agreements produced some "leapfrogging" downward in spreads after 1983. Concerted lending spreads over LIBOR declined sharply from around two points in 1983 to under a point from 1987 onwards.[3] In the case of Mexico, for example, spreads fell from 2.25 points in 1983 to 0.8125 point in 1987. Margins well below 1 percentage point had been available to Brazil until 1980, while Mexico could obtain spreads as low as half a percentage point up to June 1982.[4] In addition to lower interest charges, average maturities on rescheduled debt lengthened from six years in 1983 to eighteen years in 1988.[5] As maturities lengthened, so too did commercial bank grace periods, rising from three years in 1983 to eight years in 1988.

One casualty of commercial bank debt rescheduling was the virtual disappearance of special rescheduling fees. These had ranged up to 1.5 points in 1983 but had almost disappeared by 1986.[6] However, in efforts to persuade a critical mass of banks to make commitments to provide new money in bank restructuring agreements, early commitment fees became a feature of restructuring agreements. Banks that

Table 10.2 Medium- and Long-run Debt Restructuring, 1982–88 ($ billion)

	Official Creditors						Commercial Banks						
	1983	1984	1985	1986	1987	1988	1982	1983	1984	1985	1986	1987	1988
Major Borrowers	3.7		2.3	1.8	14.7	5.0	3.2	39.6	75.7	7.0	50.4	66.3	68.0
Argentina			2.1		1.6			14.2				29.5	
Brazil	2.3				4.5	5.0		4.5	4.8		6.7		61.0
Chile			0.2		0.1			2.2	1.2	6.0		6.0	7.0
Egypt					8.5								
India													
Indonesia													
Israel													
S. Korea													
Malaysia													
Mexico	1.4			1.8				18.8	48.7	1.0	43.7	9.7	
Turkey													
Venezuela							3.2		21.0			21.1	
17 Highly Indebted Countries	5.5	3.1	4.6	6.8	8.7	6.2		46.0	84.1	16.3	59.4	75.7	78.5
Bolivia	0.1			0.4				0.3					
Colombia			0.1										
Costa Rica								0.7		0.4			
Côte d'Ivoire		0.3	0.2	0.5	0.6	0.3			0.5		0.7		2.2
Ecuador	0.2		0.1					1.8		4.3			
Jamaica		0.1			0.1				0.2	0.2			
Morocco	1.2		1.0		0.9					0.5	2.2	0.4	
Nigeria				3.7				1.9			4.3		
Peru	0.4	1.0						0.4	0.5				
Philippines		0.9			0.9				5.9			9.0	
Uruguay			0.6	0.4					0.1		2.0		1.8
Yugoslavia	0.8	0.8				0.9		1.0	1.3	3.9			6.5

Sources: M. Watson et al., International Capital Markets: Developments and Prospects, in IMF World Economic Outlook, January 1988, Tables 28, 37; December 1986, Table 49; P. M. Keller and N. E. Weerasinghe, Multilateral Official Debt Rescheduling: Recent Experience, IMF World Economic Outlook, May 1988, Table 1; World Bank, World Debt Tables 1988–89 Vol. I, Table III-5. Bank data includes deferments but excludes new money and short-run debt. Official creditor data include agreements concluded outside Paris Club. 1988 data through September.

made early commitments to provide new money in the 1987 Argentinean and Ecuadorean restructuring agreements received a fee of three eights of a percentage point. In addition to renegotiating the terms on existing debt, commercial bank debt renegotiations also involved the issue of "new money." The amount of new long-term bank credit disbursed under concerted lending programs was $13 billion in 1983. It fell sharply thereafter, to $3.5 billion in 1986, rising to under $5 billion in 1987.[7]

Paris Club reschedulings displayed a similar relaxation of terms, particularly for Sub-Saharan Africa. Some debtors had maturities and grace periods extended to twice the conventional Paris Club limits of ten-year maturities with five-year grace periods. An earlier Paris Club prerequisite that an upper credit-tranche IMF standby arrangement be in place throughout the period covered by a rescheduling was relaxed as consolidation periods in serial agreements outran the typical life of a Fund standby arrangement. Instead, in a number of instances, Paris Club creditors were satisfied by debtor country acceptance of Fund enhanced surveillance. Eventually, in 1988, the Paris Club introduced a menu approach. The Paris Club devised its own conditionality for non-IMF members such as Cuba, Mozambique, and Poland (the latter two are now members), or IMF members in default on IMF loans.

The second round of debt restructuring saw the introduction of MYRAs. Commercial bank MYRAs were introduced in 1985 for Ecuador, Mexico, and Côte d'Ivoire. By September 1988, ten countries had negotiated bank MYRAs. Paris Club MYRAs included Turkey (1980), Ecuador (1985), Côte d'Ivoire (1986), Yugoslavia (1986), and Brazil (1987).[8] The three-tranche MYRAs for Ecuador and the Côte d'Ivoire required IMF standby arrangements for the first two tranches and either a standby or enhanced surveillance in the final tranche. The Yugoslav MYRA did not require an IMF standby for any stage of the MYRA and became an exception to the general Paris Club rule that a standby be in place as a precondition to a Paris Club agreement. Instead, enhanced surveillance was required. The precedent established with Yugoslavia was also applied to Brazil.

Commercial bank MYRAs were usually accompanied by a commitment to submit to Fund enhanced surveillance if a standby arrangement was not in place or required by the banks. The introduction of multiyear agreements without the umbrella of an IMF adjustment program during each year of the term of the loan agreement led banks to include suspension or default clauses in the MYRAs. These called either for the suspension of the restructuring agreement or for the original loan to be declared in default if it was the judgment of a sufficiently large number of the participating banks that the policies of the country were not likely to produce a balance-of-payments position capable of maintaining debt service.[9] Not until 1989 did banks formally recognize the need for debt reduction through a voluntary write-off of a fraction of outstanding loans. The Miyazawa-Brady proposals were first implemented in the Mexican debt reduction agreement of 1989.

DEBTOR COUNTRY ATTITUDES TO DEBT RENEGOTIATIONS

In approaching debt renegotiations, countries attempted to obtain agreements that would minimize debt burdens and maximize the financing of imbalances in their external accounts. This approach emphasized demands for new money and a reduction in payments on existing debt through a lowering of spreads, a lengthening of maturities, and, eventually, a reduction in debt through creditor acceptance of secondary market discounts. Individual countries sought to obtain spreads equal to, or lower than, those obtained by the last government to negotiate.

Despite highly charged domestic political problems, debtor solidarity did not extend to the formation of a debtors' cartel. In the early years of renegotiation, joint action at the regional level was largely confined to the issuance of a number of statements calling for a common analysis of the crisis and the exchange of information. There were, of course, individual calls for the formation of a debtors's cartel. More extreme calls for a debt moratorium, as proposed by Fidel Castro in 1985, received no endorsement from other Latin governments.[10] In the years from 1982 through 1988, the one factor that would have affected all debtors equally and that might have elicited a concerted debtor country response did not materialize, namely, a dramatic increase in LIBOR.

A variety of regional statements were issued by Latin American debtors, particularly by the Cartagena Group of Finance and Foreign Ministers of eleven Latin American countries.[11] Regional statements included the Quito Declaration and Plan of Action of January 1984, the Cartagena Consensus of June 1984, and the Mar del Plata and Santo Domingo Communiques of September 1984 and February 1985. The Plan of Action that accompanied the Quito Declaration of 1984 had called for a debt-service cap under which "export earnings income should not be committed beyond reasonable percentages consistent with the maintenance of adequate levels of internal productive activity, taking into account the characteristics of the economies of each country."[12] The Cartagena group also used the occasions of the summit meetings of the industrialized nations to address letters of concern to the seven heads of government. The 1987 letter to those attending the Venice economic summit called for new financial resources, lower interest rates, and long-term reschedulings while seeking to have developed country governments accept co-responsibility for the crisis.[13] In late 1988, Latin American regional efforts were intensified in preparation for the change in U.S. Administration. The new efforts included the Declaration of Uruguay, issued by the Presidents of Argentina, Brazil, Colombia, Mexico, Peru, Uruguay, and Venezuela in October 1988, calling for debt reduction.[14] Among the Presidents were the two recently installed Presidents of Mexico and Venezuela and a number of others, in Argentina, Brazil, and Peru, who had suffered severe erosion of popular support in run-ups to elections.

Discussions on common action among debtor governments had often settled on limitation of debt service burdens as an area in which such action might be feasible. A factor that had mitigated against common action had been the timing of debt renegotiations. The renegotiations of individual countries were often out of phase with each other, leaving one or two countries always at a critical juncture in their renegotiations. Each Cartagena group meeting seemed to coincide with commercial bank or Paris Club debt negotiations of one or two members reaching a final stage. These members would then be unwilling to jeopardize the negotiations by agreeing to common action. Similarly, Brazil's moratorium announcement coincided with Argentinean IMF negotiations that Argentina did not jeopardize by supporting Brazil.

Prior to 1989, the most confrontational approach to debt was adopted by countries that imposed unilateral limits on debt servicing. In some instances, these actions were attempts to reduce the domestic political pressures associated with austerity by using existing foreign exchange for uses other than debt servicing. In other instances, the actions were aimed at improving bargaining power in debt negotiations. When the newly elected President of Peru, Alan Garcia Perez, announced in his inaugural address in July 1985 that he would limit debt servicing to 10 percent of export receipts for twelve months, his action was seen as a daring challenge to existing monetary rules.[15] A similar announcement had been made in 1984 by Bolivia when it announced that it would impose a unilateral 25 percent cap on the proportion of its export receipts to be used for debt service.[16] However, as Bergsten, Cline, and Williamson point out, the Bolivian statement was rather moot as it had not previously been paying even this limited amount.[17]

In monetary terms, the unilateral decision of Peru did not present much of a challenge to its commercial bank creditors. In 1985, the Peruvian external debt of $14 billion amounted to a mere 5 percent of the more than $300 billion in outstanding loans to Latin America. Moreover, Peruvian loans had already been severely discounted in the secondary market where they were traded at less than 40 percent of face value. One year after Garcia's announcement, the discount on Peruvian loans stood at 78 percent.[18] In February 1987, Peru took a further step when it announced that it was unable to repay $252 million in past-due payments on its $782 million IMF debt.[19] Ineligible for further IMF credit until it made good on its old IMF loans, Peru continued to borrow from the World Bank until declared ineligible for further loans in June 1987 when it fell more than 90 days in arrears in payments on old loans.[20] With all financing ended, the Peruvian economy was in shambles by 1988. The confrontation policy was reversed in December 1988 and Peru began discussions with the IMF in early 1989.

Other nations followed the path blazed by Peru. At the end of 1985, Nigeria became the third country to make a unilateral announcement that it would limit its debt servicing to a fixed proportion of exports.[21] The 30 percent limit announced by Nigeria for its debt-service ratio for 1986 was considerably below its reported actual ratio in 1985 of 42 percent.[22] In November 1986, Zaire threatened to introduce a 10 percent of exports limitation on debt repayments.[23] In January 1987, Ecuador announced that, because of falling oil revenue, it was suspending interest payments to commercial banks for six months. Two months later it suspended all debt payments after devastating earthquakes and floods halted petroleum production, its main source of foreign exchange.[24] In May 1987, Zambia announced that it was limiting its debt payments to 10 percent of its exports.[25] The Côte d'Ivoire also suspended payments in May 1988.[26] At the end of 1988, Venezuela and Colombia announced suspensions of debt payments.[27] The Venezuelan suspension of principal payments on public sector debt in January 1989 preceded devastating riots in March and an emergency financing package.

The most important debt limitation was made in February 1987, when Brazil announced a unilateral and indefinite suspension of interest payments on its $68 billion medium- and long-term bank debt and froze $15 billion of short-term and interbank credits that might otherwise have been withdrawn. It took these actions prior to beginning negotiations with commercial banks on a new loan restructuring.[28] Shortly before, the Paris Club had agreed to reschedule $4.12 billion of Brazil's official creditor debt without the usual Paris Club requirement that the debtor adopt an IMF program. Instead, the Paris Club agreement required Brazil to request enhanced surveillance from the Fund. In July 1987, Brazil suspended payments of principal but not interest on official creditor export-import debt.[29]

The commercial bank response to Brazil's action left Brazil in a weaker long-term negotiating position. Although it had been able to impose short-term costs on its bank creditors, it ultimately faced banks with reinforced reserves and capitalization. By late 1987, Brazil's confrontational policy had been ended and discussions were being held with commercial banks on finding ways to pay overdue interest. Interest payments were resumed in December 1987 when Brazil made a $1.1 billion payment, using $357 million of its own money and $715 million from new bank loans as part of a November agreement.[30] The partial moratorium had lasted less than a year. By February 1988, Brazil's fourth Finance Minister in less than three years of civilian government had negotiated a preliminary provisional commercial bank agreement under which banks would provide new money of $5.8 billion to help in paying current interest through mid-1988 and paying off interest arrears from 1986 and 1987.[31] Though denied by Brazil, the new money was provisional on Brazil's resuming relations with the IMF. Brazil's three-year boycott of the IMF ended with acceptance of a standby arrangement in August 1988. However, disbursement was suspended when Brazil fell out of compliance and in July 1989 debt payments were once more suspended.[32]

The failure of the individual confrontational tactics of Brazil and Peru is instructive. Negotiating strength was weakened rather than improved. After the announcement effects wore off, domestic political pressures increased rather than diminished. The costs of reducing interdependence through cutting off credit supplies proved excessive.

BANK ATTITUDES

Commercial banks also lacked a common negotiating strategy. Throughout the crisis, there have been considerable differences among banks as to how best to proceed. Conflicting pressures on individual banks in banking consortia of several hundred banks arose from dissimilarities in national tax and regulatory treatments, country-exposure, and capitalization ratios as well as long-term strategic objectives.

The wide variation in national tax and regulatory treatment influenced the manner in which banks in each country responded to pressures for larger loan-loss provisions, loan write-offs, interest capitalization, and so forth. Loan-loss provisions reduce pretax profits, but the regulatory and tax implications vary enormously from country to country. Specific, that is, allocated, loan-loss provisions are loan-loss reserves against previously identified future losses. Such reserves are not considered part of a bank's capital by bank regulators and tax laws usually allow some offset against tax liability, reducing the extent to which a pretax loss is converted into an after-tax loss. General, that is, unallocated, loan-loss provisions are contingency provisions against possible future losses that have not yet been identified. Bank regulators usually treat these loan-loss provisions as additions to a bank's capital, but the losses produced by these provisions are usually not favorably treated by tax laws, so they produce after-tax, as well as pretax, losses. European banks traditionally have carried specific loan-loss provisions against developing country loan losses while U.S. banks had traditionally relied on general loan-loss provisions unless required to carry ATRRs by U.S. bank regulators. With the notable exception of the United Kingdom, the more highly capitalized European banks received more favorable tax treatment for their increased loan-loss reserves than their U.S. counterparts.

The wide difference between the tax and regulatory treatment of continental European banks and their British, Japanese, and U.S. counterparts produced a situation in which European loan-loss provisions in early 1987 averaged between 30 percent and 70 percent of all problem debtor country loans while the provisions of the other three countries were closer to 5 percent.[33] This situation changed abruptly with the 1987 build-up of bank reserves. Once the losses associated with sharp increases in loan-loss provisions were accepted, a wider range of debt restructuring options was available to banks. Menu items that involved losses from swaps or trade-ins of debt at discounts became feasible for banks with large loan-loss provisions.

Differences in country exposure also influenced the attitudes of individual banks toward bank renegotiations with a particular country. A bank with a large exposure in a country seeking new terms might be expected to be more conciliatory than a bank consortium member with minimal exposure. Sometimes, differences in exposure fostered "clientism" within banking consortia, with the more heavily exposed members of a bank steering committee being prepared to accept less stringent terms than would other members of the committee.[34]

Among U.S. banks, there were considerable differences in country exposure and capitalization ratios. These differences were apparent among individual money center banks and between money center banks and regional banks. Although all major U.S. banks reported significant exposure in both Brazil and Mexico, significant exposure to Argentina, Chile, and Ecuador appears to have been heavily concentrated among a smaller group of banks.[35] Notably absent from the list of banks with significant exposure in Argentina was BankAmerica, which, with Chase Manhattan, also did not disclose significant exposure in Chile.[36]

In addition to differences in absolute exposure, there were very considerable differences in exposure-to-capital ratios and exposure-to-loan-loss-reserve ratios. These produced great variation in individual bank ability to weather any losses at a time when the U.S. banking system was under great stress from deregulation and large domestic loan losses in real estate, agriculture, and energy. The top nine money center banks had 1982 exposure-to-capital ratios of 2.29 for loans to all nonoil developing countries and 1.76 for loans to Latin America and the Caribbean. The 1982 ratios for regional banks were much lower at 0.69 and 0.57. By the end of 1988, the money center ratios had been reduced to 0.91 and 0.84, respectively, while the regional ratios were 0.18 and 0.14.[37]

There were also differences in strategic attitudes between larger and smaller banks. United States money center banks have long-term objectives of remaining in developing country lending. United States regional banks may have originally participated in syndicated lending in an effort to develop better relations with money center banks rather than as part of any long-term strategy to penetrate developing country banking markets. The divergent perspectives of money center and regional banks widened as the crisis developed. The rivalry became more intense with the increased competition accompanying deregulation. Money center banks invaded the client base and home markets of regionals while also buying substantial interests in regionals in anticipation of nationwide banking.

U.S. regional banks were particularly resentful of involuntary lending and were the source of shortfalls in new money pledges in a number of reschedulings. The larger U.S. banks had occasionally been required to provide some regionals' share of new money in loan restructuring. United States regional banks, which had accounted for roughly 15 percent of U.S. bank lending to Heavily Indebted Countries, were not receptive to the Baker Plan and had already engaged in extensive writing off of previous loans prior to the 1987 money center bank build-up of loan loss reserves.

The February 1987 confrontation by Brazil imposed short-term costs on its bank creditors and produced a predictable defensive response. With the passage of 90 days of arrears on interest payments, Brazil's U.S. bank lenders reclassified their loans as nonperforming and placed them on a nonaccrual basis, reducing bank earnings.[38] On May 19, Citicorp announced an increase in its existing $1.7 billion loan loss reserve by a further $3 billion.[39] Brazilian interest payments to Citicorp were reported to have amounted to $1.35 per share, a little under 20 percent of estimated 1987 net earnings prior to the quarterly loss of $2.5 billion generated by the increase in loan-loss reserves.[40]

Other banks followed Citicorp's lead. In the second quarter of 1987 U.S. banks announced dramatic loss-producing increases in loan-loss reserves for their developing country debt. An additional $17.5 billions was added to reserves, producing record losses.[41] The losses wiped out approximately one quarter of shareholders' equity in banks. Foreign banks followed suit. In June, a British bank, National Westminster announced bad debt provisions of 466 pounds sterling, amounting to one third of its developing country loans, and in July Midland Bank announced that it was raising its loan loss reserves by 916 million pounds ($1.48 billion) to 25 percent of its troubled Third World Loans.[42]

The 1987 Brazilian payments suspension provided the incentive to build up loan-loss reserves quickly. This defensive reaction to Brazil's effort to improve its bargaining strength placed banks in a position where they could contemplate the writing off of any debtor country loan with greater equanimity. Bank attitudes to debt changed thereafter and voluntary debt reduction became more commonplace. However, rather than accept the losses entailed by its principal or interest-reduction options, some U.S. banks with low loan-loss reserve ratios opted for the new money provisions of such Brady Plan debt reduction packages as the 1989 Mexican agreement. This reduced the debt reduction capability of the plan.

THE MENU APPROACH

The emergence of steep discounts on the face value of debt presented opportunities for debtor countries to capture some of the discount through debt-reduction schemes to buy or swap old debt. The persistence of the need to reschedule debt provided sufficient time for a variety of rescheduling options which recognized debt discounts to emerge. The wide range of options produced the "menu" approach to rescheduling, which explicitly recognized the variety of interests among members of international banking consortia. Components of the menu approach have included debt-equity swaps, debt-bond swaps, currency redenomination, debt-buy backs, performance incentives, interest capitalization, and a variety of other mechanisms including debt-environment and debt-football player swaps.[43] Some of these components became prime vehicles for voluntary debt reduction. The 1987–88 build-up of bank loan-loss reserves provided the foundations for voluntary debt reduction even prior to the Miyazawa-Brady proposals of 1988–89.

DEBT-EQUITY SWAPS

Debt-equity swaps involve converting bank debt into direct foreign investment. For potential investors in a debtor country, it may be cheaper to buy some of the country's discounted foreign loans from commercial banks and present it to the sovereign government for redemption in local currency rather than obtain local currency through normal foreign exchange transactions. Debt-equity swaps serve the interests of the debtor countries by converting a foreign-currency denominated liability into a domestic currency liability. They serve the needs of banks by reducing their exposure in debtor countries and, by accepting some loss on swapped debt, increase the likelihood that the nonswapped proportion of their exposure will retain its existing value. And, of course, debt-equity swaps serve the needs of the equity investors by reducing the costs of investment projects.

Debtor countries have closely controlled the volume of swaps, showing preference for new projects that would generate export earnings and resisting swap proposals that would place domestic firms in foreign hands. As a result, the swap market grew slowly. IMF staff estimates place 1987 debt-equity conversions at $3.2 billion, with $4.3 billion of swaps from 1983 to 1986.[44] Five countries (Argentina, Brazil, Chile, Mexico, and the Philippines) account for almost all of the swaps during this period. By mid-1988, Chile had been the most active participant, converting approximately $4 billion, almost 25 percent of its total bank debt.[45] The Chilean scheme included arrangements for Chileans to participate in debt conversions.

The incentives for debt-equity swaps are provided by the discounts from face value on Third World debt. These have been enormous. The general pattern of 1987–89 discounts is contained in Table 10.3. By July 1988, the two extremes in discounts were represented by Peruvian debt, which carried a 94 percent discount, and Turkish debt, which carried a slight 1.5 percent discount. Debtor countries have an obvious ability to influence the discount on their outstanding debt through their posture on repayment and domestic adjustment. While Sachs and Huizinga drew attention to the moral hazard dimension of debt relief schemes built upon debt discounts if debtor countries use their ability to drive down the market value of their debt as a way of gaining greater relief, experience has shown that most large-discount schemes failed to attract bank participation.[46]

Participants in swaps have been varied. In some schemes, residents with assets abroad as well as foreigners seeking local currency to finance investment projects have participated. As Chile showed, permitting residents to participate provides a mechanism for recovering

Table 10.3 Discounts on Developing Country Bank Debt
(% of face value)

	1987	1988	1989
Major Borrowers			
Argentina	53	76	83
Brazil	43	49	70
Chile	32	40	35
Egypt	NA	NA	NA
India	NA	NA	NA
Indonesia	NA	NA	NA
Israel	NA	NA	NA
S. Korea	NA	NA	NA
Malaysia	NA	NA	NA
Mexico	46	48	58
Turkey	3	2	NA
Venezuela	31	45	62
17 Heavily			
Indebted Countries			
Bolivia	90	90	89
Colombia	19	34	43
Costa Rica	67	89	86
Côte d'Ivoire	40	71	94
Ecuador	55	74	84
Jamaica	63	63	58
Morocco	34	50	56
Nigeria	72	73	77
Peru	89	94	97
Philippines	32	46	50
Uruguay	30	40	45
Yugoslavia	27	54	49

Source: Salomon Brothers Inc. Based on indicative bid
cash prices, early July each year.

capital flight. Some banks have swapped their own loans for equity investment in debtor countries. Among nonbank multinational corporations, U.S. and Japanese auto corporations have used swaps to expand their Latin American manufacturing operations while insurance- and tourism-oriented corporations have used swaps to expand Latin American operations.

The successful design of debt-equity swap schemes eluded many governments in the early years of swaps. The thin secondary market for developing country debt produced great uncertainty in the general applicability of quoted discounts on what were often very small transactions. Swap schemes that called for banks to sell their debt at too great a discount failed. Debt-equity swaps also raised new questions of national sovereignty and the appropriateness of privatization. There was fear of much greater foreign control of domestic industries. The small size of the stock market in developing countries means that entire stock markets could be purchased with only a fraction of foreign debt. There were also fears that central banks would be unable to sterlize increases in the money supply needed to pay for debt-equity swaps. These inflationary fears were used to justify Mexico's negotiating tactic of excluding debt-equity swaps from the 1989 debt reduction menu. Finally, although swaps reduced immediate foreign currency debt payments, the amount of future drains through repatriation of profits from swap-financed investments is uncertain.

Some governments designated key sectors of the economy as areas in which investment would be permitted under debt-equity swaps. Although this restriction on investor's choice was presumably dictated by development planners' sense of social rates of return, the unenthusiastic response to many debt-equity schemes suggests that the designated sectors offered low private rates of return.

The absence of well-developed stock markets, limits on foreign participation, and the general level of government restrictions on all private enterprise greatly limited the attractiveness of most early debt-equity swap schemes. The only notable instance in which demand exceeded the supply of swaps was in Chile. In other countries, the demand for swaps was so low that governments were forced to reevaluate the terms they had imposed on swaps. The schemes of Argentina, Brazil, and the Philippines were recast as governments reacted to the unenthusiastic response to their early debt-equity schemes.[47] Restrictions on the sectors in which investment could occur were relaxed and conversions at less than par were abandoned. Ecuador introduced a debt-equity swap program in January 1987 but suspended it in August after only $42 million had been converted out of the target $100 million. Most of the Ecuadorean conversions had been used to finance real estate investment rather than manufacturing investment.[48] Venezuela's debt-equity swap program, introduced in April 1987, was also poorly received. The exchange rate used in conversions was not as attractive as the free exchange rate.

Even prior to the Brady Plan, the limited size of foreign direct private investment flows to most developing countries made it unlikely that debt-equity swaps to finance foreign direct private investment would have had much impact on the debt overhang of developing countries. An alternative source of funding for debt-equity swaps is the pool of capital held abroad by residents of indebted nations. Debt-equity swaps offer a potential mechanism to reverse capital flight while simultaneously reducing foreign debt. Of course, this requires that local investment opportunities appear sufficiently attractive and that participation by nationals is not motivated by "round-tripping" for exchange rate speculation.

DEBT-BOND SWAPS

Prior to the Brady Plan, efforts to persuade banks to swap debt for longer-term bonds were not very successful. A September 1987 trial balloon proposal for an unconventional Brazilian debt-for-bonds conversion scheme originally called for mandatory conversion of $35 billion of Brazil's $68 billion bank debt into thirty-five-year, 6 percent fixed rate bonds.[49] The bonds were to be discounted at less than the then secondary market discount on Brazilian debt of 45 percent. The proposal was withdrawn when banks objected to being forced to exchange assets in a scheme that would have required them to write off up to $20 billion if bank auditors forced them to value both converted and remaining Brazilian debt at the swap discount.[50]

In December 1987, the Morgan Guaranty Trust Company announced an innovative scheme that called for Mexico to pay off as much as $20 billion of its debt by issuing twenty-year government bonds that would be swapped for bank debt at existing market discounts on Mexican debt.[51] The scheme contained a U.S. government guarantee in the form of a special issue of zero-coupon U.S. Treasury bonds issued to back the Mexican bonds. The U.S. bonds were bought by the Mexican government at the deep discount found on zero-coupon bonds and are held as collateral by the Federal Reserve Bank of New York until the Mexican bonds mature. The discount would have permitted Mexico to buy $10 billion worth of U.S. bonds for $2 billion. A 50 percent discount on Mexican debt, as then existed in the thin secondary market, would have permitted $10 billion of Mexican bonds to retire roughly $20 billion of bank debt for an initial cash outlay of $2 billion.

The novel scheme was not the success its designers anticipated. Bids to swap debt with a face value of $6.7 billion were received, of which only $3.67 billion contained discounts deep enough to be accepted.[52] The $3.67 billion of bank debt was swapped for $2.56 billion in new bonds, reducing Mexico's external debt by a mere $1.11 billion. The average discount on the accepted tenders was a little over 30 percent, far short of the sought-for 50 percent. The scheme's designer, Morgan Guaranty, itself ended up with 30 percent of the swaps. The other major participants were Japanese banks, under pressure from the Ministry of Finance.

There were several explanations for the failure of the early Mexican scheme. Although the principal of the Mexican bonds was guaranteed by the U.S. bonds held as collateral, there was no guarantee that the interest on the Mexican bonds would be paid if Mexico ran into further payments difficulties. Participation in the swap made less economic sense for money center banks than for regionals who could use the bonds as "exit bonds" by swapping their entire portfolio of Mexican debt, thus escaping the need to meet "new money" requirements in any future rescheduling.

For banks not seeking exit bonds, two risks were associated with the Mexican scheme. The absence of an interest guarantee would cause the new Mexican bonds to be immediately discounted. Also, since the Mexican authorities had limited the bond sales to $10 billion, and had reserved the right to reject low discount bids, wide participation in the swap auction would result in tenders for more than $10 billion of bonds. The staff of U.S. regulatory agencies had recommended that all unswapped tendered debt must be written down to the tender price. Thus, an unsuccessful tender would generate immediate losses for banks.[53]

Prior to the 1989 Brady proposals, the possibilities presented by the Mexican arrangements were not open to all indebted countries. In the first place, substantial foreign exchange reserves were needed to be able to buy the U.S. zero-coupon bonds. In addition, the approach required U.S. acquiescence through its issuance of the required zero-coupon bonds. More general bond-backed debt-reduction schemes had included calls for the establishment of an international agency to buy debt at a discount, and proposals for an IMF-managed debt buy-back scheme. The Robinson plan of the head of American Express suggested a new debt agency. The Miyazawa Plan of Japan's Finance Minister proposed using an IMF-managed escrow fund along the lines of the Fed-managed escrow fund in the Mexican debt-bond swap.[54]

Under the Miyazawa plan, debtor countries would deposit part of their foreign exchange reserves in the escrow fund and these deposits would be used to guarantee the value of bonds issued in a discount auction swap for bank debt. In an effort to overcome the problem, which surfaced with the Mexican scheme, of unsecured interest payments on bonds swapped for debt, debtor countries would agree to set aside a percentage of export receipts to make interest payments. The unswapped bank debt would be rescheduled as before.

DEBT BUY-BACKS

Debt buy-back schemes are a further way of reducing external indebtedness by recognizing secondary market discounts. In this instance, debt is exchanged for cash rather than assets such as bonds or equity. Bolivia, Chile, and Mexico have been among the countries proposing or using debt buy-back schemes. In the highly successful Bolivian case, a special account was established by the IMF for donations from countries wishing to help Bolivia buy back its commercial bank debt under the terms of an agreement that Bolivia had made with the banks in February 1987.[55] Commercial banks insisted that Bolivia's foreign exchange earnings should not be diverted from servicing its debt. This insistence made it necessary for Bolivia to rely on foreign aid to implement the buy-back scheme. A number of developed countries, including Holland and Sweden, deposited enough foreign aid in the IMF special account to permit Bolivia to buy back 55 percent of its outstanding bank debt at seventeen cents on the dollar.

The magnitude of the Bolivian buy-back scheme was relatively insignificant in the global debt crisis. The face value of the debt bought back was less than $400 million. However, it was an important precedent for other countries with sufficient foreign exchange reserves. In November 1988, Chile announced that it had accepted bids from banks to sell $299 million of face value debt to the central bank for $168.4 million at an average discount of 56.3 cents on the dollar.[56] The buy-back auction involved the repurchase of 2.3 percent of Chile's bank debt.

OTHER DEBT SWAPS

The debt swap mechanism has provided the financing for a number of innovative deals while also reducing debt. In one of the more unusual debt swaps, the Dutch electronics multinational, Philips, strengthened the Dutch league prospects of its soccer team, PSV Eindhoven, by using $4 million of profits generated in Brazil to buy Brazilian debt at a 25 percent discount; the debt was exchanged for sufficient cruzados to persuade Brazil's soccer club, Vasco de Gama, to transfer center-forward Romario Farias to Eindhoven.[57] In 1987, one of Peru's British bank creditors agreed to accept copper, iron, and other raw materials in a debt-for-commodities swap.[58] The preferential arrangement between Midland Bank and Peru avoided a common syndicated loan agreement clause that requires any cash repayment to be divided equally among all creditors. Under the swap arrangement, Midland Bank would act as selling agent for Peru, remitting part of the cash proceeds from the sale of the raw materials to Peru while keeping a share in partial payment of its loans to Peru. The arrangement involved trivial sums. Midland was to receive $8.8 million. Peru's total foreign debt at the time was $14.6 billion and it had been reduced to barter approaches as its debt policies caused all foreign financing to dry up. The international environmental movement has also used swaps. Costa Rican debt was reduced by $5.4 million, purchased at over 80 percent discounts by environmentalists who exchanged the debt for local currency to finance conservation projects in Costa Rica.[59] In 1989, $9 million of Ecuadorean debt was bought from American Express and Morgan Guaranty by the World Wildlife Fund and the Nature Conservancy. The environmentalist organizations paid 11.875 cents on the dollar and converted the debt into local currency bonds, which were to finance environmental protection of Ecuador's rain forests.

THE BRADY PLAN

The Brady Plan of 1989 was a major advance on the Baker Plan. It was initially used to reduce Mexico's $54 billion of medium- and long-term public sector commercial bank debt. Other early candidates for the plan included the Philippines, Venezuela, and Costa Rica. Debt reduction talks have used a menu approach which included principal reduction, interest reduction, and new money as menu items. The principal reduction option involved the swapping of bank debt for bonds at a discount from the face value of existing debt but at market interest rates. The interest reduction option involved swaps at no discount but the bonds would carry much lower interest rates. Some financial backing for the bonds was provided by financing made available by the IMF, The World Bank, and Japan. The Bank and the Fund agreed to set aside about $10 billion each over three years. Member-country borrowing of these funds provided collateral for several years of interest payments on the bonds and some of the principal. The arrangement involved a transfer of risk from commercial banks to multilateral institutions, and ultimately to taxpayers. Japan promised $4.5 billion to support debt-reduction efforts.

In the Mexican negotiations, the participants agreed to a menu which contained a 35 percent principal reduction option, a fixed 6.25 percent interest rate option, and a new money option under which banks would provide new financing equal to a third of the existing exposure.[60] IMF and World Bank financing of the agreement included $375 million of a $1.5 billion World Bank loan package, 30 percent of a SDR 2.8 billion IMF extended arrangement and up to 40 percent of Mexico's IMF quota. Japan agreed to provide a further $2 billion in supporting loans.

THE PARIS CLUB'S MENU APPROACH

In 1988, the desperate plight of Sub-Saharan African countries led the Paris Club to introduce greater differentiation in the treatment of debtors and substantial easing of terms. A number of past practices were relaxed in the process, including a general principle that excluded from future reschedulings all debt incurred after a cut-off date established at the first rescheduling. Other relaxations included the subordination of longer-term debt to the servicing of short-term debt such as trade credits. Differentiation in the treatment of Paris Club debtors included particular relief for the poorest debtor countries, acceptance of SAF arrangements with the Fund rather than the previously required upper credit tranche arrangements, twenty-year rescheduling maturities and debt forgiveness by some creditor governments including Canada and EC Member States such as France, Germany, and the United Kingdom. By 1986 EC cancellations approached $4 billion.[61] In early 1988, Germany announced a plan to forgive a further $1.6 billion in addition to its previous cancellations of $2.53 billion of official debt.[62] In July 1989, the U.S. announced that it would follow other aid donors and forgive $1 billion of development loans to sub-Sahara Africa.

In September 1988, the Paris Club introduced a menu approach containing three rescheduling options.[63] A partial cancellation option allowed cancellation of one-third of consolidated debtservice obligations and an eight-year grace period, fourteen-year maturity, and rescheduling of the other two-thirds. An extended maturities option offered a fourteen-year grace period and a twenty-five year maturity. Finally, a concessional interest rate option offered an eight-year grace period, and fourteen-year maturity with rescheduled debt carrying interest-rate concessions of either 3.5 points or 50 percent.

CONCLUSION

Until the Brady Plan's recognition of the need for debt reduction, a common predicament had faced all debtor countries which have sought to renegotiate their debt: how to maximize bargaining power in order to obtain the most favorable terms. Despite their collective plight, debtor countries shied away from the formation of a debtors' cartel and, instead, negotiated individually. Banks also faced common predicaments, seeking to avoid the moral hazard that would follow any debt forgiveness while attempting to minimize losses on loans to patently uncreditworthy clients. As the rescheduling process dragged on without any global relief scheme, the terms of rescheduling were gradually relaxed. The build-up of bank capital, the large discounts on Third World debt, and the easing of bank regulations regarding foreign investments all combined to create conditions favorable to debt conversion schemes.

Despite the variety of menu options available, the Baker Plan's failure to generate the requisite new money in concerted lending packages and the absence of any far-reaching multilateral debt relief scheme left debtor countries starved of further international liquidity. The continued financing squeeze gradually forced a readjustment of debtor country economic policies away from ones that undervalued foreign exchange. Debt reduction through a variety of debt conversion schemes gathered steam in 1988 but a rising political backlash to continued austerity in debtor countries threatened political stability after only a few years of democracy in some countries. The Bush Administration's Brady Plan, introduced in 1989, sought to provide debt-reduction relief before this backlash engulfed the young democracies.[64]

NOTES

1. World Bank, *World Debt Tables 1988–89*, Vol. I, p. xliv.

2. The Fund's approach to concerted lending often made Fund disbursement of its own funds conditional on a "critical mass" of bank creditors agreeing to the terms of a restructuring.

3. World Bank, *World Debt Tables 1988–89*, Vol. 1, p. xlvi.

4. M. S. Mendelsohn, *Commercial Banks and the Restructuring of Cross-Border Debt* (New York: The Group of Thirty, 1983), p. 8.

5. World Bank, *World Debt Tables 1988–89*, Vol. 1, p. xlvi.

6. United Nations Economic Commission for Latin America and the Caribbean, "The Economic Crisis: Policies for Adjustment, Stabilization and Growth", LC/G.1408(SES.21/7), April 8, 1986, Table 10, p. 102; Maxwell Watson et al., *International Capital Markets: Developments and Prospects*, IMF, *World Economic and Financial Surveys*, January 1988, p. 33.

7. World Bank, *World Debt Tables 1988–89*, Vol. 1, p. xliv.

8. K. Burke Dillon and Gumersindo Oliveros, *Recent Experience with Multilateral Official Debt Rescheduling*, IMF World Economic and Financial Survey, February 1987, pp. 14–16.

9. Maxwell Watson et al., "International Capital Markets" p. 53.

10. Despite his own calls for a debt moratorium, Cuba reached agreements with commercial banks on debt restructuring in 1983 and 1985.

11. Drago Kisic, *Reflexiónes en Torno al Proceso de Cordinación Latin Americano sobre la Deuda Externa*, CEPEI Documentos de Trabajo No. 1 (Lima; Centro Peruano de Estudios Internacionales, 1985).

12. Sistema Economico Latin Americano (SELA), *Declaration of Quito and Plan of Action* (Caracas: mimeo, 1984) p. 2.

13. Reprinted in *Capitulos del SELA*, No. 16 (April/June 1987), pp. 75–76.

14. IMF *Survey*, November 14, 1988, pp. 354–55.

15. Alan Riding, "Peru's Debt Plan Challenges World Lending System," *New York Times*, July 29, 1985.

16. *New York Times*, June 11, 1984, p. D8.

17. C. Fred Bergsten, William R. Cline, and John Williamson, *Bank Lending to Developing Countries: The Policy Alternatives*, Policy Analyses in International Economics No. 10 (Washington, D.C.: Institute for International Economics, April 1985), p. 162.

18. Richard S. Weinert, "Swapping Third World Debt," *Foreign Policy* No. 65 (Winter 1986/87), p. 85.

19. *New York Times*, February 19, 1987, p. D6.

20. *New York Times*, June 4, 1987, p. D10.

21. *The Economist*, January 4 1985, p. 56.

22. *New York Times*, January 15, 1986, p. D6.

23. Clyde H. Farnsworth, "Plea by Zaire on Debt Seen," *New York Times*, November 17, 1986, p. D2.

24. *New York Times*, March 14, 1987 p. 1.

25. *New York Times*, June 17, 1987, p. A18.

26. James Brook, "Ivory Church to Tower Over St. Peters," *New York Times*, December 19, 1988, p. A1.

27. "Venezuela Suspends Payments of Debt Principal," *New York Times*, January 1, 1989, p. 5.

28. *New York Times*, February 21, 1987, p. 1.

29. Roger Cohen, "Brazil Halts Payments to Paris Club on $1.05 Billion of Debt Principal," *Wall Street Journal*, July 2, 1987.

30. *New York Times*, December 31, 1987, p. D3.

31. Alan Riding, "Brazil Debt Agreement is Reached," *New York Times*, February 29, 1988, p. D1.

32. James Brooke, "Brazil Says There is No Moratorium," *New York Times*, July 8, 1989, p. 42.

33. World Bank, *World Debt Tables 1987–88*, Vol. I, p. xxv.

34. A dispute between Citicorp and Manufacturers Hanover over rescheduling terms for Chile, in which Citibank had relatively small exposure, was reported by Peter Truell, "Borrowing Trouble," *Wall Street Journal*, July 2, 1987, p. 10.

35. Public disclosure is not required for loans which are less that 0.75 percent of bank assets.

36. Data from Bear Stearns Inc., reported in *New York Times*, May 21, 1987, p. D6.

37. U.S. Federal Financial Institutions Examination Council, *Country Exposure Lending Survey, Statistical Release E 16 (126)*, various years.

38. Interest on loans placed on a nonaccrual basis cannot be considered as bank income until it has been physically received in cash and interest generated in the past but not yet actually received must be deducted from earnings.

39. *Business Week*, June 1, 1987, pp. 42–43.

40. *The Economist*, February 28, 1987, p. 86.

41. Richard B. Schmitt and Christian Hill, "Banks to Post Record $10 Billion Loss for 2nd Quarter," *Wall Street Journal*, July 20, 1987.

42. *The Economist*, June 20, 1987, p. 80; *New York Times*, July 8, 1987, p. D18.

43. For details of the menu approach see Maxwell Watson et al., International Capital Markets: Developments and Prospects, pp. 54–63.

44. Michael Blackwell and Simon Nocera, "Developing Countries Develop Debt-Equity Swap Programs To Manage External Debt," *IMF Survey*, July 11, 1988, p. 226.

45. Shirley Christian, "Chile's Debt-Swap Plan Cuts Loans by $4 Billion," *New York Times*, July 18, 1988, p. D10.

46. Jeffrey Sachs and Harry Huizinga, "US Commercial Banks and the Developing-Country Debt Crisis," *Brookings Papers on Economic Activity*, No. 2 (1987), p. 564.

47. For country details see Salomon Brothers Inc., *Debt-For-Equity Swaps: A Country-By-Country Update on Market Characteristics and Regulatory Initiatives*, Stock Research Report: Banks, May 6, 1988.

48. *Business Latin America*, September 7, 1987, p. 288.

49. Anne Swardson, "Brazil Abandons its Unusual Debt Proposal," *Washington Post National Weekly Edition*, September 21, 1987, p. 24; Alan Riding, "Brazil's Finance Minister Under Attack for Changing Stance on Debt Plan," *New York Times*, September 14, 1987, p. D4; Peter T. Kilborn, "Brazil Debt Plan Barred by Baker," *New York Times*, September 9, 1987, p. D1; Alan Riding, "Brazil's Debt Plan Takes an Odd Tack," *New York Times*, September 4, 1987, p. D1; *The Economist*, September 19, 1987, p. 87.

50. Eric N. Berg, "Banks Cool to Brazil Debt-for-Bond Plan," *New York Times*, September 28, 1987.

51. Robert A. Bennett, "New Way Offered to Relieve Crisis in 3rd World Debt," *New York Times*, December 30, 1987, p. A1.

52. *New York Times*, March 3, 1988.

53. Eric N. Berg, "Banks Vary in Mexican Debt Views," *New York Times*, January 12, 1988, p. D1.

54. Steven Greenhouse, "Japan is Seeking Larger Role in World's Financial System and Debt Crisis," *New York Times*, September 26, 1988, p. D6; Susan Chira, "Third World Debt Plan is Defended by Japan", *New York Times*, October 28, 1988, p. D2.

55. World Bank, *World Debt Tables 1987–88*, Vol. I, p. xvii.

56. *New York Times*, November 10, 1988, p. D9.

57. *New York Times*, October 22, 1988, p. 37.

58. Eric N. Berg, "Peru to Pay Part of Debt in Goods," *New York Times*, September 17, 1987, p.D1.

59. Paul Simons, "Putting Debt to Productive Use," *Manchester Guardian Weekly*, December 4, 1988, p. 24.

60. Peter Truell, "Lack of Results on International Debt Could Prove Embarassing for Bush at the Economic Summit," *Wall Street Journal*, July 7, 1989, p. A10.

61. Commission of the European Communities, *The Courier*, May–June 1986, p. 96.

62. *New York Times*, March 17, 1988, p. D21.

63. IMF, *IMF Survey*, April 3, 1989, p. 103.

64. Peter T. Kilborn, "Debt-Policy Set Shift on 3d World," *New York Times*, March 11, 1989, p. 35.

11

Conclusion

The debt crisis has been an instructive case study in development strategies and in international public policy. The crisis showed that development strategies being followed in some countries in the late 1970s and early 1980s were unsustainable. A combination of over-valued real effective exchange rates, internal inflation, and large public sector borrowing proved incompatible with an external environment of volatile commodity prices, interest rates, and exchange rates. Some debtor countries, following less inflationary and more export-oriented policies, escaped the worst of the crisis, which was largely located in Latin America and Sub-Saharan Africa.

The crisis also showed that there are major costs to all parties when international public policy is incompletely formulated. The crisis owed some of its origins to debtor country penchants to avoid multilateral lending agencies. It owed some of its longevity to the unwillingness of developed countries to use these agencies in global debt relief schemes.

Much change has occurred in the economic policies of debtor countries. The case-by-case approach adopted by creditor countries, multilateral institutions, and commercial banks permitted them to maintain pressure for policy changes. The ability to exert this pressure was one reason why the case-by-case approach prevailed over proposals for generalized debt relief. However, there are obvious political constraints on economic policy and there are grounds for pessimism concerning continued reform. The reduction in state intervention sought by both the Baker Plan and the commercial banks went contrary to the dominant political philosophy in most developing countries. Although there has been considerable privatization and deregulation in recent years, skepticism surrounds governments' ability to sustain this trend. This skepticism is rooted in the politics of three areas of economic policy: trade policy, public sector deficits, and negative real interest rates.

The most drastic response of debtor countries to the debt crisis was the savage reduction in imports. Import compression is not compatible with a long-term growth strategy. Although the reduction in living standards produced by import restraint is possible for a year or two, in the longer term it must be relaxed as citizens chafe under the siege mentality it produces and as export potential is crimped through the absence of imported inputs. Shifting from import substitution to an export orientation involves fighting the entrenched power of an established industrial base already providing employment for the uncertainties of a nascent sector asked to compete in fiercely competitive world markets.

The politics of public sector deficits offer the most pessimistic outlook. The provision of a modicum of social programs for health, housing, education, and so forth invariably produces budget deficits in countries with meager tax bases and inefficient tax collection systems. The use of the state as a generator of jobs in countries with endemic unemployment adds to budget deficits.

The politics of negative real interest rates directly effects capital markets. Particularly in Latin America, negative real interest rates have been produced by a combination of pervasive inflation and credit allocation systems designed to artificially hold down nominal interest rates. The result encouraged capital-intensive rather than labor-intensive investment processes, wasted resources by channeling funds into loss-making politically connected or state-run enterprises and discouraged saving by offering negative rates of return. When combined with exchange-rate policies, negative real interest rates produced capital flight.

The unwinding of the crisis inflicted major costs on all parties, particularly debtor countries. In the developed countries, taxpayers have borne the tax expenditures produced by lower bank tax payments as bank profits fell or became losses; bank shareholders lost equity as banks increased loan loss reserves and agreed to voluntary debt reduction; export industries suffered income reductions and job losses as debtor country adjustment compressed imports. In the debtor countries, the urban poor received fewer subsidies while all suffered from the unanticipated curtailment of living standards previously financed by borrowing.

Debt is an integral part of economic development and there will continue to be external debt long after the debt crisis is resolved. In particular, the need for general balance-of-payments financing will remain. The Miyazawa-Brady proposals, coupled with quota increases for the Fund and capital increases for the Bank and regional banks, place the major multilateral lending agencies in the position of being able to reassert themselves as major sources of funds. This optimism concerning the potential long-term provision of financing flows does not extend to commercial banks. A prerequisite for a return to voluntary commercial bank lending must be the repatriation of capital. Capital flight in the late 1970s presaged the coming crisis; capital repatriation must precede new voluntary bank lending. Residents of developing countries must express confidence in domestic assets before foreigner private lenders may be expected to do so. Governments of developing countries must pursue policies that produce this confidence. Domestic conditions necessary for capital repatriation include monetary, fiscal, and exchange rate policies permitting real private rates of return appropriate to capital scarce countries.

By 1989, seven years after the eruption of the debt crisis with the Mexican difficulties of August 1982, all participants had muddled through the intervening years. Debt had been renegotiated. Debt had been reduced in some instances. The IMF had conducted a review of its conditionality policies and expanded the contingency element in conditionality. The crisis years had seen no debtor cartels; most countries hostile to the IMF had resumed relationships. The need for a more vigorous international public policy had again been recognized, particularly in the use of the main multilateral lending agencies. The belated U.S. recognition of this need had ultimately produced the Brady Plan of 1989.

A number of major economic changes had occurred. Debtor country macro and exchange-rate policies now recognized internal and external constraints on financing; commercial banks had ceded ground to the traditional multilateral lending agencies; and the IMF had accepted contingent conditionality, expanded its medium-term operations, and was working more closely with the World Bank since the establishment of a Structural Adjustment Facility and an Extended Structural Adjustment Facility.

There had also been political change. Between mid-1988 and late 1989 almost all of Latin America held national elections. After seven years of austerity, populist pressure was closing in on politicians. In the Philippines, Acquino had lost much of her luster. In Peru, the previously charismatic Garcia was responsible for a spectacular failure of economic policies. In Mexico and Venezuela, new Presidents sought to escape from the austerity of their predecessors. Elsewhere in Latin America, two converts to the democratic fold, Argentina and Brazil, held second-generation elections with incumbent governments suffering the unpopularity of years of austerity. All were shaken by the death toll of the austerity riots in Venezuela in early 1989.

The politics of heavy external debt is a politics of few options. The absence of further external financing reduces choices. Perhaps the greatest challenge posed by continuation of the debt crisis is the on-going threat that reduced choices pose to fledgling democratic institutions. The Brady Plan recognized an urgent need for debt reduction to protect these political gains against the ravages of austerity. There is also a need for politicians not to return to earlier, failed, policies.

Appendix:
U.S. Treasury and Federal Reserve Support Operations for Debtor Nations

1982

Mexico End of month Banco de Mexico drawings in April, June, and July, totaling $1.5 billion, on its regular $700 million swap line under the Federal Reserve Board's reciprocal currency arrangements. Repaid after one day in each case.

An August 4 $700 million drawing repaid in February 1983.

A new temporary special $1 billion swap facility of Treasury Department's Exchange Stabilization Fund (ESF) to be repaid with Department of Energy's $1 billion advance payment for oil for the strategic petroleum facility was used on August 14–15. On completion of the terms of the oil purchase, Mexico repaid the $825 million drawn on August 24.

An August special combined credit facility of Treasury ($600 million) and Fed ($325 million) as part of a joint U.S.-BIS $1.85 billion multilateral financing program. The Treasury facility was later raised to $800 million Drawings were $556 and $299, respectively, conditioned on Mexico making progress toward an agreement with the IMF on an adjustment program. Final drawings February 1983; final repayments August 1983.

Brazil Three special swap facilities totaling $1.23 billion provided in October ($500 million), November ($280 million) and December ($450 million) after Brazil had adopted a change in economic policies, and to be repaid with borrowings from the IMF Facilities fully drawn and repaid in February and March 1983.

A December $260 million ($250 million drawn) ESF swap in anticipation of a BIS multilateral financing package and a December $500 million ESF guarantee to BIS for part of the $1.2 billion (later raised to $1.45 billion) loan to the Central Bank. Brazil repaid the BIS in November 1983 and the contingent Treasury commitment ended.

1983

Argentina A January $300 million ESF guarantee for part of a $500 million BIS bridging loan to be repaid by end of May.

Brazil Two February Treasury swaps of $200 million each ($400 million drawn) in anticipation of drawings from the IMF's CFF and from an extended financing facility. Repaid on March 11.

Yugoslavia An April $75 million ESF guarantee for part of a BIS loan. Contingent liability ended with November repayment to BIS.

Jamaica A December $50 million Treasury swap agreement while negotiating with IMF. Repaid on March 2, 1984.

1984

Argentina A March Treasury $300 million ($0 drawn) temporary swap arrangement as part of a $500 million multilateral package to help pay interest arrears. The Treasury facility was conditional on the IMFs accepting an Argentinean adjustment program. The complicated $500 million package involved $300 million in credits from Mexico, Venezuela, Brazil, and Colombia with these credits to be repaid when Argentina drew on the U.S. Treasury credits; $100 million provided by the eleven banks in the Argentina steering committee; and $100 million from Argentina itself. The U.S. commitment was extended for a month and a half beyond its original thirty days but was never used and lapsed on June 15.

A December $500 million ($500 million drawn) Treasury special swap arrangement to the Argentinean central bank while awaiting Fund approval of a standby arrangement that was contingent on further private bank lending. Repaid in January 1985 after Argentina drew on the Fund's CFF and on the standby arrangement.

Philippines An October $45 million ($45 million drawn) arrangement as the Treasury's share of $80 million in short-term financing provided by the United States, Bank of Japan ($30 million) and Bank of Korea ($5 million), while the IMF awaited private bank support to supplement an IMF loan. Drawings repaid on December 28 from the IMF loan.

1985

Argentina A June $150 million arrangement ($143 million drawn) as the Treasury's share of a twelve-country $483 bridging facility to bridge the time between IMF agreement to provide a standby and the provision of the standby after introduction of the Austral Plan. Repaid in August and September from Fund drawings.

1986

Ecuador A May $150 million ($75 million drawn) Treasury ESF short-term swap facility to the Central Bank as a bridge while Ecuador completed bank debt renegotiations. Repaid August 14.

Mexico An August $545 million arrangement ($545 million drawn) as the U.S. share of a $1.6 billion bridge loan, consisting of a $1.1 billion two-tranche multilateral near-term contingency support facility and a $500 commercial bank loan. $273 million was to be provided from the Treasury Exchange Stabilization Fund and $272 million under the Fed's regular $700 million reciprocal swap arrangement with the Bank of Mexico. Other central banks (including those of Argentina, Brazil, Colombia, and Uruguay) provided $555 million, and a group of approximately fifty commercial banks provided $500 million

The bridge loan was provided until arrangements were completed on a $12 billion eighteen-month concerted lending package that included $1.7 billion from the IMF, $2 billion from the World Bank, and $6 billion from commercial banks. All of the commercial bank share of the bridge loan and $250 million of the official funds were contingent on 90 percent of the 500 bank creditors agreeing to lend the $6 billion.

Mexico drew $421.2 as the U.S. share of first tranche drawings of $850 million on August 29 and $123.8 as the U.S. share of second tranche drawings of $250 million on December 8. First trance repayments made in three payments between November 26 and January 5, 1987. Second tranche repayments made on February 13, 1987.

Bolivia A September $100 million Treasury ESF short-term bridging facility to the Central Bank.

Nigeria An October Treasury ESF contribution of $37 million ($22.2 million drawn) to a $250 million multilateral short-term bridging facility organized by the Bank of England. Repaid in November and December.

1987

Argentina A March Treasury $225 million ($225 million drawn) ESF share of a $500 million multilateral short-term facility arranged among central banks. The full amount was drawn in March and repaid in July. An October $200 million ($190 million drawn) Treasury ESF contribution to a $500 million multilateral near-term credit facility provided by the ESF, the BIS, and central banks of Mexico, Uruguay, and Colombia to Central Bank. Repaid in December

Ecuador A December $31 million ($31 million drawn) Treasury ESF short-term credit facility. The full amount was drawn on December 4, 1987 and fully repaid on January 26, 1988.

1988

Argentina A February $550 million ($390 and $160 million drawn) ESF short-term financing facility to the Central Bank. The first drawing of $390 million repaid in March; the second on May 31.

A new $500 million multilateral short-term facility was established on October 20. ESF share was $265 million. A $79.5 million drawing was repaid in 1988 and 1989.

Yugoslavia A June 10 $50 million ESF facility as part of a BIS-coordinated international short-term facility of $250 million. Repaid in installments on July 1, September 26 and 30.

Brazil A July 27 $250 million ESF share in a $500 million BIS-coordinated short-term facility, of which $232.5 million was drawn on the ESF facility on July 29 and repaid on August 26.

Mexico On August 1 the Bank of Mexico used its reciprocal arrangements to draw $700 million from the Federal Reserve and $300 million from the U.S. Treasury. Both repaid on September 15.

Sources: Sam Y. Cross, "Treasury and Federal Reserve Foreign Exchange Operations," in *Federal Reserve Bulletin*, various issues and *New York Times*, August 28, 1986, p. D13, and February 20, 1987, p. D20.

Select Bibliography

Almansi, Aquiles A. "Patterns of External Adjustment in LDC's: Do We Understand Them?" *International Economic Review* 30 (February 1989):77–84.

Avramovic, Dragoslav et al. *Economic Growth and External Debt.* Baltimore: Johns Hopkins Press for the International Bank for Reconstruction and Development, 1964.

Babai, Don. "The World Bank and the IMF: Rolling Back the State or Backing its Role?" In *The Promise of Privatization*, edited by Raymond Vernon, pp. 254–86. New York: Council on Foreign Relations, 1988.

Bacha, Edmar Lisboa, and Carlos F. Diaz Alejandro. *International Financial Intermediation: A Long and Tropical View.* International Finance Section, Princeton Essays in International Finance, No. 147, 1982.

Balassa, Bela. "Adjusting to External Shocks: The Newly Industrializing Developing Economies in 1974–76 and 1979–81." *Weltwirtschaftliches Archiv* 121 (1985):116–41.

———. "The Newly-Industrializing Developing Countries after the Oil Crisis." *Weltwirtschaftliches Archiv* 117 (1981):142–94.

———. "Policy Responses to Exogenous Shocks in Developing Countries." *American Economic Review* 76 (May 1986):75–78.

Bardhan, Pranab K. "Optimum Foreign Borrowing." In *Essays on the Theory of Optimal Economic Growth*, edited by Karl Shell, pp. 117–28. Cambridge Mass.: MIT Press, 1967.

Bergsten, C. Fred, William R. Cline, and John Williamson. *Bank Lending to Developing Countries: The Policy Alternatives.* Washington, D.C.: Institute for International Economics, 1985.

Blackwell, Michael, and Simon Nocera. "Developing Countries Develop Debt-Equity Swap Programs To Manage External Debt." *IMF Survey* 17 (July 11, 1988):226–28.

Buira, Ariel. "IMF Financial Programs and Conditionality." *Journal of Development Economics*, 12 (1983):111–36.

Chandarvarkar, Anand G. *The International Monetary Fund: Its Financial Organization and Activities.* IMF Pamphlet Series No. 42, 1984.

Cline, William R. "Economic Stabilization in Developing Countries: Theory and Stylized Facts." In *IMF Conditionality*, edited by John Williamson, pp. 175–208. Washington, D.C.: Institute for International Economics, 1983.

———. "International Debt: Analysis, Experience and Prospects." *Journal of Development Planning* 16 (1985):25–57.

———. "International Debt: From Crisis to Recovery." *American Economic Review* 75 (May 1985):185–90.

———. *International Debt and the Stability of the World Economy*. Washington, D.C.: Institute for International Economics, 1983.

———. *International Debt: Systemic Risk and Policy Response*. Washington D.C: Institute for International Economics, 1983.

———. *Mobilizing Bank Lending to Debtor Countries*. Washington, D.C.: Institute for International Economics, June 1987.

———, and Sidney Weintraub (eds.). *Economic Stabilization in Developing Countries*. Washington, D.C.: The Brookings Institution, 1981.

Cooper, Richard N. *Currency Devaluations in Developing Countries*. International Finance Section, Princeton Essays in International Finance No. 86, 1971.

———, and Jeffrey D. Sachs. "Borrowing Abroad: The Debtor's Perspective." In *International Debt and the Developing Countries*, edited by Gordon W. Smith and John T. Cuddington, pp. 21–60. Washington, D.C.: The World Bank, 1985.

Crawford, Vincent P. *International Lending, Long-Term Credit Relationships, and Dynamic Contract Theory*. International Finance Section, Princeton Studies in International Finance No. 59, 1987.

Cuddington, John T. *Capital Flight: Estimates, Issues, and Explanations*. International Finance Section, Princeton Studies in International Finance, No. 58, 1986.

de Larosiere, Jacques. "Adjustment Programs Supported by the Fund." Remarks before the Centre d'Etudes financieres, Brussels, February 6, 1984. Washington, D.C.: IMF, 1984. Mimeographed.

———. "Perspectives on the World Economy and the Role of the IMF." Speech to the Council on Foreign Relations, New York, November 29, 1984, Washington, D.C.: IMF, 1984. Mimeographed.

Dell, Sidney. *On Being Grandmotherly*. International Finance Section, Princeton Essays in International Finance No. 144, 1981.

Deppler, Michael, and Martin Williamson. "Capital Flight: Concepts, Measurement, and Issues." IMF, *Staff Studies for the World Economic Outlook* (August 1987):39–58.

deVries, Margaret G. *The International Monetary Fund, 1966–1971*. Washington, D.C.: The International Monetary Fund, 1976.

Dhar, Sanjay. "U.S. Trade with Latin America: Consequences of Financing Constraints." Federal Reserve Bank of New York, *Quarterly Bulletin* (Autumn 1983):14–8.

Diaz-Alejandro, Carlos. "Latin American Debt: I Don't Think We Are in Kansas Anymore." *Brookings Papers on Economic Activity* (1984), 335–89.

———. "Some Aspects of the 1982–83 Brazilian Payments Crisis." *Brookings Papers on Economic Activity* (1983):515–42.

———. "Southern Cone Stabilization Programs," in *Economic Stabilization in Developing Countries*, edited by William R. Cline and Sidney Weintraub, pp.

119–41. Washington, D.C.: The Brookings Institution, 1981.

Dillon, K. Burke, and Gumersindo Oliveros. *Recent Experience with Multilateral Official Debt Rescheduling.* IMF World Economic and Financial Survey, February 1987.

Donovan, Donal J. "Macroeconomic Performance and Adjustment under Fund-Supported Programs: The Experience of the Seventies." *IMF Staff Papers* 29 (June 1982):171–203.

Dooley, Michael P. "An Analysis of External Debt Positions of Eight Developing Countries through 1990." *Journal of Development Economics* 21 (May 1986):283–318.

———, et al. "Debt Relief and Leveraged Buy-Outs." *International Economic Review* 30 (February 1989):71–76.

Dornbusch, Rudiger. "Policy and Performance Links between LDC Debtors and Industrial Nations." *Brookings Papers on Economic Activity* (1985):303–68.

———. "Devaluation, Money, and Nontraded Goods." *American Economic Review* 63 (December 1973):871–80.

———. "External Debt, Budget Deficits and Disequilibrium Exchange Rates." In *International Debt and the Developing Countries*, edited by Gordon W. Smith and John T. Cuddington, pp. 213–25. Washington D.C.: The World Bank, 1985.

———, and Stanley Fischer. "The World Debt Problem: Origins and Prospects." *Journal of Development Planning* 16 (1985):57–82.

Eaton, Jonathan. "Monopoly Wealth and International Debt." *International Economic Review* 30 (February 1989):33–48.

———, and Mark Gersovitz. "LDC Participation in International Financial Markets: Debt and Resources." *Journal of Development Economics*, 7 (March 1980):3–21.

———. *Poor Country Borrowing in Private Financial Markets and the Repudiation Issue.* International Finance Section, Princeton Studies in International Finance, N. 47, 1981.

———. "The World Debt Problem: Origins and Prospects." *Journal of Development Planning* 16 (1985):57–82.

———. "Debt with Political Repudiation: Theoretical and Empirical Analysis." *Review of Economic Studies* 48 (April 1981):289–310.

Eaton, Jonathan, and Joseph E. Stiglitz. "The Pure Theory of Country Risk." National Bureau of Economic Research Working Paper No. 1894, April 1986.

Edwards, Sebastian. "Are Devaluations Contractionary." *Review of Economics and Statistics* 58 (August 1986):501–08.

Enders, Thomas, and Richard P. Mattione. *Latin America: The Crisis of Debt and Growth.* Washington, D.C: The Brookings Institution, 1984.

Feder, Gershon. "On Exports and Economic Growth" *Journal of Development Economics*, 12 (1982):59–73.

———, and Richard E. Just. "A Study of Debt Servicing Capacity Applying Logit Analysis." *Journal of Development Economics* 4 (1977):25–38.

Finch, C. David. "Adjustment Policies and Conditionality." In *IMF Conditionality*, edited by John Williamson, pp. 75–87. Washington, D.C.: Institute for International Economics, 1983.

Findlay, Ronald. "The Terms of Trade and Equilibrium Growth in the World Economy." *American Economic Review* 70 (June 1980):291–99.

Froot, Kenneth A. "Buybacks, Exit Bonds, and the Optimality of Debt and Liquidity Relief." *International Economic Review* 30 (February 1989):49–70.

Foxley, Alejandro. "Stabilization Policies and Their Effects on Employment and Income Distribution: A Latin American Perspective." In *Economic Stabilization in Developing Countries*, edited by William R. Cline and Sidney Weintraub, pp. 191–225. Washington, D.C.: The Brookings Institution, 1981.

Fraga, Arminio. *German Reparations and Brazilian Debt: A Comparative Study.* International Finance Section, Princeton Essays in International Finance No. 163, 1986.

Frenkel, Jacob A., and Harry G. Johnson (eds.). *The Monetary Approach to the Balance of Payments.* London: George Allen and Unwin, 1976.

Gale, Douglas, and Martin Hellwig. "Repudiation and Renegotiation." *International Economic Review* 30 (February 1989):3–32.

Gold, Joseph. *Conditionality*, IMF Pamphlet No. 39. Washington, D.C.: IMF, 1979.

Goldsbrough, David, and Iqbal Zaidi. "Transmission of Economic Influences from Industrial to Developing Countries." IMF, *Staff Studies for the World Economic Outlook* (July 1986):150–95.

Goldstein, Morris. *The Global Effects of Fund-Supported Adjustment Programs.* IMF Occasional Paper No. 42, March 1986.

Goode, Richard. *Economic Assistance to Developing Countries Through the IMF.* Washington, D.C.: The Brookings Institution, 1985.

Group of Thirty. *Risks in International Bank Lending.* New York: The Group of Thirty, 1982.

———. *How Bankers See the World Financial Market.* New York: The Group of Thirty, 1982.

Guitian, Manuel. *Fund Conditionality: Evolution of Principles and Practices.* IMF Pamphlet No. 38. Washington, D.C.: IMF, 1981.

Gylfason, Thorvaldur. *Credit Policy and Economic Activity in Developing Countries with IMF Stabilization Programs.* International Finance Section, Princeton Studies in International Finance No. 60, 1987.

Helleiner, G. K. *The IMF and Africa in the 1980s.* International Finance Section, Princeton Essays in International Finance No. 152, 1983.

Heller, Peter S., et al. *The Implications of Fund-Supported Adjustment Programs for Poverty.* IMF Occasional Paper No. 58, May 1988.

———, and Richard C. Porter. "Exports and Growth: an Empirical Re-investigation." *Journal of Development Economics* 5 (June 1978):191–93.

Hellwig, Martin F. "A Model of Borrowing and Lending with Bankruptcy." *Econometrica* 45 (1977):1879–1906.

Host-Madsen, Poul. *Macroeconomic Accounts: An Overview.* IMF Pamphlet Series No. 29, 1979.

International Monetary Fund. *Annual Report 1988*.

———. *Annual Report on Exchange Arrangements and Exchange Restrictions, 1988*.

———. *Direction of Trade Statistics Yearbook 1981–87*

———. *Fund-Supported Programs, Fiscal Policy, and Income Distribution*, IMF Occasional Paper No. 46, September 1986.

———. *International Financial Statistics Yearbook 1988*.

———.*The Monetary Approach to the Balance of Payments: A Collection of Research Papers of the Staff of the International Monetary Fund*. Washington, D.C.: IMF, 1977.

———. *Selected Decisions*.

———. *Theoretical Aspects of the Design of Fund-Supported Adjustment Programs*. IMF Occasional Paper No. 55, September 1987.

———. *World Economic Outlook*.

Inter-American Development Bank. *Economic and Social Progress in Latin America, 1988 Report*. Washington, D.C.: InterAmerican Development Bank, 1988.

Ize, Alain, and Guillermo Ortiz. "Fiscal Rigidities, Public Debt, and Capital Flight." *International Monetary Fund Staff Papers* 34 (June 1987):311–32.

Johnson, Harry G. "Towards a General Theory of the Balance of Payments." In Johnson, *International Trade and Economic Growth*, pp. 153–68. London: George Allen and Unwin, 1958.

Johnson, Omotunde, and Joanne Salop. "Distributional Aspects of Stabilization Programs in Developing Countries." *IMF Staff Papers* 27 (March 1980):1–23.

Kamin, Steven B. *Devaluation, External Balance, and Macroeconomic Performance: A Look at the Numbers*. International Finance Section, Princeton Studies in International Finance No. 62, 1988.

Kelly, Margaret R. "Fiscal Adjustment and Fund-Supported Programs, 1971–80." *IMF Staff Papers*, 29 (December 1982):561602.

Kenen, Peter B. *Financing, Adjustment, and the International Monetary Fund*. Washington, D.C: The Brookings Institution, 1986.

Keynes, John M. "The German Transfer Problem." *Economic Journal* 39 (March 1929):1–7.

———. *The Economic Consequences of the Peace*. London: Macmillan,1919.

Khan, Mohsin S., and Malcolm D. Knight. *Fund-Supported Adjustment Programs and Economic Growth*. IMF Occasional Paper No. 41, November 1985.

Kharas, Homi. "The Long-Run Creditworthiness of Developing Countries: Theory and Practice." *Quarterly Journal of Economics* 99 (August 1984):415–39.

Kravis, Irving B. "Trade as the Handmaiden of Growth: Similarities Between the Nineteenth and Twentieth Centuries." *Economic Journal* 80 (December 1970):850–72.

Krugman, Paul, and Lance Taylor. "Contractionary Effects of Devaluation." *Journal of International Economics* 8 (November 1978):445–56.

Machlup, Fritz. "The Transfer Problem: Theme and Four Variations." In Machlup, *International Payments, Debts, and Gold*, pp. 374–95. New York: Scribners, 1964.

McDonald, Donogh C. "Debt Capacity and Developing Country Borrowing." *International Monetary Fund Staff Papers* 29 (December 1982):603–46.

McFadden, Daniel, et al. "Is There Life after Debt? An Econometric Analysis of the Creditworthiness of Developing Countries." In *International Debt and the Developing Countries*, edited by Gordon W. Smith and John T. Cuddington, pp. 179–212. Washington D.C.: The International Bank for Reconstruction and Development, 1985.

Meade, James E. *The Theory of International Economic Policy*. Vol. I, *The Balance of Payments*. London: Oxford University Press, 1951.

Mendelsohn, M. S. *Commercial Banks and the Restructuring of Cross-Border Debt*. New York: The Group of Thirty, 1983.

Morgan Guaranty Trust Company. *World Financial Markets*.

Mosely, Paul. *Conditionality as a Bargaining Process: Structural-Adjustment Lending, 1980–86*. International Finance Section, Princeton Essays in International Finance No. 168, 1987.

Nowzad, Bahram. *The IMF and its Critics*. International Finance Section, Princeton Essays in International Finance No. 146, 1981.

O'Cleireacain, Seamus. "Current U.S. Policies Toward International Financial Institutions." *CUNY Bildner Center for Western Hemisphere Studies Policy Paper* No. 6 (September 1983).

Polak, J. J. "Monetary Analysis of Income Formation and Payments Problems." *IMF Staff Papers* 6 (November 1957):1–50.

Prebisch, Raul. "Commercial Policy in the Underdeveloped Countries." *American Economic Review, Papers and Proceedings*, 49 (May 1959):251–73.

Reynolds, Lloyd G. "The Spread of Economic Growth to the Third World." *Journal of Economic Literature* 21 (September 1983):941–80.

Riedel, James. "Determinants of LDC Borrowing in International Financial Markets: Theory and Empirical Evidence." World Bank, International Trade and Capital Flows Division, Division Working Paper No. 1983–82, February 1983.

Robertson, D. H. "The Future of International Trade." *Economic Journal* 48 (March 1938):1–14.

Sachs, Jeffrey D. "The Current Account and Macroeconomic Adjustments in the 1970s." *Brookings Papers on Economic Activity* (1981):201–82.

———. "External Debt and Macroeconomic Performance in Latin America and East Asia." *Brookings Papers on Economic Activity* (1985):523–74.

———. *Theoretical Issues in International Borrowing*. International Finance Section, Princeton Studies in International Finance No. 54, 1984.

———. and Daniel Cohen. "LDC Borrowing with Default Risk." National Bureau of Economic Research Working Paper No. 925, July 1982.

———, and Harry Huizinga. "US Commercial Banks and the Developing-Country Debt Crisis." *Brookings Papers on Economic Activity* (1987):555–607.

Saini, Krishan G., and Philip S. Bates. "A Survey of the Quantitative Approaches to Country Risk Analysis." *Journal of Banking and Finance* 8

(1984):341–56.

Salomon Brothers. *Debt-For-Equity Swaps: A Country-By-Country Update on Market Characteristics and Regulatory Initiatives,* Stock Research Report: Banks.

Schuker, Stephen A. *American "Reparations" to Germany, 1919–33: Implications for the Third-World Debt Crisis.* International Finance Section, Princeton Studies in International Finance No. 61, 1988.

Simonsen, Mario Henrique. "The Developing-Country Debt Problem." In *International Debt and the Developing Countries,* edited by Gordon W. Smith and John T. Cuddington, pp. 101–28. Washington, D.C.: The World Bank, 1985.

Singer, Hans W. "The Distribution of Gains between Investing and Borrowing Countries." *American Economic Review, Papers and Proceedings* 40 (May 1950):473–85.

Smith, Gordon W., and John T. Cuddington (eds.). *International Debt and the Developing Countries.* Washington D.C.: The World Bank, 1985.

Solomon, Robert. "A Perspective on the Debt of Developing Countries." *Brookings Papers on Economic Activity* (1977):479–510.

Southard, Frank A., Jr. *The Evolution of the International Monetary Fund.* International Finance Section, Princeton Essays in International Finance No. 135, 1979.

Spraos, John. *IMF Conditionality: Ineffectual, Inefficient, Mistargeted.* International Finance Section, Princeton Essays in International Finance No. 166, 1986.

———. "IMF Conditionality—A Better Way." *Banca Nazionale del Lavoro Quarterly Review* (December 1984):411–21.

Stern, Ernest. "World Bank Financing of Structural Adjustment." In *IMF Conditionality,* edited by John Williamson, pp. 87–108. Washington: Institute for International Economics, 1983.

Stiglitz, Joseph E., and Andrew Weiss. "Credit Rationing in Markets with Imperfect Information." *American Economic Review* 71 (June 1981):393410.

———. "Incentive Effects of Terminations: Applications to the Credit and Labor Markets." *American Economic Review* 73 (December 1983):912–27.

Taylor, Lance. "IS/LM in the Tropics: Diagrammatics of the New Structuralist Macro Critique." In *Economic Stabilization in Developing Countries,* edited by William R. Cline and Sidney Weintraub, pp. 465–506. Washington, D.C.: The Brookings Institution, 1981.

Tinbergen, Jan. *On the Theory of Economic Policy.* Amsterdam: North-Holland, 1952.

Tyler, William. "Growth and Export Expansion in Developing Countries: Some Empirical Evidence." *Journal of Development Economics* 9 (August 1981):121–30.

Ungerer, Horst, et al. *The European Monetary System: Recent Developments.* IMF Occasional Paper No. 48, December 1986.

United Nations Economic Commission for Latin America. *The Economic Development of Latin American and its Principal Problems.* New York: United Nations, 1950.

————. *The Economic Crisis: Policies for Adjustment, Stabilization and Growth.* April 8, 1986. LC/G.1408(SES.21/7). Mimeographed.

————. *Preliminary Overview of the Latin American Economy 1987.* Santiago: United Nations, 1987.

United Nations Conference on Trade and Development. *Handbook of International Trade and Development Statistics, 1988.* Geneva: United Nations, 1988.

U.S. Department of State. *Report to Congress on Foreign Debt in Latin America.* December 1985.

U.S. Federal Financial Institutions Examination Council. Country Exposure Lending Survey, Statistical Release E 16 (126).

Watson, Maxwell, et al. *International Capital Markets: Developments and Prospects.* IMF, World Economic and Financial Surveys, January 1988.

Weinert, Richard S. "Swapping Third World Debt." *Foreign Policy* (Winter 1986/87):85–97.

Wiesner, Eduardo. "Latin American Debt: Lessons and Pending Issues." *American Economic Review,* 75 (May 1985):191–95.

Wilcox, James A. "Why Real Interest Rates were so Low in the 1970s." *American Economic Review* 73 (March 1983):44–53.

Williamson, John. *The Lending Policies of the International Monetary Fund.* Washington, D.C.: Institute for International Economics, 1982.

————. *The Open Economy and the World Economy.* New York: Basic Books, 1983.

————, and Donald R. Lessard. *Capital Flight: The Problem and Policy Responses.* Washington D.C: Institute for International Economics, 1987.

World Bank. *Annual Report 1988.* Washington D.C.: The World Bank, 1988.

————. *World Debt Tables 1988–89.* Washington D.C.: The World Bank, 1989.

————. *World Development Report 1988.* Washington D.C.: The World Bank, 1988.

Yagci, Fahrettin, Steven Kamin, and Vicki Rosenbaum. *Structural Adjustment Lending: An Evaluation of Program Design.* World Bank Staff Working Papers No. 735. Washington D.C.: The World Bank, 1985.

Index

ABOUT THE AUTHOR

SEAMUS O'CLEIREACAIN is Associate Professor of Economics at the State University of New York at Purchase and Adjunct Associate Professor of Economics at Columbia University. He is Associate Director of the Center for Labor-Management Policy Studies at the Graduate School and University Center of the City University of New York, and Director of US-EC Seminars at the Institute on Western Europe, Columbia University.

A specialist in international economic policy, he graduated from University College Dublin, Ireland, in 1963 and received his Ph.D. from the University of Michigan in 1971.